FALL OF CAPITALISM

and Rise of Islam

FALL OF CAPITALISM

and Rise of Islam

Mohammad Malkawi

Copyright © 2010 by Mohammad Malkawi.

Library of Congress Control Number: 2010904648
ISBN: Hardcover 978-1-4500-7486-5
Softcover 978-1-4500-7485-8
Ebook 978-1-4500-7487-2

All rights reserved. No part of this book may be reproduced or transmitted in any form or by any means, electronic or mechanical, including photocopying, recording, or by any information storage and retrieval system, without permission in writing from the copyright owner.

This book was printed in the United States of America.

To order additional copies of this book, contact:
Xlibris Corporation
1-888-795-4274
www.Xlibris.com
Orders@Xlibris.com
75395

TABLE OF CONTENTS

i Acknowledgment 11
ii Preface 13

Introduction 17
    Financial and Economic Crisis 19
    Moral Crisis behind the Financial Crisis 21
    The Rise of Islam 23

PART 1: The Fall of Capitalism

1.1 Capitalism: A Historical Perspective 29
1.2 Capitalism: The Complex System and the Fault Model 33
1.3 Flaws and Defects: Dormant Faults in the System of Capitalism 36
    1.3.1. The Relative Scarcity Principle 38
        Relative Scarcity Breeds Poverty 41
        Economic System versus Economic Science 43
        Materialistic and Nonmaterialistic Human Needs 44
        Economic Products and Social Responsibility 45
        The Myth of Resources Scarcity 48
    1.3.2. The Value of Products 50
        Is the Value of a Product Virtual or Real? 51
    1.3.3. The Price Mechanism 54
        Price Mechanism: Does It Really Regulate the Market? 57
    1.3.4. Private Ownership in Capitalism 60
1.4 Capitalism in Action: Performance Scoreboard 64
    1.4.1 Poverty and Gross National Product 66
        Hunger: Food Insecurity 70
        Hunger in the World 72
        Poverty and Education 74
    1.4.2. Health Insecurity 76
        Health Catastrophes in the Developing World 78
    1.4.2. Life Insecurity 81
        Insecurity: Atrocities of Wars and Terrorism 82
        Insecurity: Assaults on Human Rights 85

1.5 Capitalism: Signs of Failure 92
    1.5.1 Virtual Economy 95
        Stock Markets and the Virtual Economy 100
        Banks, Usury, and the Virtual Economy.................................... 104
        Gold/Silver Standard and the Virtual Economy....................... 112
    1.5.2 State and Public Ownership: Conflict with Capitalism 120
1.6 What Is Next?... 123

References (Part 1)... 128

PART 2: The Rise of Islam

1 Introduction... 137
2 The Ideology of Islam 140
    The Foundation of Islam: Historical Perspective 141
    The Structure of Islam: Historical Perspective 146
3 The Rise and Decline of Islam.. 150
    The Expansion of Islam... 150
    The Decline of Islam 155
    The Second Rise of Islam.. 158
    Semi-Islamic Models... 167
4 The Economic System in Islam 170
    4.1 The Development of the Economic System in Islam 171
        Rizq (Wealth) and Its Role in the Islamic Economy................. 171
        Abundance of Resources 174
        Poverty... 178
        The Value Definition in Islam 181
    4.2. The Political Economy in Islam... 185
        4.2.1 Property Ownership 188
            Private Ownership 191
            Human Labor... 195
            Inheritance 197
            Wealth Provided to Poor 198
            State Grants.. 200
            Public Property 201
            State Property 204
        4.2.2 Productivity.. 209
            The Prohibition of Usury.. 211
            The Prohibition of Hoarding.. 214
            Partnership between Labor and Wealth (Mudharabah).... 216

II.4.3 The Monetary System in Islam	218
Benefits of the Gold Standard	223
The Methods of Issuing Currency	227
Exchange Rate of Currencies	230
5 Satisfaction of Basic Needs	234
Children, Parents, and Relatives Support	236
Zakah: A Fund for Satisfying the Needs of Individuals	239
Public and State Property: No Human Needs Remain Unsatisfied	241
Private Property: Beyond the Basic Needs	243

PART 3: Is Islam a Threat or Benefit?

1	Unfounded Fear	247
2	Theoretical Foundation	254
3	History of Implementation	259
4	Final Word	268

References (Part 2 and 3)	269
Index	281

Dedication

In memory of my father Isam Malkawi 1930-2005

I

Acknowledgment

I would like to acknowledge the great effort and support I received throughout the period of writing, editing, and publishing of this book. Many thanks are due to the professional editors of this manuscript. I sincerely acknowledge the comments, suggestions, and feedback of scores of friends, colleagues and scholars around the world who provided invaluable contribution to the wealth of information provided in this book.

I humbly acknowledge the continued and significant support of Dr. Mohammad Alweh for his endless contribution and feedback. My daughter Fatima deserves my best appreciation and love for designing the cover of the book.

I certainly acknowledge and appreciate the enduring support and encouragement I received from my family, especially my mother, who continues to nourish me with her prayers, advices and wisdom. I certainly appreciate the great love, support, and understanding of my wife, my daughter and five sons. My seven brothers and three sisters have provided me with all the support and encouragement. I am especially indebted to my brother Ahmad who encouraged me to write this book and provided most helpful advices and support.

Without the support and help from God, I could not have accomplished this task. I am always in deep remembrance to the bounties he bestowed upon me.

II

Preface

When I first arrived at the land of the largest capitalist nation in the world, I was amazed by the power of capitalism productivity in the United States of America. As a young teenager, less than 16 years old, I saw huge tractors and combines cultivating hundreds of acres and producing tons of corn and soybean grain; all operated by a single family. I saw the hands of a farmer hardened by the land he cultivates and softened by the money his land generates. I did not see then the invisible hands of the banks financing all that operation. I could not see any signs of failure then.

A year later, my education fate flew me to the other extreme. I arrived at the land of the largest socialist nation in the world to spend the next 6 years studying while observing socialism in the Union of Soviet Socialist Republics (USSR). I recall how often I had to stand in line to buy a grocery product, only to be disappointed an hour later because the item I waited for is no longer available. That system would not last; my instincts told me. I recall having to buy a communist publication as a condition for buying a book of math or computer science. That system would not last for long; I felt it.

I recall having to step over people laying drunk in my morning journey to school and on my way back. I recall scores of students graduating from medical, law, and engineering schools without attending classes; they were political activists or rich foreign students. I recall people having to go through surgery only to fulfill the quota plan for the surgeon at a given hospital. I recall the primitive radio fixed on the wall of my dorm room, which must have been a two way radio. Every time I disabled the radio, technicians would show up at my room to fix it; although, I never asked for the service; that system could not last for long; I knew it. My guts feelings, my instincts, and simple analysis turned out to be true only 10 years after I graduated. Socialism collapsed and the Soviet Union was dismantled by 1991.

The 6 years I spent in the Soviet Union gave me an experience of a lifetime. For one thing, I can not experience the life under socialism today even if I want to. Most importantly, I learned the principles of economy, political economy, and social structure of both socialism and capitalism. The teachings of Karl Marx, Vladimir Lenin, and Friedrich Engels were as important part of the curriculum as the subjects of math, physics, and engineering. The theory of historic materialism developed by Marx and later refined by Lenin suggested that capitalism would fade away only to give rise to socialism. That view was dead beaten in real world when socialism fell first. Marx's theory of the "surplus value" was correct only in the sense that under capitalism the wealth tends to accumulate in the hands of the few. But the other part of the theory that the poorer classes of workers and farmers would revolt for their stolen rights of ownerships never materialized.

When I arrived at the land of capitalism for the second but longer period of time, I observed what I could not have observed during my first trip when I was a young boy. The farm I lived in during my first trip was no longer the same. It was confiscated by the bank which, few years earlier had financed its production, in exchange of the debts which my host family failed to pay. The hard working farmer lost his land as well as the seed company he co-owned with his brothers. This system would not last; my instincts told me.

The same monster, the bank, swallowed the machine factory owned by one of my friends in the city of Milwaukee in Wisconsin. I recall how my friend traveled to my home country in attempt to setup a factory to help industrialize a developing country. I recall how the owner (my friend) was enthusiastic about helping people get jobs, supporting education, and how much he detested laying people off their jobs. Just like every other business under capitalism, his was owned by the Bank. Typically, businesses in capitalist countries are indebted to one or more banks. I still recall the words of an investing bank representative to the owner of a small technology company "you can not be in businesses without being in debt". My machine factory owner friend lost his machine shop, the one that produced real products right here in the land of capitalism. It was making products and generating profit when it was confiscated by the bank. The banks for sometime were going after the life insurance policy of my friend as a guarantee for their supposedly lost wealth! I knew then that this system would not last.

During my tenure at one of the largest corporations in the world (more than 160000 employees at the time), I witnessed how scores of the best engineers and technicians were escorted out of the building under the auspices of layoff. The first round of layoffs which eliminated more than 50,000 jobs were done at a time when the company was profitable and making lots of money. The layoffs were necessary to boost the stock prices of the company which have soared over the roof.

I admit that these are just stories, instincts, and guts feelings. So where are the signs of failure if there are any? After all, capitalism has gone through several rounds of recessions, depressions, downturns, low productivity and corporate failures in the past. It has always emerged as strong or even stronger. Why is it different this time?

The first part of this book "The Fall of Capitalism" addresses this question and provides a thorough analysis of the deeply rooted defects in the core theory of capitalism and how these defects can lead to a total collapse, if not properly contained and removed.

The six years I spent in the Soviet Union helped shape my world view in another direction. They helped me to discover the power of the religion of Islam, which until that time I knew very little about. I grew up as a Muslim by the virtue of being born to a Muslim family. I had no choice to be a Muslim, a Jew, a Christian or an atheist. My knowledge of Islam was limited to the teachings and daily rituals, which I learned in school or observed in mosques. The moment I stepped foot in the land of communism, I felt the challenge against the core of my beliefs. Signs and slogans of atheism were displayed all over the place. To believe in God was considered a reactionary practice, and for locals was against the law.

For the first time in my life, I had to face the question whether "God" was a reality or a fiction. The principles of atheism and communism, the dialectic and historic materialism, and the communist political economy all were part of a systematic mind cleansing I had to face for the whole period of my stay. This had placed a tremendous pressure on my inner feelings as well as on my inherited belief. I soon discovered that feelings alone coupled with the love for heritage can not sustain my belief. I had one of two options: either surrender my faith or prove it correct. I took the second option.

My investigation of the core ideas underlying the belief in my religion created in me a stronger belief, supported not only be feelings but also by reason and rational. What I discovered through my journey looking for proofs is that Islam not only provides a solid foundation for faith, but most importantly it provides a complete structure for life. Equipped with proofs, evidences, and knowledge I was able to conduct dialogue and debate with my communist professors. By the end of my stay in the Soviet Union, and through extensive readings and arguments, I had convoluted in my own mind the full image of the ideology of Islam.

After returning from the Soviet Union to my home country, I realized and discovered the second major fact about Islam. That was the fact that Islam as an ideology lives only in the heritage books or in the minds of few people who took the time, effort and challenge to discover the reality of Islam. Since then, I participated in thousands of events, lectures, conferences, and seminars worldwide advocating the need to revive the ideological structure of Islam and to install it in the real world.

Thirty years after graduating from the Soviet Union, and twenty years after the collapse of the Soviet socialism, a historical phenomenon has been depicted in the world affairs; that is the phenomenon of the "rise of Islam" to resume its role as a universal ideology. The second part of this book "The Rise of Islam" is devoted to the discussion and analysis of this phenomenon.

Along with the rising Islam trend, the notion of terrorism had clouded the atmosphere of Islam and the historical movement for its revival. When I was asked to speak at a conference in London in 1994 about the rise of Islam, I had to address the concern people may have regarding the links between Islam and terrorism. The first attempt to blow the world trade center in 1993 had been connected to Muslims. The bombing of the federal building in Oklahoma was first attributed to a Muslim terrorist before Timothy McVeigh was convicted. Then the catastrophic terrorist event of 9/11/2001 spurred the most serious fear ever towards Islam and the potential rise of Islam. My first public lecture after the 9-11 attacks was under the title "The Islamic Perspective on Terrorism," where I tried to prove that Islam as an ideology is not responsible for terrorism; on the contrary, Islam is part of the solution to this outrageous and horrific problem. The third part of this book "Is Islam a Threat or Benefit" provides evidence that the implementation of Islam is in the benefit of people, and the fear from the Islamic ideology is unfounded.

"The Fall of capitalism and the Rise of Islam" is a historical record of two major and massive historical events, which are unfolding in front of us today, and may have the greatest impact on the life of peoples and nations around the world.

INTRODUCTION

Top leaders of the world acknowledge the fact that a deep economic depression is encompassing the entire world and scores of economists and politicians cite the core ideas of the economic system of capitalism as a root cause of the problem. The G8 leaders in their meeting in Italy in July 2009 stated in the G8 Leaders Declaration: Responsible Leadership for a Sustainable Future: "We remain focused on the economic and financial crisis and its human and social consequences"[1]. This crisis prompted scholars like Francis Fukayama to blow the siren on capitalism and democracy. He wrote in his article "The Fall of America, Inc."[2]:

> *Along with some of Wall Street's most storied firms, a certain vision of capitalism has collapsed. How we restore faith in our brand. The implosion of America's most storied investment banks. The vanishing of more than a trillion dollars in stock-market wealth in a day. A $700 billion tab for U.S. taxpayers. The scale of the Wall Street crackup could scarcely be more gargantuan. Yet even as Americans ask why they're having to pay such mind-bending sums to prevent the economy from imploding, few are discussing a more intangible, yet potentially much greater cost to the United States—the damage that the financial meltdown is doing to America's brand.*

University of Massachusetts economics professor Richard Wolff breaks down the root causes of today's economic crisis, showing how it reflects seismic failures within the structures of American style of capitalism itself[3]. Professor Wolff declares that the current crisis is the greatest crisis of capitalism in his lifetime. He suggests that more fundamental changes need to be made to avoid future catastrophes.

The current economic crisis and the score of criticisms targeted at capitalism point to one important trend in the contemporary history of systems and ideologies; that is the downfall of capitalism.

Yet another trend which captures the attention of scholars as well as politicians is the one related to the rise of political Islam and the quest for the reestablishment of an Islamic model of governance and economy in a large geographic span of the world. The most explicit reference to this trend is made by Noah Feldman in his book *The Fall and Rise of the Islamic State*[4]. Feldman argues that the Islamic state which fell in 1924 is being reconstructed today. He states:

> In both symbolic and practical terms, the Islamic State died in 1924. Yet today, the Islamic State rides again . . . The trend is with them. In Muslim countries running the geographical span from Morocco to Indonesia, substantial majorities say that the Shari'ah should be the source of law for their states. (Feldman, pp. 2)

Another account of the "rising Islam" trend is depicted in a recent article published by Patrick Buchanan in the *Townhall.com* online magazine under the title "An Idea Whose Time Has Come"[5]. Pat Buchanan wrote:

> But today, tens of millions of Muslims appear to be . . . returning to their roots in a more pure Islam. Indeed, the endurance of the Islamic faith is astonishing. Islam survived two centuries of defeats and humiliations of the Ottoman Empire and Ataturk's abolition of the caliphate. It endured generations of Western rule. It outlasted the pro-Western monarchs in Egypt, Iraq, Libya, Ethiopia and Iran. Islam easily fended off communism, survived the rout of Nasserism in 1967 and has proven more enduring than the nationalism of Arafat or Saddam. Now, it is resisting the world's last superpower.

The published material on either of the issues—the fall of capitalism or the rise of Islam—is notably large. What is not common in the literature is to have both issues discussed in the realm of the same platform. Recently, the "fall of capitalism and the rise of Islam" was a title of a conference convened in the Chicago area. The conference generated mixed reactions from both Muslim and non-Muslim communities. It is interesting to note that when each dimension of the subject is discussed separately, the reaction is far less dramatic than when both issues are addressed simultaneously. The combination of both topics provokes scores of Blogs, Twitters, Web sites, and media commentaries. It is this combination which will be the subject of this book.

It is also uncommon for Muslims to be involved in the political discussion on the fate of capitalism. Students of political science, history, theology, and global movements are accustomed to reading the accounts of socialists, communists, academics, and think tank politicians on the plight of capitalism. But rarely we find Muslims addressing this issue from an Islamic perspective. This book will provide an account of capitalism from the perspective of a Muslim and the viewpoint of Islam.

The most recent crisis of the capitalist economic world did provoke several inquiries into the Islamic economic alternatives. But those inquirers continue to be made in search of temporary fixes for an ailing economy instead of looking for a comprehensive economic system with different foundation and structures than those exhibited by capitalism and socialism. One objective of this publication is to present a comprehensive view of Islam as an ideology which comprises economic, political, and social system as well as a system of values and ethics, all coupled with a spiritual filling of the human soul.

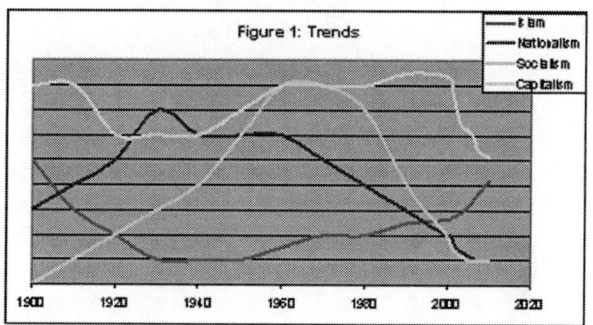

This book is not an outgrowth of the "clash of civilizations" as prophesied by Samuel Huntington[6]. Rather, it is a depiction of an ongoing trend in the global arena; see figure 1. On one side, the ideologies of nationalism, socialism, and capitalism either have faded or are still fading. On the other side, the grounds for the rebirth of an Islamic state governed by the Shari'ah of Islam continue to strengthen.

Financial and Economic Crisis

The financial crisis is not a new phenomenon in the world of capitalism. The United States and Europe have gone through several recessions and/or depressions for the last hundred years. Unlike all crisis and turmoil of the past, this time around, the financial crisis raised serious concern about the plight of capitalism, the backbone infrastructure of the current financial and economic system. When stock and commodity markets hit rock bottom in 2008, capitalism was viewed as seriously sick. As astonishing as history could be, the Islamic Ottoman State was viewed as the sick man of the world in the late nineteenth century; then, capitalism was emerging as the healthy splendid one. Today and after a long century of success, capitalism is becoming the sick man of the world; Islam, now, is emerging as the healthy and splendid one.

The *Financial Times* ran a series of articles titled "The Future of Capitalism." Economists, politicians, and philosophers saw the Great Recession of 2007-09 as a historic watershed and produced new visions of a changed capitalism. Chief economics commentator at the London *Financial Times* Martin Wolf makes the following conclusion in his article "This Crisis Is a Moment, but Is It a Defining One?"[7]:

> *My guess is that this crisis accelerated some trends and has proved others unsustainable. It has damaged the reputation of economics. It will leave a bitter legacy for the world. But it may still mark no historic watershed. To paraphrase what people said on the death of kings: "capitalism is dead; long live capitalism."*

Leszek Balcerowicz, a former Polish deputy prime minister and governor of the National Bank of Poland and a professor at the Warsaw School of Economics, believes that the current crisis points to a potential weakening of capitalism. He concludes in his article "This Has Not Been a Pure Failure of Markets"[8] that capitalism's most serious enemy is from within. In his words, "Dynamic, entrepreneurial capitalism has nowadays no serious external enemies; it can only be weakened from within." This is a direct reference to inherent defects at the core foundation of capitalism which can turn into a failure. A failure, as is the case in complex systems, results from a fault, which is activated by a trigger, and, if not contained or isolated in due time, will lead to a failure. In this sense, dormant faults or defects are the enemies from within.

Perhaps, the most intriguing argument in favor of capitalism was made by Edmund Phelps, director of the Center on Capitalism and Society, Columbia University, and winner of the 2006 Nobel Prize in Economics[9]. Nevertheless, Edmund recognizes that a serious damage has been impacted against capitalism, such that "restructuring is required to make capitalism work well again."

Sir Martin Sorrell, chief executive of the world's leading advertising and marketing services group WPP, makes the following conclusion in the *Financial Times* article "The Pendulum Will Swing Back"[10]: "It must be said plainly that capitalism messed up or, to be more precise, capitalists did." He claims, however, that "just as the crash was inevitable, so will be the pendulum swinging the other way."

It is clear that the current crisis has spurred numerous studies addressing the plight and future of capitalism. This is a major deviation from previous crisis, where the emphasis has been on recovery, risk analysis, and damage assessment. In part 1 of this book, we will address this issue in a greater detail.

Moral Crisis behind the Financial Crisis

It has become customary for economists, politicians, and thinkers to claim that traits such as greed and fear were behind the current financial crisis and economic downturn. In a more general case, prominent thinkers and politicians put the moral crisis behind failure at a larger scale. Zbigniew Brzezinski, the former national security advisor in the Carter administration, warns that the United States has lost the moral compass which is necessary for the United States to sustain its world leadership. In Brzezinski's own words, "The moral standing of America has been tarnished . . . the absence of moral convictions leaves opportunities for demagogy that exploits sudden crises and new fears"[11].

Jimmy Carter addresses the deepening moral crisis in the United States in his book "Our Endangered Values: America's Moral Crisis"[12]. His theme is summarized in the following words: "Extensive and profound are the transformations that are now taking place in our basic moral values, public discourse, and political philosophy."

Scores of economists, politicians, and commentators attributed the current financial crisis and economic downturn to lack of moral values and ethics in the market. According to Barack Obama, "we excused and even embraced an ethic of greed . . . we encouraged a winner-take-all, anything-goes environment"[13]. GOP presidential candidate John McCain said the financial crisis was caused by "greed, corruption, and excess . . . as Wall Street treated the American economy like a casino"[14]. George Bush cited corporate greed and market excesses when he claimed that *"Wall Street* got drunk"[15]. Ralph Nader says he predicted the current Wall Street crisis, which he believes to be caused by "pure greed"[25]. Reflecting on events taking place on Wall Street, a reporter for CNN made an unusually bald statement: "Markets are run by two things: fear and greed."

Oskari Juurikkala, a researcher at Institute of International Economic Law in Finland, wrote "Greed Hurts: Causes of the Global Financial Crisis"[16]. Oskari states that the current economic crisis proves that "greed is evil," in reference to the fact that greed is one of the main causes of the current crisis. John Steele Gordon, an author who specializes in financial and business history and the author of *An Empire of Wealth: The Epic History of American Economic Power* sites greed, stupidity, and delusion as main factors in the current financial crisis[17].

In an article published by the Wharton School of the University of Pennsylvania, the following account was given to the root cause of the crisis: "To explain the current economic crisis, the world of finance has a particular lexicon—including, for example, credit default swaps, mark-to-market and securitized subprime mortgages. Psychologists, on the other hand, might use very different terms: hope, greed and fear"[18]. The archbishop of Canterbury Dr. Rowan Williams blamed "human greed" for the financial crisis. He joined Muslim leaders from around the world in calling for world leaders to work together to prevent the burden of the financial crisis from falling on the weak and the poor[19].

The *Inner Projection Journal* published an article on May 23, 2009, under the title "Financial Downfall a Moral Not Financial Crisis" and gave this account: "Regardless of where you look—the sports arena, business room, political meetings, school and college campuses, places public and private—people have become predominantly less civil and moral. The 'Express Yourself' 80s has turned into the 'Just Yourself' 2000s." The article continues to explain, "We have fallen on hard times economically, for sure. But morally, we have not only fallen harder but deeper"[20].

Jeffrey T. Kuhner, a columnist at the *Washington Times*, in his article "Our Moral Crisis" published by the *Washington Times* on October 5, 2008, explains the deepening moral crisis in the world of capitalism. He says,

> We must address the deeper roots of this financial crisis. There is a moral crisis that infects every aspect of our society ... In short, our culture has done everything to destroy what used to be called character. What happened to individual restraint, thrift and personal responsibility? These are the virtues that built the most impressive capitalist economy the world has ever created.

Kuhner believes that the moral crisis is threatening all institutions; he continues to express the extent of the moral crisis:

> We are now facing more than just a financial mess; almost every other major institution is under threat. The political system is adrift; public schools are failing; the borders are porous; the intelligence agencies are dysfunctional; the inner cities are infested with drugs and gangs; the family is broken; and millions are fleeing their churches.

The Russian minister of cultural affairs also attributed the current financial crisis in the world as well as in Russia to a deeper moral crisis. He says, "During any tough times the first thing that suffers is our culture, youth, and education"[22].

Suite101.com online magazine published the article "Moral Crisis & Problems with Modern Capitalism," authored by Irish writer Timothy Woods, where he wrote: "The financial crisis has laid bare the pitfalls of modern capitalism. The current generation is dangerously close to losing forever a sense of values, of a moral code . . . we unwittingly maintain, strengthen the inherent greed produced by free markets the world over"[23].

"The Deeper Roots of Our Financial Crisis" is an article written by Theodore Roosevelt Malloch (former president of the World Economic Development Congress sponsored by CNN). The article appeared on February 11, 2009, in the online journal *Another Perspective*. In his article, Malloch insists that the moral crisis behind the current financial crisis is serious and should be accordingly addressed: "Unless those (Moral) causes are addressed, all the finger pointing and all the proposed solutions will be like putting band-aids on a tumor"[24]. He concludes that the moral, essentially embedded in the "virtue," is literally and figuratively missing from our public vocabulary and the idea of "the moral" has been either "trivialized or totally relativized." Furthermore, the moral values behind the economic system of capitalism cannot be restored or revived through "training session or quick executive briefing, because they are habituated over years and years. At the very root of the financial crisis is a moral vacuum, which can only be filled with true virtue."

Numerous politicians, thinkers, religious leaders, and economists continue to predict that moral crisis and lack of fundamental ethics and virtues can lead to serious failures in the financial and economic arena. How can greed bring down a powerful system like capitalism? What role moral plays in the production of wealth and in its distribution? These questions and others will be addressed in the subsequent chapters of this book.

The Rise of Islam

How could Islam be an alternative to capitalism? In what capacity is Islam being investigated? Isn't Islam just another religion like Christianity and Judaism? What type of "rise" are we talking about if Islam has been with us for the past fourteen hundred years? These and many more questions will be addressed in this book in part 2. But before we do so, let's see how Islam has been directly tagged and brought into the picture since the financial crisis began to sweep the world over. In so many reports, discussions, and forums, the Islamic financial practices have been cited as the most stable and immune in the current crisis.

Perhaps the work of Charles Tripp *Islam and the Moral Economy: The Challenge of Capitalism* is the most relevant in this respect, since he places Islam in a direct contrast with capitalism[26]. His argument is that capitalism has greatly influenced the Muslims' behavior in the past few decades. Today, the trend is in the opposite direction. Islam is sought to modify practices in the world of capitalism. The intrinsic properties of Islam will be explored to see why and how Islam can contrast capitalism.

In an article published by the *New York Times* on December 24, 2008, James Joyner reports that the global financial crisis has been a boom for Islamic banks, which avoided much of the damage from the subprime mortgage crisis by following strict principles laid out in the Quran. French finance minister Christine Lagarde has promised to make adjustments to the regulatory and legal arsenal to enable Paris to become a major marketplace in Islamic finance; she said, "Western financiers could learn a thing or two from the Islamic world as global leaders try to establish new principles for the international financial system, based on transparency, responsibility and, moderation"[27]. The US deputy treasury secretary Robert M. Kimmit, during a visit to Jiddah in Saudi Arabia, was quoted to have said that experts at his agency have been learning the features of Islamic banking[28]. Islam is being considered more of a solution than a problem. Majed al-Refaie, the head of Bahrain-based Unicorn Investment Bank, explains the reason for this shift: "The beauty of Islamic banking and the reason it can be used as a replacement for the current market is that you only promise what you own"[28]. Although this is too simple as an explanation to the phenomenon of the rising of Islam, it does point to the direction of a new trend.

The Islamic Development Bank organized a forum on the global financial crisis on October 25, 2008. The forum debated whether the Islamic finance can help inject greater discipline into the current financial system and reduce financial instability[29]. It has become customary for international forums and organizations to discuss the potential contribution of Islam to the stability of the current financial systems.

Ossi V. Lindqvist, former rector of the University of Kuopio in Finland, argues that Islam has in the past contributed to the advancement of science and technology in Europe[30]. His presentation at a conference held in Finland in October 2008 provoked a debate on the ability of Islam to contribute to the current financial crisis in the Western world.

With the financial crisis reaching its peak, more and more politicians and economists point to the direction of Islam as a potential source of stability. Germany's president Horst Köhler said that a new codex is needed. He says that the world needs a second Bretton Woods, referring to a global monetary system based on the gold standard and on fixed exchange rates, as the Islamic financial system ordains. Bretton Woods ceased to exist in 1971, when President Richard Nixon nullified the gold standard[31].

There is no doubt that the Islamic financial system is more stable than the current one based on capitalism. However, I should warn that the current practices of Islamic financial system poorly function and operate in a non-homogenous environment. The Islamic financial system will not be able to provide the full expected results from an Islamic system, unless the environment in which it operates is cooperative and homogenous from the Islamic perspective. What the current financial crisis has shown is that Islam has a different way of organizing the financial matters of a society. It has also shown that it has the potential of building a more stable financial system. Such a stable system can only be fully functional when the other systems in the society which have a direct impact on the financial system are in line with the financial system. This book argues that the rise of Islam is a comprehensive rise which brings up the economic system together with the political system, and the moral system together with the legal system. This will be discussed in greater details in part 2 of this book.

This book is organized in three parts. Part 1 deals with capitalism. This part answers the basic question, is capitalism failing, and why? Part 2 deals with Islam. This part answers the basic question, is Islam rising again, and how? Part 3 answers the basic question, is the rise of Islam a threat to world order, or is it a benefit?

PART 1

The Fall of Capitalism

كَلَّا بَل لَا تُكْرِمُونَ الْيَتِيمَ
وَلَا تَحَاضُّونَ عَلَى طَعَامِ الْمِسْكِينِ
وَتَأْكُلُونَ التُّرَاثَ أَكْلًا لَمًّا
وَتُحِبُّونَ الْمَالَ حُبًّا جَمًّا
(سورة الفجر: 17–20)

Nay, nay! But ye honor not the orphans
Nor do ye encourage one another to feed the poor
And ye devour Inheritance; All with greed
And ye love wealth with inordinate love!

—Quran 89: 17-20

1

Capitalism: A Historical Perspective

Capitalism, in the context of this book, refers to the system which is responsible for organizing the economic and financial affairs of a society on the basis of theories of capitalism. As such, it should be immediately noted that the failure of capitalism does not necessarily mean the failure and collapse of the society or state which adopts capitalism as an economic system. Societies and states can adopt other systems and can adapt to a new environment without capitalism. However, the failure of the economic system will have a great impact on the ability of the state and the society to carry their normal functions and to satisfy the needs of the society and the individuals until a new system is created and stabilized.

Another issue to note before we proceed is that capitalism means different things to different people. Various definitions and characterization of capitalism can be found in numerous books and references. The most widely accepted definition of capitalism is an *"economic system based on private ownership."* It is defined in the *Merriam-Webster* dictionary as *"an economic system characterized by private or corporate ownership of capital goods, by investments that are determined by private decision and by prices, production, and the distribution of goods that are determined mainly by competition in a free market."*

In the more general sense, capitalism typically refers to a system in which the means of production are privately controlled; labor, goods, and capital are traded in a market; profits are distributed to owners or reinvested by the investors; and wages are paid to labor. Proponents and advocates of capitalism in this capacity include Adam Smith, Francis Bacon, David Hume, David Ricardo, Max Weber, John Maynard Keynes, Milton Friedman, and many others. Opponents and critiques of capitalism include Karl Marx, Friedrich Engels, Vladimir Lenin, and many others.

Karl Marx believed that capitalism was destined to rise as one of the evolutionary cycles of a society as dictated by "historical materialism inevitability"[32]. Using the same theory, Marx also believed that capitalism will eventually decay and vanish, leaving the way for the rise of socialism and communism. This theory was put to an end before the end of the twentieth century when socialism collapsed in the Soviet Union. Relying on Marx's own theory of the development of societies, Francis Fukayama concluded that the end point of mankind's ideological evolution was liberal democracy (including capitalism) rather than communism[33]. However, this final end as detected by Fukayama turned out to be only a soft and temporary one when the markets began to collapse and banks began to fail and "a certain vision of capitalism has collapsed," using Fukayama's own words in his article "The Fall of America, Inc."[2].

Adam Smith's reasoning for "the system of natural liberty" in *The Wealth of Nations* (1776) is usually taken as the beginning of classical political capitalist economy. Smith devised a set of concepts that remain strongly associated with capitalism today. He argues that the pursuit of individual self-interest unintentionally produces a collective good for society. In support of free enterprise, Smith criticized monopolies, tariffs, duties, and other state-enforced restrictions and believed that the market is the most fair and efficient arbitrator of resources. David Ricardo, in *"The Principles of Political Economy and Taxation"* (1817), shared Smith's views and further developed the theories of capitalism.

The rise of the theories of capitalism in the mid-eighteenth century coincided and in some ways was preceded by other phenomena, namely, "the separation of church and state" and the "era of Enlightenment." Ideas derived from these phenomena had a great impact on the development of capitalism as a means of organizing the financial and economic transaction in the society. In fact, it can be argued that capitalism has emerged as one of the natural consequences of the separation of church and state. The separation between church and state dictates that man becomes *free* from the religious doctrines outside the scope of the church. This freedom manifests itself in four major areas, namely, the freedom of speech, the freedom of ownership, the freedom of worship, and the personal freedom. The freedom of speech, once fully utilized and developed, defines the political system of a society and leads to various forms of democracies.

The freedom of ownership, once fully utilized and developed, defines the economic system of a society and leads to various forms of capitalism. The other two forms of freedom define and shape the individual characters in the society giving rise to various forms of religion, customs, traditions, morals, ethics, and physical outlook; once fully utilized and developed, they define the shape of the social system. The political system of democracy, the economic system of capitalism, and the social system of individualism, together with the idea of the separation of the church and state, forms the structure of a complete and comprehensive ideology.

This ideology is interchangeably referred to as the ideology of Democracy or capitalism. Both refer to the same structure. The proponents of the ideology use the name "Democracy" when they want to emphasize the political freedom aspect of the ideology. In trying to justify the recent wars and invasions of Iraq and Afghanistan, US politicians emphasized the need to export "Democracy" to these nations. Of course, along with democracy go capitalism and the social individualism. In trying to understand the current financial crisis and their impact on the society, the economists and politicians used the name "capitalism." The point is that "Democracy" and "capitalism" refer to the same ideological structure.

This ideology originally emerged when the emperors and kings of Europe and Russia were using religion as a means to exploit the peoples and transgress against them. They used the clergy as an instrument for this exploitation. This led some philosophers and thinkers to deny religion completely. Others acknowledged religion but called for its separation from the people's daily life affairs. Eventually, the opinion of the majority of the philosophers and thinkers settled on one idea, which is the separation of religion from life and state. That was a compromise solution between the clergy who sought to control everything in the name of religion and the philosophers and thinkers, who denied religion and the authority of the clergy. Consequently, the main doctrine, which underlines the ideology of capitalism/democracy, is the separation of religion from life. In a letter to the Danbury Baptists in 1802, Thomas Jefferson wrote that the American constitution should build a wall of separation between church and state[36].

Understanding the effect of the separation of church (religion) from state and the life affairs will be quite necessary when discussing the moral and ethic crises which stand behind the current financial crisis. It helps understanding the background for conclusions such as the one made by Milton Friedman: "The only common interests shareholders have is to maximize profits"; "Any commitment to fulfilling social responsibilities other than making money is an illegitimate tax, or even theft"[37]. The historic development of capitalism, as one that emerged from the separation of church and state, also allows one to understand the dynamics of capitalism in societies where Christianity was not the dominant religion.

2

Capitalism: The Complex System and the Fault Model

Capitalism is a complex socio-politico-economic system. As in any other system, mechanical or social, failure modes follow certain models. In order to understand the nature of failure or to detect a failure once it occurs, it is very important to understand the model in which failures occur and manifest themselves. One of the most general models used for describing system failures is depicted in figure 2. At the core design of the system, there could be one or more defects or faults. These faults, if detected in the early stages of the system development, are removed and/or fixed. If a fault remains in the system due to oversight by the designers or lack of complete knowledge, it becomes a dormant fault. A dormant fault will not do any harm to the system until

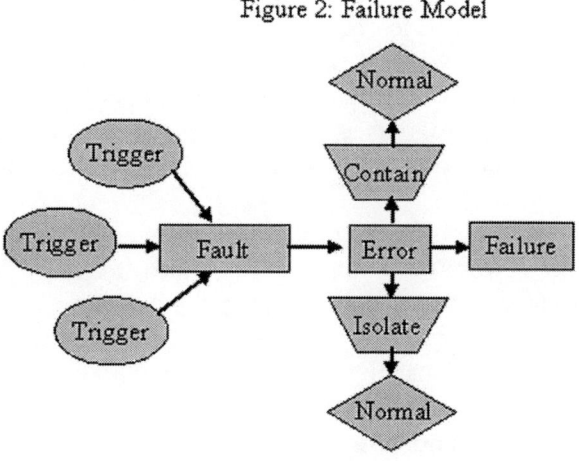

Figure 2: Failure Model

it gets excited or provoked by a trigger. A trigger is a certain condition or environment which provokes or excites a certain fault in the system. In physical systems, dormant faults are uncovered and detected through extensive testing which exposes the system to all types of conditions and environments. Unfortunately, social-political-economic systems cannot be tested in a lab! Therefore, dormant faults in such systems can only be exposed when the system is actually implemented and practiced over a long period of time and the proper conditions occur at a given time within a given environment. Once a fault is triggered, the system will experience an error which causes the system to deviate from its normal behavior. An error can lead to complete system failure if not contained and isolated in due time. The failure of the system renders the system unable to provide its main functions or achieve its objectives.

As an example, think of a weak spot in the design of a house basement as the defect or fault. The weak spot is where excessive water due to rain or floods can penetrate the house. The triggering condition for this fault is too much rain in a short period of time. The flow of water into the house through the basement is the error, because in normal circumstances water should not come into the house. This error (water in the house) can be detected by people living in the house or some monitoring device. This is how the error is identified and isolated. To contain the error such that it does not lead to damage, a water pump is used to remove the excess water from the basement and push it outside. If there is no water pump, or the pump fails to kick in for some reason, the error will not be contained and the floodwater persists in the house. This may lead to serious damages, including the collapse of the house.

This failure model is very common in our life. A weak heart or partially blocked arteries or defective lungs or unhealthy kidneys cause all types of sicknesses and pains, which if not treated and contained in due time may lead to death. Mechanical defects in our cars (leaky parts, unbalanced wheels, irregular electric voltage) can cause all types of problems in the car which can lead to total damage of the vehicle or even to catastrophic accidents.

The political, economic, and social systems are not much different. All systems may have defects and dormant faults. It is more difficult to diagnose and define these faults and detect than it is in physical systems. Part of the problem of the analysis is the fact that political, economic, and social systems are usually supported by people with strong convictions and sometimes by people with power and authority. While the Soviet Union was well and powerful, it was almost impossible to point to any defect within the socialist system, leave alone to errors and problems arising from these faults. This dogmatic view allowed the errors to propagate without proper containment, which eventually led to the failure of the system altogether. The case of the Soviet Union and socialism is an interesting case and an excellent example for understanding the fault-error-failure model in socio-politico-economic systems.

What is more interesting, however, is the application of this model to capitalism. Socialism has passed through all the stages of the model and finally experienced a major collapse and failure. It is an interesting case from the historical perspective. Capitalism is going through the second stage of the model. Dormant faults have produced erroneous financial and economic behavior. Policies and strategies such as bailout and government intervention have been exercised to isolate and contain the errors; attempts are being made to return the system to normalcy or normal functionality. Hence, the case of capitalism is important from a practical perspective.

In the discussion to follow, we will address the following questions: What are the defects or dormant faults of the capitalist system? What are the conditions that triggered these faults? What are the errors that resulted from triggering the faults? Were the errors correctly identified within a reasonable time frame? Could these errors be resolved? Are the faults being eliminated from the core of the system? Is failure imminent? What is the impact of the errors on the life of people? What is the impact of the failure of capitalism?.

3

Flaws and Defects: Dormant Faults in the System of Capitalism

Since its inception, capitalism and its main principles have been under scrutiny, criticism, and attack. Among the most serious attacks are those that came from socialist and communist philosophers such as Marx, Engels, and Lenin. Some Islamic thinkers provided criticism from a different perspective.

But it was Marx who provided one of the most thorough criticisms of the basic principles of capitalism. Marx, in his account of capitalism, focused on the definition of "value" and thought to have found a major and fundamental defect in the theory of capitalism. Marx redefined the "value" and used his own definition of "value" to attack the core ideas of capitalism. Marx defined value as "the amount of labor invested in the process of producing a product." He claims that whatever benefit a product has is a direct result of the labor invested by a laborer. This applies to products of lands made by farmers as well as products of industry made by workers. Marx defined the "surplus value" to be the amount of labor (or its monetary equivalent) retained by the capitalist after the consumption of the product. This surplus value, Marx maintains, is a direct theft of the labor of workers by the ones who own the means of production (the land or factory). Marx predicted that the surplus value will result in a massive accumulation of wealth in the hands of the owners of the means of production at the expense of those who exert their labors to produce the value in the first place. Eventually, this process should lead to a clash between the class of laborers who produce the value and the class of capitalists who retain the value to themselves[32].

The main contribution of Marx is the fact that he directed his criticism to the core principles of capitalism, namely, the value and the price of goods. Marx's analysis is inherently flawed. His major error is that he based his discussion and analysis on his own definition of the value. The "surplus value" concept is at once the point of strength and the point of weakness in Marx's theory of anti-capitalism; in this respect it resembles the Achilles' heel. It is sufficient to point out that the farmer may cultivate and farm two pieces of adjacent lands with the same type of crops, using the same tools, and still receive two different results for his products. Obviously, the value of the products, which may be different in quantity and quality, cannot be equal to the labor of the farmer which is the same in both cases. Many examples of the like can be cited to show the inaccuracy and flaw of the surplus value concept.

More recently, Sorin Cucerai makes the following comments on capitalism in his article "The Fear of Capitalism and One of Its Sources"[39]:

> *Paradoxically, the "freedom and prosperity of capitalism" are possible only by denying people direct access to food and shelter. In order to have this capitalist freedom, we must be alienated from our own nature. Any individual that lives in the capitalist order is a fundamentally precarious being, of a radical frailty.*

The main criticism that came from scholars within the framework of capitalism focused on the level of government intervention in the economics affairs of a society. The purest form of capitalism calls for the least government involvement where equilibrium is achieved through the price mechanism; this is the laissez-faire capitalism (translated to "leave it to be"). Laissez-faire capitalism comes under severe attack and criticism during financial and economic crisis, recessions, and depressions. The *Forbes.com* online magazine published an article on Feb 19, 2009, under the title "Laissez-Faire capitalism Has Failed" authored by Nouriel Roubini, where he writes, "There is now a rising risk that this crisis will turn into an uglier, multiyear, L-shaped, Japanese-style stag-deflation (a deadly combination of stagnation, recession and deflation."

Serious and significant criticisms of the fundamental principles of capitalism were made by prominent Islamic thinkers, namely, Taqiuddin al-Nabhani and Mohammad Baqir Al-Sadr. Al-Nabhani detailed his critique of capitalism in his book *The Economic System in Islam*[41]. Al-Sadr provided a detailed account of the errors of capitalism in his book *Our Economy—Iqtisaduna*[42]. Al-Nabhani focused on the three principles of capitalism (relative scarcity, value, and price mechanism). Al-Sadr's main focus was on the private property and ownership.

In the following sections, we will investigate some of the major flaws within capitalism and then show how these flaws have led to the creation of erroneous behavior over the years of capitalism application. These flaws have remained as dormant faults and have caused serious errors time and time again. Government intervention had been utilized to contain the impact of these flaws and errors and have attempted to prevent a complete failure of the systems. In a statement made to a congressional committee on April 3, 2008, the Fed Reserve chief Bernanke said that "if Bear Stearns had been allowed to fail, the adverse impact of a default would not have been confined to the financial system but would have been felt broadly in the real economy through its effects on asset values and credit availability"[47].

The main flaws and defects within capitalism are embedded within its main principles, which were developed by Adam Smith and David Ricardo (34, 35). These principles are the "relative scarcity," the "value of a product," and the "price mechanism." We will discuss each one of these principles and the flaws within them in the following sections.

3.1. The Relative Scarcity Principle

The relative scarcity principle establishes a relation between the needs and the desires of people on one hand and the means necessary to satisfy these needs and desires on the other hand. The scarcity principle asserts that man has certain needs, which require satisfaction, and there must be some means to satisfy these needs in order for man to survive. The needs recognized by capitalism are the materialistic ones, such as the need for food, clothing, medicine, education, and security. The moral needs and values such as pride, honour, and social responsibility, or spiritual needs such as the sanctification of God's will, are not acknowledged by the capitalist system. Nonmaterialistic needs are disregarded and have no place in the economic studies. Milton Friedman confirms this view when he says, "Making money is the only social responsibility for an economic entity"[37].

The relationship between commodities and services on one hand and the needs on the other hand is straightforward. Commodities and services embody within them certain benefits. The benefit is what makes something desirable; because the benefit inherent in a product is what enables that product to satisfy a human need. Therefore, a product (anything) is considered beneficial from the economic perspective if some people have a desire for the product, because it satisfies some of their needs. An economically beneficial product can be essential or marginal, useful or harmful. The only criterion for a commodity or service to have an economic value is the benefit embedded within the commodity or service which enables them to satisfy one or more of the human materialistic needs. Thus wine, tobacco, drugs, guns, and apples are considered to be beneficial because there are people who desire them. Stocks, derivatives, interest (usury) are also beneficial as long as there is someone who would benefit from their use. Electric cars carry great benefits to the society in terms of energy saving and environment friendliness. However, the economic benefit of these products is far less than the economic benefit of petroleum-based vehicles; hence, electric cars may become economically feasible only when the price of oil soars so high.

The capitalist looks at the means of satisfaction, that is, the commodities and services, from the viewpoint that they satisfy a need, without taking any other factor into consideration. Capitalism considers wine a beneficial product with economic value because it satisfies the needs of some people. The winemaker is perceived as one who provides a service with an economic value because he satisfies the need of some people.

Capitalism, as such, does not concern itself with the nature of society, but rather with the economic material resources (economic commodities and services), as means of satisfying human materialistic needs. This view in essence defines the primary function of the capitalist economic system: *supply commodities and services* to *satisfy man's needs, irrespective of any other consideration*. Note that the moral factor is absent from the core foundation of capitalism.

Capitalism believes that the commodities and services are limited relative to the human needs. The human needs are thought to be unlimited and constantly growing. Capitalism also believes that besides the basic and primary needs, which must be satisfied, there are other non-essential needs and desires which continue to increase as man proceeds to a higher level of urbanization. Satisfying all these needs which continue to multiply and increase is a goal that cannot be completely fulfilled, no matter how much commodities and services are produced. In other words, the commodities and services will always be scarce relative to the needs which require these commodities and services.

This principle provides the basis for defining the main objective of the capitalist political economy and it formulates the main problem addressed by capitalism. In particular, this problem is defined by the following question: how to satisfy ever-growing human needs using insufficient resources and means of satisfaction? This is the essence of the principle of "relative scarcity of products" (34, 35). Scarcity of means to satisfy ends of varying importance is an almost ubiquitous condition of human behavior[46].

From this perspective, the society faces an economic problem, which is the relative shortage of commodities and services. The inevitable result of this shortage is that some needs are either partially satisfied or not satisfied at all. If the means are scarce, they cannot all be achieved, and according to the scarcity of means and their relative importance, the achievement of some ends has to be relinquished[46]. In this case, it is necessary that the members of society agree on rules that decide which needs have to be satisfied and which needs are to be deprived. In other words, it is necessary to set a rule that decides the manner of distributing the limited resources over the unlimited needs. These rules are further defined by the other two principles, namely, the value of the product and the price mechanism.

Note that the main problem addressed by capitalism is the needs and resources in general and not the specific needs of a man or human. The problem is to make resources available to satisfy the needs, but not necessarily the needs of John or Hasan. The natural and straightforward solution for this problem is to achieve the highest level of production, in order to supply the highest level of goods and services to the nation as a whole. This does not mean the supply of resources to individuals per se.

The problem of distributing the goods and services is closely connected to the problem of production. The objective of economic studies and research is to increase the supply of goods and services which are consumed by the society. Under capitalism, the economic health indicators include the gross domestic or national product (GDP, GNP) and stock market indexes which measure the rate of production in a society. Thus the problem of increasing the national production is one of the most important studies related to the economic problem under capitalism: "the scarcity of the commodities and services in relation to the needs."

In short, the relative scarcity defines the problem and dictates the solution. Needs and desires are growing. Resources are not sufficient. Produce more and more of the resources. This is the solution to the economic problems of the society including the problem of poverty and deprivation. The principle of relative scarcity has several defects, which are bound to cause serious errors in the societies living under capitalism and could eventually cause the collapse of the system.

Relative Scarcity Breeds Poverty

The main objective of the capitalist economic system is to increase the country's wealth as a whole, and it strives to achieve that through the highest possible level of production. This is a direct result of the theory of "relative scarcity of products." To compensate for the shortage of products, it is required to maximize the production of products (commodities and services). The highest level of satisfaction of the needs of the people results from increasing the national income, or the gross national product. This is achieved by raising the level of production in the country, and by enabling individuals to acquire the wealth as they are left free to work and produce. It is not the objective of the economy to satisfy the needs of the individuals or to facilitate the satisfaction of every individual in the community; rather capitalism concentrates on satisfying the needs of the community as a whole by raising the level of production and increasing the national income of the country. The distribution of income among the members of society occurs by means of freedom of possession and freedom of work and by the utility of the "price mechanism". It is left to the individuals to acquire whatever wealth they can get from the total sum of the national wealth. Everyone strives to get his/her share of the wealth using whatever means, skills, or tools he/she can afford. Whether the individual is or is not able to satisfy his/her needs is not of concern to the economy, as long as the production of goods continues to grow, and the wealth continues to grow.

Consequently, the poverty of the individuals is not considered a problem for the economic system to resolve. This view of poverty is inherently wrong because it does not improve the life of individuals, and does not fulfil the basic needs of every individual. In fact, the very definition of relative scarcity opens the door wide open for the poverty of individuals. Since it is recognized that the resources that exist in a society are not enough to satisfy the needs of all, it is only natural for the ones who have faster and more access to wealth to acquire more of it. There will always be a segment of the society which will lag behind, acquire less, and consume less, and eventually fall below poverty lines.

The relative scarcity view does not lead to the resolution of people's poverty, despite the massive increase in the production of goods and services. The hard fact is that the needs, which require satisfaction, are needs of individuals. They are the needs of particular people such as George, Maria, Hassan, Omar, and the like. The fact that the needs of George are satisfied does not make Maria any better, unless her needs are also taken care of. The needs (materialistic and nonmaterialistic) are needs of individual people; they are not needs of a group of individuals, a group of nations, or a group of people. It is true that capitalism addresses the hunger as a need and food as a means of satisfying the hunger. But capitalism estimates the total amount of food to be produced in a given society and provides the incentives to produce it. Once the estimated amount of food is produced, capitalism does not ensure that George or Maria has obtained their share to eliminate their hunger. In fact, it is very likely that George acquires much more resources than he needs, thus leaving nothing for Maria. Over time, it is natural to see the wealth accumulation moves in the direction of a fewer number of people who have managed to surpass others in the process of wealth accumulation. We will later show how the increase in production had not helped the elimination or even the reduction of poverty rates in capitalist societies.

The economic system must be concerned with distributing the means of satisfaction for all the individuals of a society. In other words, the distribution of goods and services must be in a way that they reach every member of the nation or people, not necessarily in equal terms. It is not sufficient to increase the wealth of the group, irrespective of the plight of every individual. Although the economic system is meant to organize the economic transactions in a society, the people who live in the society (one individual at a time) are concerned about their own life. That is why it is imperative for the economic system to enable each and every individual to satisfy his/her basic needs. The fact that capitalism does not address the specific needs of individuals is a major flaw and defect at the core of the ideology that is bound to generate and sustain poverty under capitalism.

The study of the factors that affect the size of national production differs from the study for satisfying all the basic needs of all individuals personally and completely. The first one falls within the scope of the economic science, while the second one belongs to the economic system. The subject of the economic system should be the basic human needs of man, as a human being, and the distribution of wealth to the members of society to guarantee the satisfaction of all their basic needs. This should be the subject of study, and should be considered at the foundation of the system. The treatment of the poverty of a country as a whole does not solve the poverty of individuals. On the contrary, the treatment of the poverty of the individuals may lead to increasing the national wealth by motivating people to work and produce more. It is not surprising then, that the stimulus and tax incentive packages are used by governments to stimulate the economy and increase production rates.

Economic System versus Economic Science

The economic system addresses the needs of people and the means of satisfying these needs. The production of commodities and services, which are the means of satisfying the needs, together with the distribution of these commodities and services, are treated by capitalism as one subject, inseparable from each other. The subject matter of the distribution of commodities and services is embedded within the subject of the production of commodities and services. Capitalism as a system does not distinguish between production on one hand and possession of products on the other hand. Consequently, the capitalists integrate the economic science and the economic system within the scope of one subject without differentiating between both.

In reality, though, there should be a clear difference between the economic system and economic science. The economic system (its principles, laws, regulations) deals with the issues of wealth possession, expenditure, and distribution. Possession, spending, and distribution of wealth vary according to the viewpoint about life or ideology. Islam, for example, differs from socialism/communism and capitalism in issues related to possession, ownership, spending, and distribution. Each of these systems has its own ideological viewpoint of life. For example, each ideology treats the issue of ownership in a different manner. While capitalism emphasizes private ownership, socialism/communism utilizes public ownership, and Islam uses both private and public ownership.

Economic science deals with production, product improvement, invention, and the means of production. Economic science, like any other sciences, is universal to all nations and is not particular to any one ideology. The improvement of production, for instance, is a technical scientific issue and can be adopted by people irrespective of their ideology or life view. For example, automation as a means of product improvement can be used by capitalists, socialists, or Muslims without any ideological barriers.

The integration between the production of the economic resources and the manner of their acquisition and distribution is a fundamental fault in the capitalist system which is bound to cause errors and potential failure in the economy of capitalism. When capitalists face the issue of poverty, they resort to produce more products instead of focusing on distributing the ones which they already have and might be more than enough to feed the hungry and house the homeless and treat the ill.

Materialistic and Nonmaterialistic Human Needs

Capitalism views the materialistic needs as the only ones which need to be satisfied. This is a serious flaw in Capitalism because it violates the natural composition of a human being which exhibits both materialistic and non-materialistic needs. Besides the material needs, humans have instincts, emotions, feelings, intellect, and mind. Each of these units requires satisfaction and/or organization. Hunger is an example of a material need which requires food for its satisfaction. Fear is an example of nonmaterial needs which is a manifestation of the survival instinct. Greed is another manifestation of the instinct of survival. Both needs should be addressed and taken care of. It is almost unanimous that greed and fear had the greatest impact on the most recent financial crisis. Ignoring the nonmaterialistic needs can easily allow traits such as greed to dominate the production and acquisition practices. As a result, poverty becomes irresolvable problem with epidemic proprtions. The nonmaterialistic needs also include the needs to worship and sanctify a God, the needs of love and hate, the needs of pride and patriotism, and may many more.

Failure to address these needs or considering them irrelevant at the time of production and consumption of products create a great disparity in the society. It has become widely known under capitalism that the only role of a stakeholder in a company is to make money. Social responsibility of corporates is known to be a problem with epidemic scale. The absence of moral values in the market (production and consumption) has serious impacts on the overall well-being of the society, which invariably affects the well-being of the economy. As discussed earlier, moral crisis had been widely acknowledged to be a major factor behind the financial crisis which led to the collapse of major financial institutions. The decay of moral values over time is a natural and expected consequence of the fact that capitalism focuses and concentrates only on materialistic needs during the cycle of production and consumption.

Discrimination in the workplace based on gender, race, color, and ethnicity is a direct result of such separation between material and nonmaterial needs. Until the government intervened in 1963, corporations under capitalism in the United States were able to pay women less than what they paid men for the same job. The Equal Pay Act[43] was signed in 1963 by former president J. F. Kennedy, making it illegal for employers to pay unequal wages to men and women who hold the same job and do the same work. In 1963, a woman earned fifty-nine cents for each dollar a man earned; and in 2009, a woman still earns seventy-eight cents for each dollar a man earns. African American women and Hispanic women continue to be paid much less than white men and white women (sixty-four cents and fifty-four cents on the dollar respectively).

Perhaps patriotism provides the most interesting paradox when it comes to nonmaterialistic needs. The defense of a land or nation needs to be translated into measurable materialistic needs under capitalism. The problem becomes more visible and serious when a higher price is offered for a counterobjective, which could amount to treason. This is exactly how treason is committed by those who sell off the patriotism of their nation in favor of a higher price. Patriotism is a nonmaterialistic need. It is a genuine feeling that normal people carry within their own self which motivates them to stand up in defense of the land they live on. Compensation paid to soldiers should not be looked at as a compensation for patriotism; it is a compensation for the time spent in duty which prevents a soldier from earning money doing another job.

Another example is the case of lawsuits. Lawsuits are filed for material objects such as physical injuries and property damages, as well as for nonmaterial objects such as character, pride, and honor. Amazingly, the lawsuits for nonmaterial objects usually cost much higher than those for material objects. There is a visible disparity when it comes to lawsuits related to people's feelings and honor. The price placed on feelings or honor can range from nothing at all to hundreds of millions of dollars! It is also interesting to note that the number of lawsuits soars during financial and economic crisis. In the US districts, the number of lawsuits increased from 150 per month in 2003 to 650 per month in 2009. This large variance in the price of nonmaterial injuries reveals a defect at the core of the economic system, which only deals with material objects. As such, the estimation of the price of a nonmaterial injury is left to the discretion of the arbitrators in each case.

Failure of capitalism to consider and address the nonmaterialistic needs of people is a serious flaw and defect within the system. This defect is bound to lead to major errors and potentially a collapse of the system.

Economic Products and Social Responsibility

As noted above, capitalism does not give weight to any value, except to the material value of the product and the material nature of the human need. According to Milton Friedman[37], the social responsibility of business is to maximize profits and any commitment to fulfilling social responsibilities other than making money is an illegitimate tax, or even theft; maximizing profits will produce the best overall consequences for society.

It is interesting to note that the study of business ethics did not emerge as a field of study in the United States until the 1970s; international business ethics emerged in the late 1990s[45]. This is a clear indication that the ethical aspects of the economy are not based in the core theory of capitalism. The ethical aspects in the business world emerged as a result of unethical practices, which no longer could be ignored.

The absence of the ethical and moral aspect of the business and the absolute focus on making money and profit is a major flaw in the origin of the theories of capitalism. This is bound to create a myriad of unethical practices, which adversely impacts the stability of the economy at large. According to Theodore Roosevelt Malloch[24], the moral values cannot be reinstated through training sessions, course development, or executive summaries. Morality has been detached from the system the moment the nonmaterialistic needs were ignored.

Under capitalism, feeding a poor (a form of wealth distribution) may be done only if it brings a material benefit, such as tax break. But it will not happen in response to an order from God or in pursuit of God's pleasure and satisfaction. It is not surprising that most of the effective charity organizations in the capitalist world are religion based.

Besides the absence of the moral and ethical factor in the production and consumption process, capitalism fails to recognize the fact that the society as a whole has certain needs which are different from those of the individuals. Capitalism, as discussed earlier, is based on the principle idea of separation of church and state. Further, it is built upon the freedom of ownership which emphasizes the private ownership principle. This foundation has led the capitalists to believe that the society is made only of the people who interact with each other in order to satisfy each other's needs through the exchange of their efforts and/or products. The main component of the society in the capitalist's view is the people. The main transactions, which occur between people, are those related to the exchange of products and efforts. The state in the society is a tool, whose main function is to guarantee the free execution of transactions. In order to accomplish its task, the state needs to be paid by the people (through taxes) in return to the services provided by the state to individuals in the society. Such view of the society is flawed.

The people alone cannot form a society until and unless permanent relations persist among them. Note that a group of individuals travelling on an aeroplane or a ship do not form a society, although the travellers may interact with each other and execute various types of transactions while on the ship or on the plane. The people in a town, city, or region would, however, form a society when the relations between them become more stable and permanent. The relations between people take place in response to their needs and desires. The needs and desires of men and women for progeny lead to relations of marriage. The needs and desires of people for safety and security lead to bonds of patriotism. The needs and desires of people for pride and identity lead to bonds of tribalism and nationalism. The needs and desires of people for sanctification lead to bonds of religion. The needs and desires of people for food, clothing, and health lead to financial and economic relations. These relations and bonds will take one form or another based on what type of ideas, concepts, and emotions the people have towards these relations and bonds.

The belief in the separation of religion from state and the emotional feelings toward freedom will eventually shape the various bonds and relations in a particular way, which is different from that one shaped by the belief in the historical materialism evolution, or from that one shaped by the belief that God is the source of all legislations. What distinguishes societies one from another is not the people who live in the society; rather it is the shape of the relations and bonds that exist between the people. When the Russian society recently was transferred from a society of socialism to a society of capitalism, the individuals did not change; their needs did not change. Alexander, Peter, and Katrina continued to have the same needs and desires. What required the change, however, were the means and ways they satisfy their needs, and the nature of bonds and relations between them, and the laws and regulations which protect these bonds and relations. Similarly, in the society of Egypt, the majority of people are Muslims. However, the financial relations between them are conducted according to the principles of capitalism. The political relations are conducted according to local nationalism. The society of Egypt cannot be characterized as an Islamic one, although the majority of the people are Muslims. It cannot be characterized as a democratic one, although part of the relations is done according to capitalism.

Using computer analogy, the society is similar to a network of computers. Each computer in the network is a stand-alone unit which has its own specifications, needs, and problems. But the network as a whole has its own specifications, needs, and problems. The most prominent piece of the network is what the computer people call the network protocol. It is not acceptable to address the needs of each node in the network and assume that the protocol of the networks will automatically be satisfied and the network will function as well.

In summary, the society is not simply a collection of individuals. There is a protocol in the society that has its own requirements and needs, which are different from those of the individuals. Morality, ethics, respect of the order, spirituality, laws and orders, ideas and themes, public opinion and awareness are all part of the needs of the society. Ignoring these needs and limiting the economic problem to profit making by individuals is a serious defect. It is incorrect to consider a thing beneficial simply because it generates profit to someone, or because somebody likes that product, whether it is harmful or not and whether it affects the relationships among people or not, and whether it is prohibited or permitted in the belief of the people in the society.

Capitalism considers alcoholism, tobacco, cannabis, opium, explosives, and the like as economic commodities just because there is somebody who wants them. These commodities cannot be considered of benefits and value when their negative effects on the relationships between people in the society are taken into consideration. It is wrong to look at a product merely as it is, regardless of its impact on the society. The growing problem of global warming due to increased output of carbon products in the sphere is another example, where the profitability of individuals clash with the society's well-being.

The Myth of Resources Scarcity

The capitalists claim that the economic problem which faces any society is the scarcity of commodities and services. They also claim that the steadily increasing needs and the inability to satisfy all of them, i.e., the insufficiency of commodities and services to satisfy all of man's needs completely, is the basis of the economic problem. This view is erroneous and and may well collide with the human nature. The needs which must be met are the basic needs of the individual as a human (food, shelter, health, and clothing), and not the luxurious ones, although they too should be pursued. The basic needs of humans are limited, and the resources and the efforts which they call the commodities and services are certainly sufficient to satisfy the basic human needs; it is possible to satisfy all of the basic needs of mankind completely. In other words, it is not the unavailability of the resources that creates the problem; rather it is the distribution of these resources. The economic problem should, therefore, be the distribution of the resources in a manner to enable every individual to completely satisfy their basic needs and to help them to strive for attaining their luxurious needs.

The reference to the steadily increasing needs is not accurate. The basic needs of man as a human do not increase. They are fixed and well defined. The luxurious needs may increase and vary. It is true that the advancement in various levels of urbanization increases demands for luxuries; but certainly the basic needs remain the same irrespective of urban development. The inability of a person to satisfy his luxurious non-essential needs does not cause a problem in the society; what causes a problem is the inability to satisfy the basic needs such as the needs for food, shelter, clothing, and health. Prophet Mohammad (PBUH) is reported to have said, "He who has security at his home, a healthy body, and food for his day, indeed has attained all the needs for his life"[67].

Moreover, the question of the increasing luxuries is a question which is related to some people and not to all individuals in a country. This question is solved through the natural motivation of a human to satisfy his needs. This motive drives man to work towards satisfying these luxurious needs. People in a given country may meet these demands by expanding the resources of the country, working in other countries, or improving the quality of products, goods, and services. This is a matter related to the means and ways of increasing and improving the quality of production, which is an issue of economic science rather than economic system. That is different from the issue of completely satisfying the basic needs of each and every individual in society, which is a problem of the economic system rather than the economic science.

A typical example cited in the economic studies of resource scarcity is related to the scarcity of time. It is claimed that within the twenty-four hours of the night and day, we are unable to satisfy all our needs that arise within the day. This may be true in general, but when we consider hunger in particular, we must realize that the twenty-four hours' time frame should be sufficient to feed each and every individual. Islam, for example, makes it categorically prohibited for anyone to remain hungry within the day and the night[55].

Peter Rosset, director of Institute for Food and Development Policy in California and the coauthors of *World Hunger: Twelve Myths* explore the myth of scarcity and confirm that the food resources of the world are abundant rather than scarce, and that millions are starving even in countries with excess food production[82]. He concludes that the claim that world hunger can be solved by increasing food production is an unsubstantiated myth. The scarcity myth has led to production of expensive export foods on the expense of production of basic foods for the population. Such policies have been widely supported by international organs such as the G8, IMF, and the World Bank. According to Peter Rosset, "The true source of world hunger is not scarcity but policy; not inevitability but politics. The real culprits are economies that fail to offer everyone opportunities, and societies that place economic efficiency over compassion."

3.2. The Value of Products

The second major principle of capitalism is the principle which defines the value of the product. The value of the product is the degree of its importance, relative to a particular person or relative to another thing. When the value is used relative to a person, it is called "the value of the benefit," or simply the "benefit." When measured against another thing, it is called the "value of exchange" or simply the "value."

Under capitalism, the value of the benefit of a thing is evaluated by its marginal benefit. The marginal benefit of a unit is that benefit which satisfies the weakest need. This is known as "the diminishing marginal utility" theory[38]. According to this theory, the benefit is not evaluated from the viewpoint of the producer and the costs of production only; this would only consider supply but not demand. Nor is it evaluated from the viewpoint of the consumer alone (benefit, desirability, and relative availability or shortage); this would imply the consideration of demand without supply. The benefit value should be observed and evaluated from the viewpoint of both supply and demand.

Marginal utility states that the benefit of a thing should be assessed at the least or minimum point of satisfaction. For example, the value of a loaf of bread should be assessed at the least point of hunger and should not be assessed when everybody is hungry or when the one who needs the bread is too hungry. In other words, the benefit value of the bread is measured at a time when bread is abundant in the market, not at a time when there is a shortage of bread. The law of diminishing marginal utility does not always hold as we shall see later; this could very well be one of the sources of defects and dormant faults in the foundation of capitalism.

The exchange value is an attribute which makes a thing suitable for exchange with other products. The strength of exchange of a thing is measured relative to another thing. For example, the value of exchange of wheat relative to corn is estimated by the number of units of corn which should be conceded to obtain one unit of wheat.

Exchange occurs between two commodities or services which are similar or close in their values. The study of the exchange value is necessary for economists because it is the basis for the exchange of products. It is a utility which can be measured; it also serves as a scale with which commodities and services are measured and by which the productivity of actions can be measured.

Production is defined as the work invested for creating benefit or increasing benefit in a thing. In order to identify whether a work is productive or not or to determine which work has greater productivity, there must be an accurate scale by which productivity can be measured. This scale is the societal value of the various products and services. In other words, it is the collective evaluation of the work spent and the service provided. Such an evaluation is necessary because in the modern time, production for the purpose of exchange has dominated and almost replaced production for consumption. In today's economy, virtually every person exchanges his/her production with other people's production. The proper way of exchanging products and services is through compensation. In order to estimate the amount of compensation for a product or service, the value of exchange needs to be estimated. Hence, the knowledge and definition of the "value" is an essential factor in production and consumption; it is essential for all the studies leading to the satisfaction of the needs.

In modern history, this value of exchange has been dominated by one type of exchange, the exchange of a product or service for money. The exchange value of a commodity or a service for money is called the "price." The price, therefore, is the amount of exchange of a commodity or a service relative to money. The difference between the value of exchange and the price is that the value of exchange is the exchange ratio of one thing related to (any) other thing, while the price is the exchange ratio of one thing related to money. It is perceivable that the prices of all goods rise or fall at the same time. It is impossible, however, for the exchange values of all commodities relative to each other to rise or fall at the same time. It is also possible for the prices of commodities to change without resulting in a change in their value of exchange or value of benefit. The price of a commodity is only one of its values; it is the value of a commodity relative to money. Naturally, the price has become the de facto scale for deciding whether a thing is beneficial or not and for defining the degree of benefit of that thing. The commodity or the service is considered productive or beneficial if the society puts a high price for this commodity or service. The degree of benefit of this commodity or service is measured by the price which the majority of the consumers agree to pay for possessing or utilizing it. Products and services evaluated by a price can be any commodity or service: agricultural or industrial product; the service is that of a trader or transportation company, doctor or engineer.

Is the Value of a Product Virtual or Real?

The value of a commodity under capitalism is a relative (virtual) one and not absolute. The value of a loaf of bread, for example, is its marginal benefit assuming that the bread is abundant in the market; this is based on the diminishing marginal utility concept. When the loaf of bread is offered to one who is hungry and the bread is scarce, the value of the bread is too high. The value diminishes until it settles down when the people demanding the bread are no longer hungry and there is enough bread for those who want to acquire it. So the value (which is the benefit of the product) needs to be estimated at the time when the demand for the product is the lowest and the supply of the product is plentiful.

The product also has another value, which is the exchange value. The exchange value is the quantity of commodities and efforts that could be exchanged in return for the loaf of the bread. The value becomes a price if what is obtained for the loaf of the bread is money. These two values, under capitalism, are separate, and have two distinct names, benefit and the value of exchange or money.

This definition of value is inaccurate. Note that in both views of the value (benefit and the price), the estimator is measuring the value relative to the consumer. This view does not provide any measure of the benefit of the product itself. In case of the loaf of bread, the definition of value does not refer to the inherent benefit in the bread in the sense that bread has a property of satisfying the hunger. In reality, the value of the bread is the quantity of benefit in it. When this quantity is measured, the element of scarcity should be taken into consideration, but it should not define the value. This view of the value (quantity of benefit embedded in the product) holds whether the product is possessed through hunting, manufacturing, farming, selling, or buying. The benefit remains the same whether this was related to the person or related to another thing, whether the product is plentiful or scarce. Indeed, value is a name for a specific thing which has a specific reality; it is not a name for a relative thing, which varies over time and from one condition to another. In other words, the value should be an objective measurement of benefit and not a relative one.

The capitalist definition of value is a major flaw and it is fundamental to the political economy of capitalism. This view has led to the creation of a virtual economy which gives the illusion that the economy is far greater in size than what the real economy is or should be. The phenomenon of virtual economy will be further discussed in subsequent sections.

The marginal utility value is an estimation which is used to help regulate production on the basis of the worst-case scenario of distributing the commodities. Thus the value of a commodity is estimated based on the lowest limit of its consumption so that production proceeds on a guaranteed basis. The marginal utility is not really the value of the commodity; it is the market estimation of the need for that product, so it is a measure of the demand for the product rather than a measure of the benefit of the product, which is the real value. The value (benefit) of a product would not drop if its price decreases, nor would it rise if its price increases; that is because the value should be estimated at the time of evaluating the product's value.

The capitalist definition of the value according to the diminishing marginal utility creates the illusion that the value of a product increases as its price increases and conversely, it decreases when its prices decreases. This illusion has helped create a category of customers willing to pay high prices for products under the assumption that the value of the products is high. Therefore, the marginal utility theory should be viewed as a theory for price rather than a theory for value. Advocates of capitalism recognize the difference between price and value, although they claim that price is just another type of value. The estimation of price is governed by the abundance of demand together with the shortage of supply or the abundance of supply together with the shortage of demand; thus price is related to the level of production of a commodity. However, the value of a product should be defined and estimated by the quantity of benefit present in the commodity at the time of evaluation, bearing in mind the element of scarcity; so supply and demand do not utterly affect the value; rather they affect the price.

As such, the subject of value as discussed in the political economy of capitalism is flawed at the level of its definition. Any subject based on this definition will be flawed as well since the basic concept is false.

Note that the benefit of a product can be measured in terms of the benefit of another product or effort; such an evaluation would be correct and would lead to much greater stability over the short term. If the value is estimated by the price, then the evaluation would be relative, not real, and may fluctuate over time according to the market. What fluctuates is the price only, not the value of the product. The use of the price is a means to obtain money according to the market and not according to the benefit inherent in the product.

The capitalists as well as communist scholars claim that benefits are the result of the labor which man exerts. This view is also incorrect because it totally ignores the initial benefit inherent in the raw materials. Raw materials such as oil, gas, gold, silver, and many others have inherent benefits which distinguish their values from other materials irrespective of the human efforts. A jeweler spends the same effort making rings out of silver and gold. The value of the gold ring and the silver ring are different; the benefit of the gold and the silver rings is estimated collectively by the society. Obviously, the effort of the jeweler is not a factor in the process of estimation.

Rivers, forests, oceans, wind (for wind energy), sun (for solar energy) all carry benefit which can be recognized and evaluated by the people in the society. The ability of wind to produce energy is a benefit that has been recognized and utilized for centuries. Human did not contribute to this benefit. The same applies for the energy internally present in the sun heat. All of these are examples where the real value of things is inherently built in the objects as they were created by God. The Quran depicts this inherent benefits in certain things allowing them to be of a certain value for people (Quran14:32):

> *Allah is He Who created the heavens and the earth, and caused water to descend from the sky, thereby producing fruits as food for you, and made the ships to be of service unto you, that they may run upon the sea at His command, and hath made of service unto you the rivers*

3.3. The Price Mechanism

The price (the monetary exchange value of a product) plays an important role in the process of production, consumption, and distribution of products and services through what capitalists call "the price mechanism." This is another fundamental principle of capitalism. Adam Smith was the first to refer to the price mechanism when he wrote of the "invisible hand of the price mechanism"[34]. He described how the invisible or hidden hand of the market operates in a competitive market through the pursuit of self-interest to allocate resources in society's best interest. This remains the central view of all free-market economists, i.e., those who believe in the virtues of a free-market economy with minimal government intervention. This is the essence of the political economics of capitalism.

The price mechanism decides which of the producers will enter the production race and which will be excluded. In the same manner, it decides which of the consumers will satisfy their needs and which consumers will not be able to do so. The production cost of a commodity is the principal factor which controls its supply to the market. The benefit of the commodity is the principal factor which controls the market demand for the product. Both values are measured by the price. The supply and demand concept thus becomes a cornerstone in the study of capitalism. Supply refers to the supply of the market, and demand refers to the demand of the market. Both supply and demand are tightly coupled with "price"; hence, the price mechanism is fundamental to the economy of capitalism. Demand changes inversely proportional to the change in price. If price increases, then demand decreases; if price decreases, then demand increases. This is contrary to supply which changes directly proportional to the price. The level of supply increases as the price increases and it drops as price decreases. In both cases, price has the greatest effect on supply and demand; consequently, it has the greatest effect on production and consumption.

The price mechanism under capitalism plays a major role as well in the distribution of commodities and services amongst individuals in a society. According to the "price mechanism," the ideal method to distribute commodities and services in a society is that which guarantees the highest possible level of production, which also guarantees the highest level of compensation for the efforts of production. When this relationship between production (supply) and consumption (demand) is violated, an imbalance occurs in the system; this could be a dormant fault of the capitalist political economy.

Capitalism claims that the price mechanism produces economic equilibrium automatically. It gives the consumers the choice to decide for themselves the distribution of the resources owned by the society over the various economic activities. This is accomplished when the consumers demand some commodities and turn away from others. The consumers spend their income (which they obtained by means of exchanging their goods or efforts) by buying what they need or what they desire. Thus, the consumer who dislikes wine will abstain from buying it and spends his income on other things. If the number of consumers who dislike wine increases, or if all consumers come to dislike it, then the production of wine becomes unprofitable due to decrease in the demand. Thus, production of wine would stop in a natural way. The same rule applies to other commodities and services. By deciding what to buy and what to leave, the consumers define the level and kind of production.

The price mechanism is one of the main pillars of capitalism; it is considered to be the incentive for production, the regulator of distribution, and the link between the producer and the consumer; in essence it is the means for achieving equilibrium between production and consumption.

It is maintained that the principal motive for man to undertake any productive effort or sacrifice is his material reward. Capitalism excludes the possibility that man expends effort for a moral or spiritual motive. The moral motive, if it exists at all, is attributed to a materialist compensation (think of tax incentives).

Man expends his efforts to satisfy his materialistic needs and wishes only. This satisfaction is either through the consumption of commodities which he produces directly or through receiving a monetary reward that enables him to obtain the commodities and services produced by others.

Since man depends in satisfying most of his needs, if not all of them, on exchanging his efforts with others, then the satisfaction of needs is focused on obtaining a monetary reward for his efforts. This monetary reward allows him to obtain commodities and services, and accordingly man does not have to focus entirely on the commodities which he produces. Therefore, the monetary reward, which is the price, is the motive for man to produce. This is how "the price" is considered the incentive for production.

Besides being an incentive for production, the price also regulates distribution. In the normal case, man likes to satisfy all of his needs completely and he strives to obtain the commodities and services which satisfy these needs. If man is left free to satisfy his needs, he would not stop short of possessing and consuming whatever commodity he likes. Because of the limitation of man's capabilities and the scarcity of resources, man has to stop satisfying his needs at a certain limit. This is the limit at which he can afford to exchange his efforts with others efforts, that is, at the limit of the monetary compensation which he receives for expending his effort; this is the limit of the price.

The price provides a constraint which acts naturally to restrict man's possession and consumption to a level which is proportional to his income. The price regulates man's choice between competing needs; he proceeds to satisfy what he finds necessary and leaves what he finds of less importance. Thus, the price forces the individual to settle for partial satisfaction of some of his needs at the expense of others. This is how the price regulates the consumption of utilities by individuals. Indebtedness within capitalism has been used to expand the consumers' abilities to consume more products than they could afford without borrowing money. Indebtedness within capitalism has grown to be a dominant phenomenon after the widespread use of the credit system.

The price also regulates the distribution of limited utilities amongst the consumers who demand these utilities. The disparity between the incomes of the consumers leads to a variation in the level of consumption by people based on their incomes. More pricy commodities will be available only to those who can afford them; less pricy commodities would be consumed by people who can afford the lower prices. The price, thus, becomes the regulator in distributing utilities amongst consumers by setting a high price for some commodities and services and a low price for others.

The price mechanism is also responsible for achieving equilibrium between production and consumption by establishing a link between the producer and the consumer. The producer makes products to fulfill the desires of the consumers; he is rewarded through profits. The producer would lose if the products are not accepted by the consumers. The producer detects the desires of the consumers through the price. If the price of a commodity increases as a result of increased demand, the production increases as well.

Conversely, production decreases if the price drops due to a decrease in the market demand. The response of the market to the price increase and decrease due to variations in the demand makes the price mechanism a tool which achieves equilibrium between production and consumption and a link between the producer and the consumer; this process occurs automatically without the need of external intervention. This is the essence of the price mechanism in the political economy of capitalism. It constitutes a cornerstone of the economy. The failure of the price mechanism to achieve the desired objectives of equilibrium, wealth distribution, and balanced economy is detrimental to the foundation of capitalism.

Price Mechanism: Does It Really Regulate the Market?

Based on the price mechanism theory, the capitalist economists conclude that the ideal method to distribute the wealth among the members of society is that which guarantees the highest possible level of production; the products will naturally be distributed through the price of products. The production increases when the reward for the efforts exerted by the producer increases. The underlying assumption here is that the benefit of products is the result of man's efforts only. But this is not always true. Benefits initially are found in products in their most basic and raw form as created by God. The effort and labor of man help transfer the raw materials after certain types of processing to a form and shape usable or desirable by the consumer. It is not accurate to say that the benefit of a product is entirely created by man. In fact, there are certain raw materials which carry benefit without the least amount of efforts from man. The best and simplest examples are the air, water, meadows, forests, and many others. So, considering the benefit as a result of human efforts only is inaccurate; it neglects the raw material and other readily available resources. Then, it is not accurate to claim that the price (which is the compensation for man's efforts) is the parameter which controls the level of production.

Similarly, the decline in the level of production does not result solely from a decrease in the reward for work. Production can decline as a result of the depletion of natural resources, decline in the wealth of the country, wars, natural disasters, or other reasons.

As an example, the decline of production in both Britain and France after the Second World War did not result from a reduction of the work reward; it resulted from the shrinkage in their influence over their rich colonies. It also resulted from their involvement in the war and their loss of strategic resources. Production decline in the United States during the Second World War did not result from a reduction in rewards for work done by producers; it resulted from its involvement in the war against Germany. The decline in production in the Islamic World today did not result from a reduction in the reward to work; it is the result of the intellectual decline into which the whole Muslim nation fell. Production decline in the United States in recent years is mainly due to outsourcing of manufacturing to India and China, and so on.

Therefore, the inadequacy of the reward to work is not the only reason for decline in production; it is, therefore, incorrect to assume (based on this premise) that the ideal method of distribution is to secure a rising level of production.

The claim that the primary motive for the person to expend his effort is the material monetary reward (price) is also incorrect. Man often expends effort in return for a moral reward such as the attainment of a reward from God, or for the sake of achieving ethical merit such as returning a favor. The needs of man can be materialistic such as material profit; they can be spiritual such as sanctification or moralistic such as praise. So taking into consideration materialistic needs only is incorrect.

It has become customary, even in capitalist societies, to motivate people for innovations through means other than the material rewards of bonuses and salary increases. Carly Fiorina, former CEO of Hewlett-Packard, used historical examples from the Islamic civilization to motivate HP engineers and scientists for inventions when she noted that the Islamic civilization was driven more than anything by invention[48].

The price is not the only incentive for production as proclaimed. A man could spend his resources in satisfying a spiritual or a moral need more generously than he spends in satisfying a materialistic one. A stonemason could designate himself to work for months in cutting stones for building a mosque or a church; a factory may assign its production for one or more days of the year as charity donation to poor people; a nation could allocate some or all of its efforts on preparing to defend its territories. Such production is not motivated by price. Moreover, the materialistic reward itself is not confined to price; it could come in the form of other commodities or services. Hence, considering the price as the only incentive for production is incorrect.

One of the great anomalies of capitalism is that it considers price as the only regulator for distributing wealth amongst the members of society. Price is considered the only constraint that forces the consumer to limit his possession and consumption based on his income; it is also the price which makes some people consume more or less than others based on their income. Price regulates the distribution of wealth amongst consumers, through the rise in the price of some goods and drop in the price of others, and in the availability of money to some people and its nonavailability to others. Thus, every individual's share of the wealth of a country is not based or equal to his basic needs; it is equal to the value of the services in which he has contributed in producing commodities and services; it is equal to what he owns of land or capital, or equal to what he carried out of work, and projects.

Based on this principle, which makes price the sole regulator of distribution, capitalism has effectively decreed that man would not be able to satisfy his needs except to the limit of his ability to contribute to the production of commodities and services. A person born with a physical or mental disability will not be able to satisfy his needs simply because he does not produce and does not earn money with which he can buy products to satisfy his basic needs. The purest form of capitalism driven by the price mechanism essentially denies some people the right to live.

On the other hand, a person who was born strong or born in a rather rich environment, and who is more able to create and possess wealth, satisfies his basic and luxurious needs; furthermore, he may practice control and mastery over others with his wealth. In the race to compete for wealth, it is only natural to expect a great disparity between some who acquire much more and others who acquire much less.

The one whose motivation to seek material gains is stronger will exceed others in possessing wealth. The greedy ones will acquire more wealth and try to prevent others from acquiring wealth, thus opening the door for monopoly. The one who adheres to spiritual and moral values (in the process of earning) will acquire less wealth than others. This method of wealth distribution ignores the significance of the spiritual and moral elements from life and produces a life built upon a materialistic struggle to gain the means of satisfying materialistic needs.

Wealth imbalance based on the price mechanism eventually occurs in all countries which adopt and apply capitalism. The domination of monopolies has developed in countries adopting capitalism, where the producers of goods and services exercise control over the consumers. Over the course of years of capitalism domination, the production of goods and service tends to accumulate in the hands of fewer and fewer people. A small group of people, such as the owners of large oil, automotive, and heavy industry corporations, have come to dominate consumers, reigning over them by imposing certain prices for the commodities they produce. In the US, the top 5% of the population owns more than 50% of the total national wealth, and the top 20% owns more than 80% of the total wealth.[138].

This major flaw in the origin of the system has called for patches in order to prevent the type of failure that the communist theoreticians predicted or the ones that the old Soviet Union socialists aggravated. The state (government) was given the right to intervene for price regulation and control in special circumstances to protect the national economy, to protect consumers, to reduce consumption of some commodities, and to break monopolies. Welfare programs are temporary patches aimed at supplementing the ability of the poorest segment to satisfy their basic needs. The bailout of failing businesses and consumers is another form of fixes used in capitalist societies. More on this will be discussed later.

These measures contradict the basis of capitalism, which is based on free-market rules driven by the relative scarcity, value, and price mechanism. Several capitalism economists do not adopt this interventionist approach (conservatives) and contend that the price mechanism alone is sufficient to achieve harmony between the interest of the producers and the interest of the consumers, without any need for governmental intervention. These patchwork solutions which are recommended by the interventionists Keynesian economists (liberals) are only applied in certain circumstances and conditions, and even in these circumstances, the distribution of wealth amongst the individuals does not achieve the complete satisfaction of all basic needs for each and every individual.

The poor distribution of commodities and services, which resulted from the concept of freedom of ownership and from the concept of making the price the only mechanism for distributing wealth, will continue to dominate every society that applies capitalism.

3.4. *Private Ownership in Capitalism*

Capitalism is a system based on the recognition of individual rights, including property rights, in which all property is privately owned[49]. Freedom of ownership resulted from the separation of church and state and the consequent development of the basic freedom(s) of man. Ayn Rand,[1] author of *The Fountainhead*, describes this relationship between private property ownership and the separation of church and state: "When I say capitalism, I mean a full, pure, uncontrolled, unregulated Laissez-faire

---

[1] Ayn Rand (1905-1982), philosopher and author of numerous books on individualism.

capitalism—with a separation of state and economics, in the same way and for the same reasons as the separation of state and church"[50].

The other extreme opposite to capitalism is socialism/communism which only recognizes the public or state ownership. Communist philosophers, especially Marx, criticized the private ownership under capitalism and considered this type of ownership to be the root cause of all evils in a society. When socialism takes over a society, its first task will be the confiscation of the property of individuals and to transfer it to public property under the control of the state. The communists go all the way to deny the basic human need and aspiration for ownership; they claim that the striving of individuals to own things is a mere reflection of the bourgeois mentality and influence over the society.

The communist view of private ownership contradicts the natural behavior of humans. It is part of man's nature to work and possess property in order to satisfy his needs; hence, it is only natural to strive for the possession of property. Satisfying man's needs is an inevitable matter that cannot be denied or ignored. Any attempt to prevent man from possessing wealth would be contradictory to his nature; similarly, any attempt to restrict his possession to a certain quantity would also contradict his nature. It would, therefore, be unnatural to stand between man and his acquisition of wealth, or to stand between him and his efforts to achieve this acquisition. One obvious reason for the short-lived socialism is its conflict with the human natural strives for private ownership.

Possession and ownership is not a reflection of societal order as claimed by Marxists. Rather, it is a manifestation of the inner instinct of survival which exists within man, right at birth time. The society with all the ideas, concepts, orders, traditions, and values direct the possession quality into different directions. Agricultural societies direct the possession instinct to the ownership of land; hunting communities direct this instinct to the ownership of bows and arrows and other means of hunting; industrial societies direct the possession attribute of the instinct to own machines, factories, and other means of production. In all of these cases, the society does not create the love to own within individuals as proclaimed by Marxist theoreticians; rather it steers that love in one direction or another.

The problems associated with the private ownership as observed by many, particularly the communist philosophers, do not arise from the private possession per se, whether the possession of commodities or possession of means of production. The problem actually arises from considering private ownership to be the only form of ownership in the society[49]. Public or state ownership is not recognized in the core foundation of capitalism. Every time a need rises for the state to own property (such as land, banks, factories), a big debate takes place; on one end, purist capitalists (supporters of laissez-faire capitalism) detest such ownership. On the other end, pragmatists allow state ownership in response to crisis. The most current economic crisis led the US government to intervene and own large portions of banks, insurance companies, and auto industry.

The Capitalists' denial of public or state property is based on their view of the society as discussed earlier. This view considers the society to be composed of individuals who are allowed to live, own, speak, and behave as freely as possible. Hence, the public property under this view is meaningless. The society, however, is not merely made of group of individuals. The society structure includes, besides the individuals, the relations and the systems that link the people together and provide the society its own distinct shape. This view of the society gives rise to two other distinct entities in the society: the public as a whole with the various types of links and relations and the state which maintains these relations and links through the law and order of the society. Each of these entities—the individual, the public, and the state—has its own characteristics, needs, interest, and behavior.

The individual has needs for food, drink, safety, shelter, health, rests, and others. He needs to acquire and possess the means to satisfy these needs. The interests of the individuals are best served by the individual property ownership. The public as a whole has needs for coherency, security, unity, and others. The public needs to acquire and possess the means to satisfy these needs; the public interests are best served through the public ownership of property. The state as a unit has needs for stability, security, order maintenance, protection, balance creation, and other needs. The state must acquire and possess the means to satisfy its needs. Therefore, the main problem with the capitalist view of ownership is that it recognizes only the private ownership of individuals. The communists made the same error, except that they approved only the public ownership and denied the private ownership; they allowed the state to own in its capacity as a representative of the public. In fact, the communists believe that the state has a temporary existence in the society; at advanced stages of communism, the state should dissolve, and the only property that remains is that of the public.

Problems occur when each entity in the society violates the property rights of the other entities. For example, when the property which belongs to individuals is confiscated by the public and state under the umbrella of nationalization, problems begin to surface: fraud, corruption, and lack of productivity. When the property which should be owned by the public is overtaken by individuals, the problems of fraud, poverty, and monopoly begin to surface. When the state property is overtaken by individuals, the state becomes dependent on the wealth of individuals and falls into debt; as a result, the political decisions of the state become more biased towards those who finance the state. This phenomenon leads to oppression, corruption, and a loss of law and order.

This argument leads to the main conclusion that private ownership is a valid concept in the society; however, this ownership is not absolutely free. Private ownership should be limited to the scope of private ownership which is limited and restricted by the scope of the public and the state ownership.

Nationalization of private property as well as privatization of public property are counterproductive and constitute an invasion to the rights of individuals and to the interest of the public. Nationalization leads to illegal restriction of private property and creates a myriad of problems, the least of which is corruption and diminished productivity. Privatization of public property, on the other hand, deprives the less fortunate in the society from securing their basic needs for food, health, education, and security.

The proper way of organizing the ownership is to define the scope of ownership for each entity: the individuals, the public, and the state. A clear borderline between the ownership of these entities should be well established. Note that the borderlines define the type of ownerships for each entity; the quantity of ownership within each scope is irrelevant and should not be restricted. It does not pay to transfer ownership between the three entities based on conditions and crisis. In fact, the transfer of private property ownership to public or state ownership under the pressure of crisis leads to the situation where the state and public become the owners of property that should be owned only by individuals, and the individuals become the owners of property that should be owned only by the public.

Perhaps the most important characteristic of the Islamic political economy is that it clearly defined the scopes of the three types of ownership. It further prohibited the transfer of one type of ownership into another no matter what the conditions are. The ownership under Islamic economics will be further discussed in the part 2 of this book.

In summary, capitalism and its political economy are built upon three main principles: relative scarcity, the benefit and exchange value, and the price mechanism, the price mechanism being the cornerstone of this foundation. These principles are wrapped within the main concept of "private property ownership" which in turn emits from the idea of the separation of church and state. These principles along with the basic idea of private ownership have serious flaws and defects as discussed in the preceding sections. Next, we will explore the impact of these flaws on the well-being of the society.

4

Capitalism in Action: Performance Scoreboard

The success or failure of an economic system should be measured by the direct impact it has on the life of the people who live under that economic system. Measures of economic growth, wealth expansion, and financial stability should be correlated to the plights of people in the society. The impact of the economic system, in this case capitalism, should be measured by the level of security and satisfaction provided to the people. The security and satisfaction are further measured in terms of food security, education security, health security, and physical security. Another measure of the stability of the system is the moral, ethical, and ideological conviction and trust in the economic foundation.

Two major systems have dominated the world arena in the last one hundred years, namely, capitalism and socialism. Socialism collapsed before the end of the twentieth century with a complete failure and hence will not be discussed in this book except where it is needed to clarify a concept.

After the collapse of socialism, capitalism proceeded to dominate the entire globe; different flavors of capitalism exist in different parts of the world. Even socialist China has adopted a cocialist brand of capitalism. After the collapse of Soviet Leninist socialism, capitalism had entered the era of *global economy*, more officially known as *globalization*. Globalization extended the impact and influence of capitalism to almost every corner of the world. The most recent financial crisis, which started in the United States, rippled through Europe, Japan, China, the Middle East, and Africa. The study of the impact of capitalism is not constrained to a particular nation; rather its impact is observed globally.

The responsibility of capitalism to the economic situation of the world at large is an acknowledged fact. Globalization has made world capitalism the de facto economic system of the world. The activities of the World Bank and the International Monetary Fund (IMF), the two main instruments of the capitalist world, are directly and indirectly responsible for the economic conditions in the developing world.

The relation between poverty in the world at large and the capitalist instrument, the IMF is reflected in numerous cases and stories. One of such cases stands clear in the recent Haiti rice crisis. The Haiti rice crisis is narrated in a moving article, published by Inter Press Service (IPS), a communication institution with focus on development and globalization in the south[62].

The article reports on a woman with three children who says that she can no longer afford to purchase rice to feed her three children in a country which once was one of the largest rice producers in the world. The mother of three explains the dilemma: a little can of rice alone costs sixty-five cents, oil is twenty-five cents, and charcoal is twenty-five cents. With dollar twenty-five cents (the absolute poverty line set by the UN), you can't even make a rice meal for one child. Haiti, the hemisphere's poorest country, imports most of the food it consumes; this is the result of free-market policies that have undermined national production. The president of Haiti René Préval recognized that "cheap imported rice destroyed nationally grown rice"[62]. Thirty years ago, Haiti produced nearly all the rice it consumed. But in the late 1980s, cheap imported US rice flooded the country after a military junta began liberalizing the economy with support from the International Monetary Fund (IMF).

The first batches of imported rice were escorted by armed convoys. Rice farmers regarded the imported US rice as a threat to their production and livelihoods. As it turned out, their concerns were justified. In 1994, an IMF-sponsored plan cut tariffs on imported rice from 35% to 3%, the lowest in the region. In one year, the amount of rice imports doubled.

While the US government subsidizes its own rice farmers, its Haitian counterpart was prohibited from doing so under the terms of their agreement with the IMF. Over the last twenty years, rice production in Haiti has been cut in half, while imports now dominate the market. For many people in Haiti, undernutrition and starvation is the only remaining option.

By the end of the twentieth century, twenty to thirty million people around the world were estimated to have lost their land under the impact of trade liberalization and export agriculture[63]. The US international food aid program, formalized in 1954 as Public Law 480, dominated the food trade landscape over the next two decades. US-managed food surpluses were distributed to states regarded as future customers. This food export regime indeed undermined local farmers with low-priced staple foods[64].

The main instruments of influencing the local economies worldwide have been the World Bank and the IMF through what is known as the Structural Adjustment Programs (SAPs). Formulated as loan conditions, SAPs mandated macroeconomic policy changes that obligate recipient nations to liberalize their trade and investment policies. As a result, governments reduced tariffs on imported goods, lifted subsidies on local products, particularly food, moved large acreage land from farming into mining and oil exploration, and plunged the nations into difficulty to repay loans. The end result is dependence on imported foods and supplies by giant capitalist corporations.

The dominance of capitalism in the world and its impact on world economic conditions are observed in prevalent poverty, hunger, health epidemics, and much more.

The discussion of the basic principles of capitalism and its political economy revealed several defects and flaws at the core of the system, particularly the principles of scarcity, value, price, and private ownership. The implementation of a system with major flaws is expected to produce over time several anomalies, crises, and pitfalls in the life of people living under such system. This conclusion follows from the fault-error-failure model discussed in section.2. It is also supported by observations and real-life statistics and data.

In the next sections, we will examine actual data from the contemporary world conditions under capitalist economic system. The data shows that the theoretical flaws of the major economic principles have led to serious errors that continue to cause huge catastrophic effects on very large segment of the population in the world. Continuous attempts and forced intervention through bailouts and government buyout of failing economic entities are sought to contain the impact of the crisis, hoping to prevent a complete collapse and failure of the entire system of capitalism.

4.1 Poverty and Gross National Product

The original theory of capitalism calls for the increase in production and consequently the increase in the wealth of nations. It further claims that the increased production coupled with the dynamics of supply and demand and the price mechanism will guarantee the best distribution of the produced wealth to the members of the society. Production of wealth under capitalism has continuously risen over the past one hundred years, with few exceptions during world wars. In the meantime, the number of people who are classified as poor based on local national and international standards continued to be indifferent to the wealth growth. This phenomenon is a worldwide phenomenon which includes extremely rich nations such as the USA as well as extremely poor nations such as Haiti and the sub-Saharan Africa.

In a statement made by the heads of state and government at one of the World Food Summits of the Food and Agriculture Organization (FAO), they expressed their deep concern over the persistence of hunger which constitutes a threat both to national societies and to the stability of the international community itself[51]. According to the statement, "it is intolerable that more than 800 million people throughout the world, and particularly in developing countries, do not have enough food to meet their basic nutritional needs." The leaders confirm that food supplies have increased substantially, but poverty and hunger continue to persist. Despite their recognition that food supply has increased without reducing hunger, they insisted that the solution will be more of the same "increased food production."

In this declaration, the leaders of the world confirm the existence of a serious problem in poverty and hunger. In the meantime, they continue to declare that the solution is to increase the resources and products. They should have noted that the defect is not in the productivity of food; rather it is the mechanism of its distribution that fails to enable each and every person to have the proper access to food, commodities, and services. The mechanism of distribution of the resources remains unchanged. The end result will continue to be the same. The production of resources will increase the wealth of the already wealthy, but will not benefit those who need these resources the most.

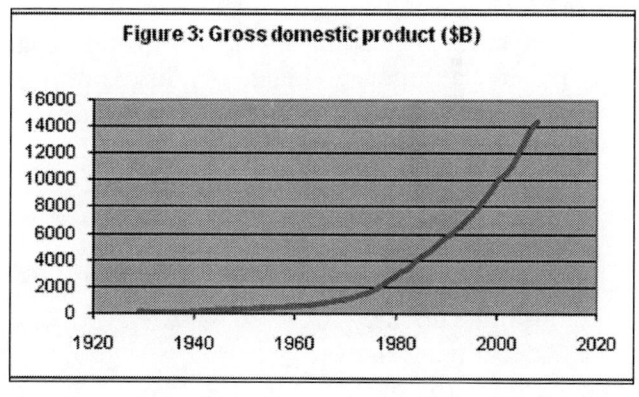

Figure 3: Gross domestic product ($B)

In fact, the gross national or domestic product of individual nations as well as of the world at large has been on the rise for decades. Figure 3 shows the increase in GNP figures for the United States since 1929[52]. Except for a short period of time, the GNP has always increased. After 1970, the GNP began to increase at exponential rates; this is the time when the United States departed away from the gold standard; more on this later. The current GNP in the United States exceeds fourteen trillion dollars.

The poverty numbers and rates in the United States are shown in figure 4. Note that the number of poor people continued to increase after 1970 despite the fact that the total wealth in the country was increasing at an exponential rate. The poverty rates continue to average around 12.5% despite the tremendous wealth increase (from $1 trillion in 1970 to $14.5 trillion in 2008).

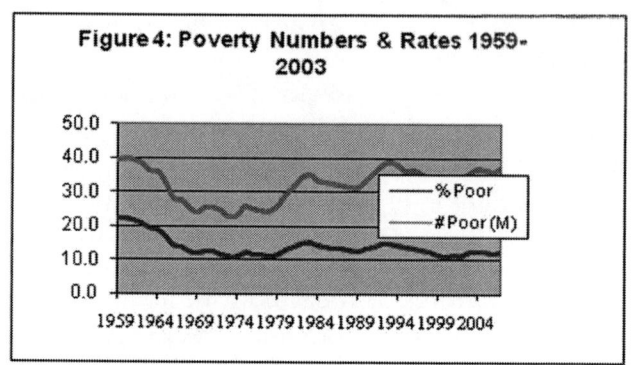

Figure 5 contrasts the wealth increase in the United States with the poverty rates. Note how the wealth continues to increase while the number of poor people remains averaged around thirty million people. These figures pertain to the United States, the richest country in the world and the leader of capitalism.

The impact of capitalism on the world at large is more devastating. The poverty numbers and rates are disheartening. This fact is recognized by world leaders, world institutions and organizations such as the World Bank, the FAO, and others.

Poverty is said to exist when a person earns less money than he actually needs to fulfill his basic needs. This definition is consistent with the capitalist view of the price and its role in determining who would be able to

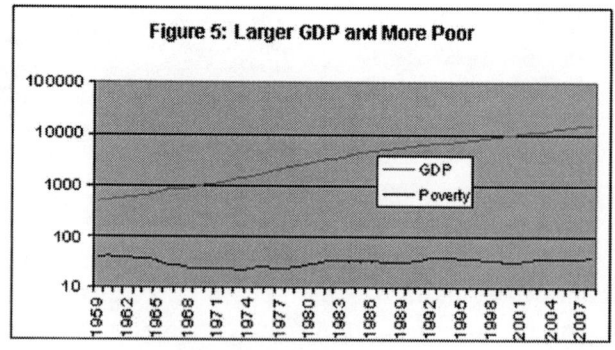

satisfy his needs and who would not. A person who earns less money (price for his efforts or trade) than the price of the goods he needs to fulfill his needs is a poor one. Hence, one way to measure poverty is to collect data on people who earn less than

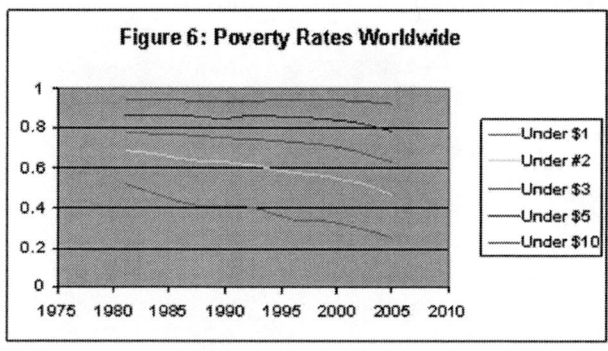

one, two, or more dollars per day. World Bank figures show that in 1981 there were 1.899 billion people whose income was less than $1 a day. This number was reduced to 1.374 billion in 2005. When the poverty line goes up to two, three, five, or ten dollars per day, the state of the world under capitalism becomes absolutely frightening. Figure 6 presents poverty data for several poverty lines[53]. Note that except for the $1 data, the number of poor people continued to stay above 40% of the world population.

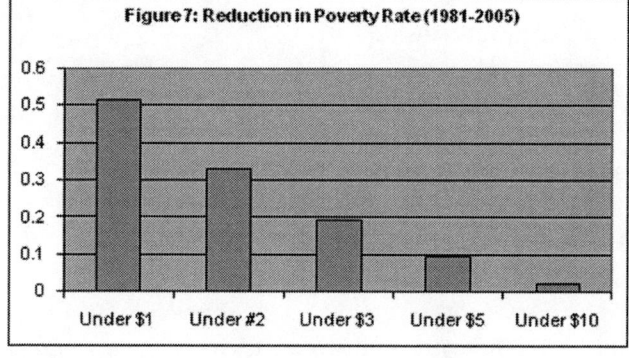

Figure 7 shows the reduction of poverty rates over the years (1981-2005). The largest reduction is in the number of people who earned less than $1 a day; the rate of people living under $1 a day was reduced by half over twenty-five years (50% to 25%). Very little improvement was observed for people who earned five or ten dollars a day. In 1981, 95% of the world population excluding the United States and Western Europe lived under $10 a day; twenty-five years later, this percentage was reduced only to 93%. Over the same period, prices and inflation have soared worldwide.

In other words, the 50% of those who used to earn $1 in 1981 and moved to the $2 bracket are not necessarily better off. The Bureau of Labor Statistics in the United States uses a calculating tool to compute the consumer price index (CPI) inflation rate[54]. Using this calculator, what $1 could buy in 1981 requires $2.15 in 2005. In other words, the people who lived under $1 in 1981 continue to be in the same poverty status in 2005 even though half of them now live on $2 a day. The consumer price index for the period 1947-2009 is shown in figure 8. Note how sharply the prices increased after 1972 (this is the time when the United States departed from the gold standard).

Peter Rosset, director of Institute for Food and Development Policy in California, clearly states that the food resources of the world are abundant rather than scarce[83]. In his book[83] he declares that "the belief that world hunger can be solved by increasing food production is an unsubstantiated myth. The real problem is poverty."

Hunger: Food Insecurity

Perhaps the most devastating result of poverty is hunger. Quite often people refer to poverty simply in terms of people who earn less than a predetermined amount of money. The problem becomes really serious when the poor actually remains unable to fill his stomach with the

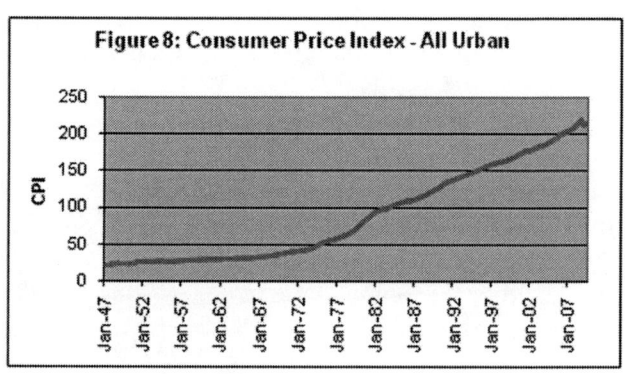

necessary food to sustain a decent life. Capitalism as a system does not address the issue of hunger. In fact, the principles of capitalism give rise to the possibility that individuals in a society will not be able to satisfy some of their needs; these needs could very well be the need for food, which is necessary to eliminate hunger. Capitalism speciously claims that there is not enough resources (in this case food) to feed each and every hungry stomach. In response to the phenomenon of hunger under capitalism, many institutions were created to fight hunger. The existence of such institutions within the societies of capitalism is a simple proof that capitalism as a system not only fails to resolve the epidemic problem of hunger, but in fact it causes this problem. Islam, on the other hand (as will be discussed later), calls for the elimination of hunger and makes this call a fundamental principle of Islam. Prophet Mohammad is reported to have said, "Allah and his Messenger will disown a community which allows one of its members to sleep hungry"[55].

Despite the tremendous growth in the economy and the wealth of the United States, the Physician Task Force on Hunger in America (established in early 1984) concluded that hunger is a problem of epidemic proportions across the nation; it is getting worse, not better. They further concluded that present policies are not alleviating hunger in America[56]. This fact can be hardly accepted by many, as argued by Ardis Armstrong Young[57]. He raises the question "Why do Americans allow people to go hungry when they can grow enough food to feed the world and they waste more food than the hungry could eat?"

Larry Brown, director of the National Center on Hunger and Poverty, summarized the hunger problem in the United States in his book *Hunger in America: The Growing Epidemic*[58], where he writes:

> *We are the richest nation in the history of the world with millions of people going hungry and wondering where their next meal is coming from and we're still unable to rid our society of this scourge.*
>
> *The U.S. is not the only nation where people go hungry but it is the only wealthy industrial nation where such a high percentage of its population suffers from nutritional deprivation due to inadequate incomes. Nearly one in five children, in our nation, lives below the poverty level—we have more than enough food to end this problem—the real issue is not whether America can end hunger, the question is whether we have the leadership to do so.*

The only issue with Brown's conclusion is that he thinks that the resolution of hunger is a political issue, where political leaders can instill programs to deal with hunger. This illusion resulted from the fact that hunger was eliminated in the 1970s due to policies adopted in the early 1960s. When those policies were either changed or removed during the Reagan administration, hunger crawled back[57]. However, what should be noted is that there is an internal and intrinsic reason for poverty and hunger to exist because of the underlying economic principles. Administrative programs, policies, and regulations as well as charity organizations can reduce the scale of the problem, suppress it for some time, or hide it. However, these policies and programs do not eliminate the root cause of the problem; so once they are lifted or reduced, hunger immediately pumps up. When the Reagan administration cut seven billion dollars from the food stamp program in 1981, hunger related problems such as anemia, tuberculosis, poor growth, and osteoporosis crawled back immediately.

The way governments in capitalist states deal with the problem of hunger is similar to someone who detects a gas leak in a house and goes to find a nice and good filter to clean up and filter out the gas from the air instead of finding the leak source and fixing it altogether. The moment the filter is removed or fails to do its job properly, the gas immediately fills the house! Using the same analogy, the policies and regulations are used to filter out hunger and feed the hungry. The cause of hunger remains dormant in the basic principles of the economic system: food is relatively scarce. Price dictates the output of the production, determines the amount of consumption, and decides who could or could not eat. It is no surprise then that one of the definitions found for hunger in the *Oxford English Dictionary* in 1971 is "the want or scarcity of food in a country."

Hunger in the World

If hunger is a problem with epidemic proportions in the United States, the richest country in the world, then what proportions does hunger have in Haiti, Bangladesh, Kenya, and the rest of the developing and underdeveloped world? The statistics on world hunger are shocking, startling, and terrifying. The magnitude of the problem is signified when we know that the wasted resources and food in the world are more than sufficient to feed the hungry. Time and again, it is clear that the mechanism of distribution that is failing; it is not the insufficiency of the resources.

According to published data and statistics on hunger by World Bank and other organizations, one person every other second dies out of hunger and malnutrition, 85% of these are children. In the Asian, African, and Latin American countries, well over 1.3 billion people are still living in what the World Bank has called absolute poverty (below $1 a day)[53], which results in various types of illnesses, malnutrition, and potential death. In a statement made by the secretary general of the United Nations Ban Ki-moon to the Millennium Development Goals report 2009[59], he says,

> We have been moving too slowly to meet our goals. And today, we face a global economic crisis whose full repercussions have yet to be felt. At the very least, it will throw us off course in a number of key areas, particularly in the developing countries. At worst, it could prevent us from keeping our promises, plunging millions more into poverty and posing a risk of social and political unrest.

The report further states that "major advances in the fight against extreme poverty from 1990 to 2005 are likely to have stalled. In 2009, an estimated 55 to 100 million more people will be living in extreme poverty."

Hunger in the developing world continues to prevail. Since 1990, more than 170 million children under five years have vanished due to poverty, hunger, undernutrition, and related diseases. The United Nations Food and Agriculture Organization (FAO) expects that more than one billion people will remain under extreme poverty and hunger conditions by 2015. Sub-Saharan Africa experiences the worst of such conditions, where 30% of its population faces the danger of hunger, undernutrition and potential death on a daily basis.

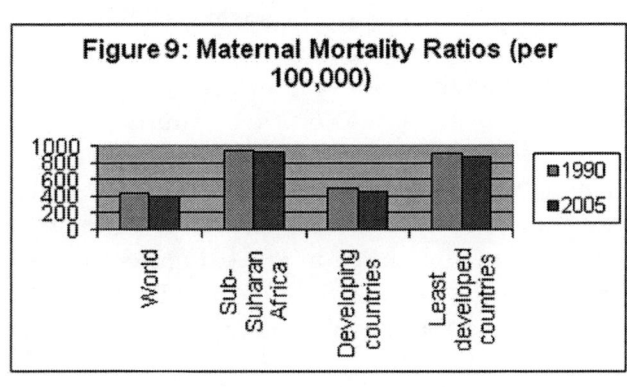

According to the World Health Organization[60], more than fifty thousand people die every day from poverty-related causes. The children are the largest segment hit by hunger with thirty thousand deaths daily according to UNICEF report[61].

Hunger deprives people, especially children, from receiving the necessary nutrition for growth. The impact of hunger on large populations is visible on the percentage of children under age five who are underweight. Thirty-one percent of children under five (that is, one out of every three children) in Asia, Africa, and Latin America were underweight in 1990. The status of children has not improved a lot since then; in 2007 more than 26% of the children in this region were still underweight and this rate is expected to rise even more due to the current financial crisis.

Footprints of poverty and hunger are visible in many aspects of the human life. Of particular significance is the maternal and neonatal (newborn babies less than twenty-eight days old) death rates shown in figure 9. The World Health Organization

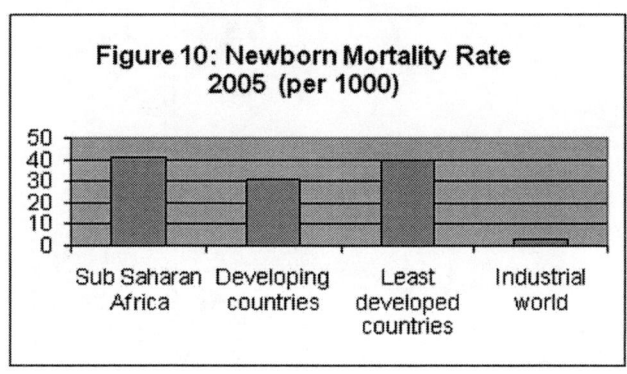

estimates more than five hundred thousand women die every year in the process of delivering children. The largest number of deaths occur in the sub-Saharan Africa (50% of the total), where the poverty rate is highest in the world.

The disparity between the well-being of mothers in industrial world and the developing world speaks for an out-of-balance distribution of resources. In Niger, for example, the country with the highest risk of maternal death, 1 out of 7 births will result in the death of the mother compared to 1 out of 47,600 in a country like Ireland.

By the same token, neonatal mortality (probability of newborn dying within twenty-eight days of birth) is expected to be very high due to extreme poverty and hunger. WHO estimates that around 3.7 million babies died after birth in 2004. Figure 10 illustrates the wide disparity between the poor and the rich worlds. Forty out of every 1,000 newborn babies die in the low-income regions compared to only 3 out of 1,000 in the industrial world.

Poverty and Education

Besides the direct impact on the life of women who give birth to children and the newborn babies, poverty and hunger impede the progress of nations by inhibiting education. Extreme poverty obstructs learning through poor nutrition, bad health, lack of books, insufficient lighting and places to do homework and parental poor education. Poverty increases the rate of dropout of schools. Lack of education constitutes an obstacle which prevents the acquisition of the necessary means for improving life quality.

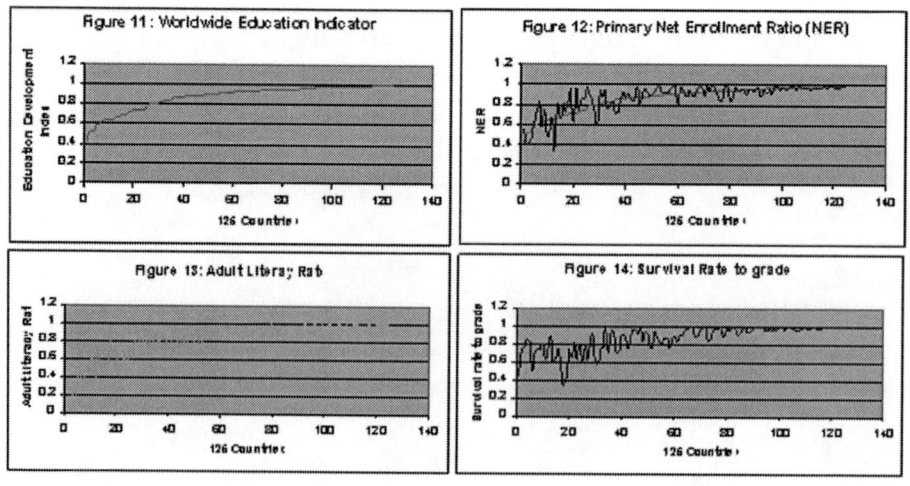

This leads to a cycle which proves to be too difficult to break: poverty impedes education, while lack of education sustains poverty. Extremely poor people have lesser chance of getting proper education, which is necessary to compete for jobs with more educated people; without proper employment, it is almost impossible to get out of the poverty plunge. Under the dominance of capitalism, the poor segments of the population are the least educated; and those with the least education are the poorest. Poverty and hunger affect the cognitive ability of children in schools. UNESCO reports show that underweight and stunted children due to poor nutrition cannot concentrate in school and are likely to drop out[61].

Current policies under the dominance of the system of capitalism have failed to break this cycle. Over the last few decades, the poor continued to lag behind in education, and the poverty rates continued to persist. Seventy-seven million children of primary school age in the developing world were not in school in 2007, 57% of them were girls[61]. Nearly a billion people entered the twenty-first century unable to read a book or sign their names.

The UNESCO Education for All (EFA) Global Monitoring Report[61] shows that "young children in greatest need, who also stand to gain the most, are unlikely to have access to education improvement programs." Coverage remains very low in most of the developing world and few programs exist for children under age three. The main barrier for education is poverty and hunger.

Figures (11-14) show education indicators in 125 countries based on UNESCO report[61]. All of the indicators show that the poorest countries lag behind in adult literacy, net enrolment ratios, and survival rate of students to grade 5; as a result, the education development indicator (EDI) for one-third of the nations of the world is below 80%, with countries like Chad, Niger, Burkina Faso, Mali, Guinea, and Mozambique having lower than 60%

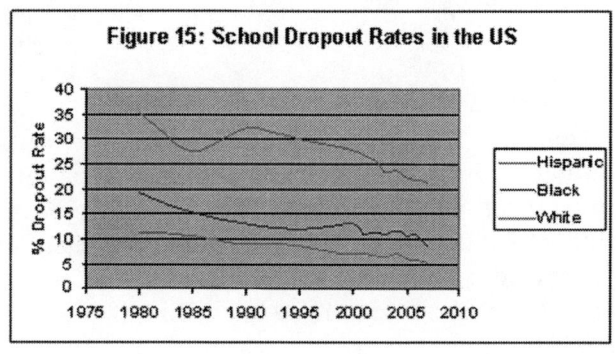

Figure 15: School Dropout Rates in the US

education index. The literacy rate in Chad and Niger is less than 30% of the total population. Given the strong correlation between poverty and education, it is very difficult to see an improvement in the well-being of the life of people in these African nations unless a serious change occurs in the method and style of wealth distribution in the world.

In the United States, the largest and richest cpitalist country, illiteracy continues to be as high as 14%, that is, one out of seven people lack the basic skills for reading[65]. Statistics show that the highest dropout rate from schools has been with the poorest communities in the United States, the Hispanic and black population. The ratio of dropouts between white, black, and Hispanics remained the same over the last thirty-five years, with Hispanics averaging 3.6 times more than whites, and the blacks are 1.5 times more than white dropouts (figure 15). This is further signified by the fact that 75% of the people receiving welfare aids in the United States cannot read[66].

4.2. Health Insecurity

Capitalism strikes again. The target this time, after hunger and education, is health. What ordinary people look for in an economic system is not the mere theories which substantiate the system and its foundation. Ordinary people at the end of the day want to be healthy with enough food on the table and a sense of security when they go to bed. A successful system is the one that removes from the people the fear of losing their ability to function due to epidemic diseases or losing their lives altogether.

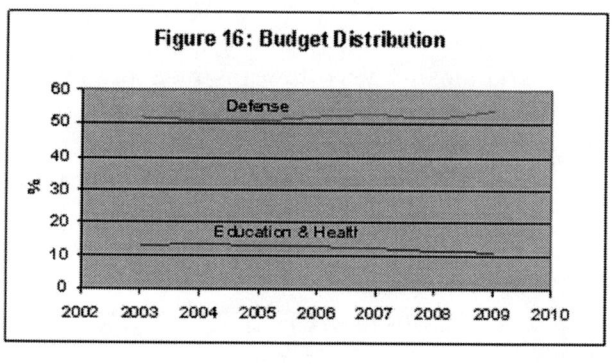

Despite the extraordinary growth in wealth and resources under capitalism, health insecurity continues to haunt individuals and nations across the globe. In America, the wealthiest capitalist nation in the world, health crisis continues to escalate over the years. Health crisis has become a permanent subject of debate during election times in the USA. It is estimated that a man during his lifetime has a chance of 44% to have one form of a cancer disease[68]. This rate is not slowing down; on the contrary, it has increased dramatically during the past few years. In other words, the tremendous growth in wealth and advancement in technology is not helping in fighting an enemy from within. Heart-related problems consume more than seven hundred thousands lives a year. According to the American Heart Association, 831,272 lives vanished due to heart related diseases in 2006. Such high rate of fatal diseases is not accidental. This is a direct by-product of systems which control wealth distribution and resource allocation. To see this imbalance of resource allocation, just look at one of the annual budgets and see how the resources are allocated. The curves in figure 16 show a breakdown of the discretionary budgets (budget subject to approval by Congress and the president) for the past seven years in the United States (69, 70). The United States spends on military more than 50% of its budget every year, whereas it spends less than 14% on the education and health needs. In the meantime, it is a well-known fact that epidemic diseases such as cancer, heart problems, diabetes, and others consume much more lives than all those who die in direct wars or indirect wars of terrorism.

Peter Jennings, the late ABC anchor, concludes in a documentary called "Breakdown—America's Health Insurance Crisis," that spiraling costs and the growing number of uninsured are all part of a health insurance system in a state of crisis[71]. According to the Agency for Healthcare Research and Quality, nearly fifty-four million Americans under age sixty-five, or 18% of the population under the age sixty-five, were without health insurance in 2007[72]. The current economic downturn will contribute seven more million to the army of uninsured Americans[73]; by 2010 there will be more than sixty million people without health insurance. The largest group of uninsured people belongs to the poorest segment of the population; 32% of the total number of people without insurance (fifteen million) is Hispanics.

The main reason for the increased number of uninsured people is poverty, which is reflected in the increased cost of health insurance and related premium compared to the wages and income of people. Even if employees are offered coverage on the job, they can't always afford their portion of the premium. Health insurance premiums have increased 119% for employees between 1999 and 2009[74], that is, three times more than the average increase in employee wages. The average wages increased only 35% between 1999 and

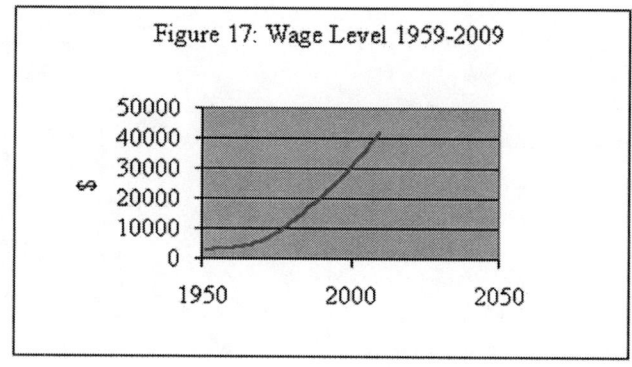
Figure 17: Wage Level 1959-2009

2008; see figure 17. Small firms refrain from offering health insurance due to rising health insurance premiums.

It is estimated that twenty-two thousand people die every year because they are unable to access reasonable health care resources. People without proper insurance receive less preventive care; they are diagnosed at more advanced stages of diseases and receive less therapeutic care. This leads to high mortality rates among uninsured individuals.

As in the case of education, lack of proper health care deepens poverty, and poverty dramatically reduces health care for individuals. In order to break this cycle, more needs to be done than simply increasing the supply of drugs, health equipment, and hospital beds. It is the mechanism for distributing these resources that enables individuals to receive the proper health care. The high cost of health care destroys the economic well-being of families. Medical bills have a major financial impact on 30% of low-income families without health coverage[75], pushing them into debt.

The disparity between those who have insurance and those who do not is growing more and more. As a result, the health divide has been widened in access to usual source of care, annual physical checkup, and preventive care.

Profits at ten of the country's largest publicly traded health insurance companies rose 428% from 2000 to 2007, while consumers paid more for less coverage. In 2008, the total profit of five insurance companies topped $7.8 billion.

Health Catastrophes in the Developing World

HIV/AIDS, malaria, and tuberculosis continue to be the most serious threat to the life of millions of people in the developing countries. The health care systems in developing countries have deteriorated to extreme levels such that these and other diseases have become so epidemic.

According to published data by UNAIDS/World Health Organization, the number of people diagnosed with AIDS in 2007 was more than 33 million people. More than 2 million of them died in the year 2007. More than

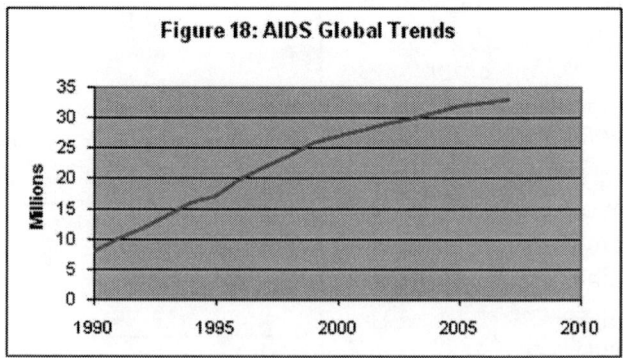

Figure 18: AIDS Global Trends

25 million people have died of AIDS since 1981. The majority of the AIDS victims are in the poorest part of the world in sub-Saharan Africa, where 22 million people live with the disease and 1.5 million have vanished as a result.

The epidemic of AIDS is growing worldwide despite the tremendous growth in wealth and health care facilities. Figure 18 shows the global trend in the AIDS epidemic. In some African countries, one out of three people carry the AIDS/HIV virus. More than 40% of the world population living in Nigeria, Ethiopia, Russia, China, and India face serious health risks due to spread of AIDS. Nigeria is projected to have 10-15 million cases by 2010, and Ethiopia 7-10 million. In both countries, the situation is likely to be aggravated by a lack of public health infrastructure due to extreme poverty. The AIDS population is expected to reach 10-15 million by 2010 in China and 20-25 million in India.

The main challenge for AIDS treatment in developing countries is the high cost of the treatment which amounts to $10,000-$15,000 per person per year. This high cost is barely affordable in highly developed nations; this is certainly the main barrier which prevents patients in the developing world from getting the proper treatment. Given the high poverty rates among the population of AIDS, it is difficult to see a break point in this catastrophic disease. Given the high poverty rate, a large percentage of the African nations will continue to face serious threats from AIDS. Unless the epidemic of poverty is resolved, the hope out of AIDS remains slim.

Poverty is also responsible for the majority of AIDS cases in the United States. Forty-nine percent of the total AIDS cases in the United States belong to the black population, which makes less than 15% of the total country's population. It is estimated that 22% of the African Americans with HIV do not have health insurance[76].

Tuberculosis (TB) is in a similar league as AIDS. One-third of the world's population is infected with TB. In 2002, there were 8.8 million new cases, and around 2 million deaths from TB. Asia and sub-Saharan Africa account for more than 84% (7.4 millions) of the new TB cases[77]. With the possible exception of measles, more persons in developing countries die from TB each year than from any other pathogen[78].

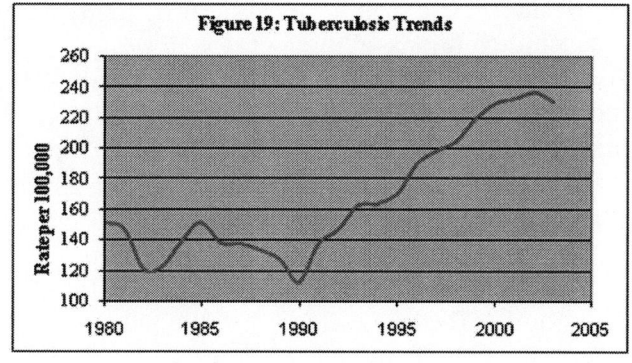

In the USA, the number of active tuberculosis cases began to rise in 1985 after it had declined continuously since the 1950s. Several factors were behind the return of tuberculosis, including the HIV/AIDS epidemic, increased poverty, IV drug use, and homelessness. It is worth noting that the Reagan administration cut 7 billion dollars from the food stamp program in 1981. Immediately after this cut, hunger-related problems such as anemia, tuberculosis, poor growth, and osteoporosis crawled back.

The Centers for Disease Control and Prevention (CDC) reported 14,093 cases of active tuberculosis (TB) in the United States in 2005, and 10 to 15 million people with latent tuberculosis. Thirty percent of those with latent TB infection will progress into active tuberculosis if they have diabetes, and almost all with HIV infection will progress into active TB. As in the case of AIDS, tuberculosis in the United States is highest among the poor population of the Hispanics (8.5 cases per 100,000) and the blacks (9.4 per 100,000) compared to whites (1.1 cases per 100,000).

There are cures, yet only around 37% of TB cases receive proper treatment due to a lack of resources and unreliable supplies of quality drugs. As a result, multidrug-resistant TB (MDR-TB) incidence is surging, with three hundred thousand new cases each year. MDR-TB is a hundred times more expensive to treat than normal TB. One more time, poverty and unbalanced distribution of resources is responsible for another disease of epidemic proportions. The World Health Organization (WHO) estimates that 36 million people will die of tuberculosis by 2020 if it is not controlled[79]. Figure 19 shows that TB cases continue to be on the rise; it is not slowing down.

Another major killer is malaria, and as with TB, drug resistance is a growing problem. WHO estimates that each year there are 300-500 million cases, with 1-3 million deaths—mostly children. The social and economic burden of such infection is catastrophic. Malaria continues to undercut sub-Saharan Africa's GDP per capita growth rates by some 1.3 percentage points per year.

Besides these main killers, there are many other diseases that continue to consume millions of human lives every year. Poverty, hunger, poor access to clean water, inadequate sanitation and malnutrition, AIDS, tuberculosis, and malaria are depriving us of several million lives, the majority of whom are children.

Disease and poverty under the dominance of capitalism are winning the war against human life. Without proper education, food security, and healthy workforce, the world has little hope of sustained economic and social development. Sick and hungry children cannot afford to attend school and, if they do, will not be able to learn well. The end result is large pools of poorly educated, unemployed, and alienated young people. This is a recipe for political instability, social incohesion, and a suitable climate for failure.

The irony is that world organizations such as the World Health Organization (WHO), the World Bank, the International Monetary Fund (IMF), and others continue to emphasize the necessity to increase the production of drugs and health care resources. What should be emphasized is the fact that the cost of treatment of any of the epidemic diseases ($15,000 per year for AIDS victims) is way beyond what many of the AIDS patients in the world can afford. What the world needs is not more of the same: increased production and resources; the world really needs a new economic infrastructure with a more just mechanism for resource distribution, a system that enables the hungry to access food resources and the sick to access drugs and health care facilities, and the illiterate to access education facilities.

The objective of providing health, food, education, and security for all cannot be treated as a patch to the economic system; rather it should be engraved in the fundamentals of the economic system. This is exactly where capitalism fails, and that is why the world is in dire need of a new system and ideology.

4.2. Life Insecurity

The terminal result of the political-economic-social system in any society should be no less than the immense feeling of security enjoyed by the group as well as by the individuals. Poverty, hunger, illiteracy, and lack of health contribute to the intensity of the people's insecurity; this is reflected in the high rate of deaths due to these serious killers. On top of these catastrophic causes of insecurity, people worldwide continue to face yet a more direct assault on their lives. These assaults come in forms of wars between nations, civil wars, tyranny of dictators, harsh treatment of intelligence apparatus, kidnapping, vandalism, and last but not least, acts of terrorism.

Some may argue that some of the assaults on human security may not be related to the underlying political or economic structure; this may be true for few sporadic incidents. But the majority of incidents with most devastating toll on the human life come from wars, civil wars, local unrest and revolts, intelligence interrogations, and acts of terrorism. Such incidents cannot be and should not be isolated from the local, regional, or world political and economic orders.

The local, regional, or world order is essentially the set of rules, regulations, and mechanisms used to deploy and maintain the relations within the country, between countries in a given region, or in the world at large. Within the country, the order is maintained by the authority of the state coupled with the underlying economic and political infrastructure. Within a given region, the order is usually maintained by regional organizations with members from the states of the region. Examples of regional organizations are the NAFTA for North American states; the European Union and its accompanying set of organization for the European states; OPEC for the oil-producing and exporting countries; the Arab League for the Arab states. The world order is maintained by world organizations such as the UN Security Council, the World Trade Organization (WTO), the World Bank, the International Monetary Fund (IMF), and others. Behind each order (local, regional, or global) stand one or few states with immense power; such powerful states use their influence and power to sustain the order or to change it when necessary.

This discussion is necessary in order to understand the relations between the lack of security and the current world, regional, and local orders. The world order today is maintained primarily by the USA, accompanied by other powerful nations such as Britain, France, Russia, and China. This order is maintained or even sometimes manipulated using instruments such as the Security Council, the WTO, the World Bank, and the IMF.

The USA is by far the country with the largest impact on the world order. The US decisive role became more distinct and apparent after the collapse of the Soviet Union and the dismissal of socialism as a world ideology in the last decade of the twentieth century. The USA practiced its decisive role in 1991 during the Second Gulf War when Iraq occupied Kuwait. The same was repeated in 2001 after the terrorist attacks on September 11 and in 2003 when the United States invaded Iraq without UN approval.

Since the end of the First World War, the order in the world (locally, regionally, and globally) had been maintained by few states which belonged to the ideology of either capitalism or socialism. This case continued until 1991 when socialism was dropped from the world order equation subsequent to the collapse of the Soviet Union. The world under the dominance of capitalism has suffered several types of atrocities and assaults against humanity.

Insecurity: Atrocities of Wars and Terrorism

The First World War ravaged through European states, which were dominated by capitalism. The war consumed seven million civilian and ten million military lives, with more than twenty-one million wounded[80]. Without going into details, it was evident at the end of the war how Britain and France spread their colonialist grip over a vast area of the world (Middle East, Africa, and Southeast Asia). Imperialism and colonialism were the most visible outcomes of the war; it is not far-fetched from the truth to claim that imperialism was a major factor of the war to begin with. Imperialism is thought of as the highest stage of capitalism according to communist theoreticians[32]. Others perceive imperialism as a method utilized by capitalism to secure sources of raw material, cheap labor, and markets (41, 42). The old colonies of European states continue to suffer until today from deep oppression, dictatorships, poverty, and backwardness.

The Second World War consumed more than sixty million lives; Forty million were civilians[81]. Many civilians died because of disease, starvation, massacres, bombing, and deliberate genocide such as the one committed against millions of Jews in Germany and Europe. The Second World War gave birth to the two competing camps, WARSAW (alliance of Soviet Union and Eastern European states) and NATO (North Atlantic Treaty Organization), and to a cold war that consumed hundreds of billions of dollars during five decades. The war also introduced globalization, which continues to increase the gap between the poor and the rich, and deepen the inequality between the people of the world.

The main two instruments of globalization, which were born in the womb of the Second World War, are the International Monetary Fund and the World Bank. These two instruments have broken the backbone of the economies of countries like Mexico, Turkey, Indonesia, and Korea. Under the policies of the IMF and the WB, the developing countries (third world countries) in Asia, Africa, and Latin America and the Caribbean continued to play the same role for the last fifty years: supply the raw material, the consuming market, and the cheap labor to the profit-generating industrial nations.

The first and second world wars produced a long-lasting problem in Palestine by creating the state of Israel. This problem has threatened the stability and security of the region as well as of the world for many decades. It has consumed hundreds of thousands of lives and continues to do so until today. It has shown the world an unprecedented form of brutality, when the tanks, machine guns, jet fighters face young children equipped only with stones. Arab as well as Jewish nations have become a fuel for imperial wars supported and sustained by Europe and then by the United States. Arms sales for the entire region of the Middle East have been sustained mainly due to the Arab-Israeli war.

The world order under the dominance of the Western superpowers led by the USA could not prevent the invasion of Afghanistan in 1979 by the Soviet Union. In the aftermath of the invasion, the *mujahideen* (Afghan revolutionary fighters) fought a proxy war on behalf of the USA for almost ten years; during this period, the United States facilitated arm supplies, intelligence, training, and international support for the mujahideen. The ten years war consumed more than 1.5 million of Afghan lives and more than 25,000 of the Soviet lives. The Afghan war culminated more than forty years of cold war between the ideologies of capitalism and socialism.

The world order under the dominance of the Western superpowers financed an eight-year war between Iraq and Iran (1980-1988) for no reason other than to sustain control over the oil fields in the Arabian/Persian Gulf and the free movement of oil to the industrial world; this objective is in complete harmony with capitalist motives as proclaimed by the Carter doctrine: "Soviet troops in Afghanistan posed a grave threat to the free movement of Middle East oil"[83]. The war consumed more than half million lives and many more wounded.

The Second Gulf War was yet another episode in the determination of the superpowers, especially the United States and Britain, to control the oil rich region. For the first time in contemporary history, Margaret Thatcher (former prime minister of Britain) and George H. Bush (former president of the USA) invoked chapter VII of the UN Charter, which allows the use of force against Iraq to force it out of Kuwait[84]. The then secretary of state James Baker was too frank when he explained the reasons for the gulf war[85]:

> *The economic lifeline of the industrial world runs from the Persian Gulf oil reserves and we cannot permit a dictator such as this to sit astride that economic lifeline; to bring it down to the level of the average American citizen, let me say that means jobs. If you want to sum it up in one word, it's jobs.*

Besides the tens of thousands of casualties (dead and wounded), the sanctions imposed upon Iraq after the end of the war consumed more than two million children's lives.

African nations suffered great pains and lost millions of lives in proxy wars between factions supported by one or another of the super capitalist nations in Europe and the United States. Millions of people continue to die in conflicts that have proven to serve only the interests of multinational corporations digging for gold, oil, and diamonds in Africa.

Diamond money paid for Unita offensives that in the 1990s elevated Angola's civil war to a new plateau of savagery. More than half a million Angolans were killed. Land mines maimed about ninety thousand.

Fighting displaced four million Angolans, and about one million continue to depend on foreign food aid. Blaine Harden[86] best describes the diamond wars in Africa in his *New York Times* 2000 publication "Africa's Diamond Wars," where he says,

> *The miseries of modern Africa are, in many ways, a legacy of its colonial history. Colonialism demolished whatever political culture may have predated the arrival of Europeans. It invented huge, largely fictive nations. To make their nation-building pay, colonialists used force to haul off everything from ivory to rubber to human beings.*
>
> *In Congo, the Belgian colonial state was famously greedy and cruel. Its agents set impossible quotas for production of rubber and ivory, killing or chopping off the hands of villagers who failed to meet them.*
>
> *In Sierra Leone, since the 1940's, predators who smuggle diamonds have warped every aspect of the nation's economic and political life. Angola, Congo and Sierra Leone had plenty of diamonds to excite greed, fuel war and to buy favors.*

The stories of millions of lives lost in wars launched for the conquest of capital are repeated in Vietnam where 5.5 million lives vanished and Korea where 3.5 million people died. Similar stories come from Columbia, Venezuela, Mexico, Guatemala, Grenada, Cuba, Chile, Argentina, and the list goes on. It is estimated that during the twentieth century alone, more than two hundred million people died in war-related activities.

Insecurity: Assaults on Human Rights

Throughout the twentieth century and well into the twenty-first one, assaults on human rights and degradation of human integrity worldwide have been a trademark of the dominant ideologies of both capitalism and communism. Within the Socialist camps of the Soviet Union and Eastern Europe, human rights were almost nonexistent except within the Socialists' definition of those rights. It is not the intention of this publication to detail the atrocities committed against human life under socialism. It is sufficient to mention (for now) that I have witnessed firsthand the life under socialism with all the sore taste of brutality, calamity, and abuse.

The plight of human dignity under the dominance of capitalism has not been any brighter. Amnesty International and Human Rights Watch organizations have reported on millions of cases of assault on human rights, human dignity, and human lives worldwide. The assaults are carried out by governments security agencies irrespective of their claimed level of civilization. The irony is that Amnesty International and Human Rights Watch organizations were initially set to monitor the human rights of people living in the Eastern Bloc of the world under the dominance of socialism. The United States and Western Europe had consistently used the reports of these organizations as a means of pressure against their counterpart socialist countries. Since the collapse of the Soviet Union and the abolishing of socialism, Amnesty International continues to report horrible assaults on human rights. The 2007 Amnesty International report[87] states:

> *Gross human right violations took place throughout much of the world. They ranged from extra judicial executions to widespread use of torture and unfair trials, harassment and intimidation of human rights defenders. Freedom of expression and association continued to be curtailed*

In 1993, two years after the collapse of the Soviet Union, Amnesty International reported acts of torture in 112 states and extrajudicial executions in 61 states.

Perhaps the most striking and astonishing assaults against human dignity in the recent history are those committed in the prisons of Abu Gharib in Iraq and Guantánamo by US intelligence authorities.

Abu Gharib prison witnessed appalling calamities of physical, psychological, and sexual abuse, including torture, rape, sodomy, and homicide held in the prison in Iraq. These acts were committed by personnel of the United States Army together with additional US governmental agencies[87].

The Guantánamo prison is another strike against human rights and dignity under capitalist democracies. The UN Commission on Human Rights reported that detainees at the US facility of Guantánamo have been subjected to force-feeding, prolonged solitary confinement, and other abuses, and have been denied the right to a fair trial, as well as religious freedom. In the view of the report's authors, "The legal regime applied to these detainees seriously undermines the rule of law and a number of fundamental universally recognized human rights, which are the essence of democratic societies"[88].

Aside from war-related human rights abuse in the United States, human rights have suffered a great deal in various forms of slavery and discrimination. Racism in the United States has been a major issue since the colonial era. Historically, the heaviest burdens of racism in the country have fallen upon Native Americans, African Americans, and Latin Americans.

Native Americans were referred to as "merciless Indian savages" in the United States Declaration of Independence. Despite all declarations of equality and equal opportunity, American Indians, Alaska Natives, Native Hawaiians, and Pacific Islanders remain among the most economically disadvantaged groups in the United States; and according to national mental health studies, American Indians are the most affected racial group to suffer from high levels of alcoholism, depression, and suicide.

The story of slaves brought from Africa against their will is even more devastating. Until 1865, there were more than four million black slaves in the United States. Postemancipation America was not free from racism; discriminatory practices continued in the United States with the existence of Jim Crow laws, educational disparities, and widespread criminal acts against people of color. One hundred years after the emancipation proclamation which officially freed the slaves, black students were not allowed until 1965 into the Mississippi State University[132]. Segregation between black and white populations in restaurants was common in Southern states in the United States until the 1960s.

Racism became a by-product of capitalism and white supremacy following the relocation of millions of African Americans from their roots in the Southern states to the industrial centers of the North after World War I, particularly in cities such as Boston, Chicago, and New York. In Northern cities, racial tensions exploded, most violently in Chicago, and lynching (mob-directed hangings) increased dramatically in the 1920s. More than 3,400 blacks were lynched between 1882 and 1968[90].

The story of racism and discrimination continue to haunt America until today. George W. Bush summed up the case for racism in a speech delivered to African citizens of Senegal in 2003[91]: "My nation's journey toward justice has not been easy and it is not over. The racial bigotry fed by slavery did not end with slavery or with segregation. And many of the issues that still trouble America have roots in the bitter experience of other times."

Indeed, blacks in America continue to be at a disadvantage compared to their white counterparts despite civil rights movement, equal opportunity acts, and affirmative actions. Racial gap between blacks and whites is

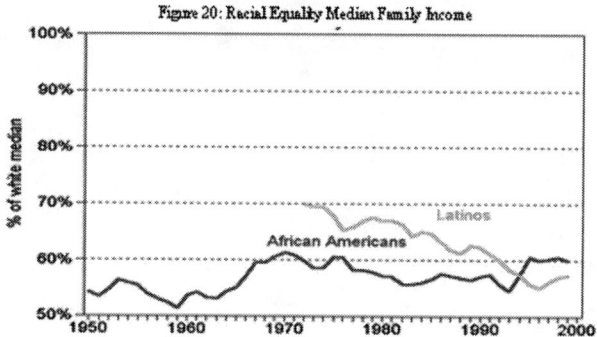

Figure 20: Racial Equality Median Family Income

visible in so many aspects of life. The family income of a black family has been significantly less than that of a white family for the last sixty years. Throughout the 1980s, the median black family income was barely 55% that of a white family[92]; see figure 20.

The poverty rates among blacks continue to be much higher than that for whites in the United States. Figure 21 shows that blacks were twice as much likely to be poor than whites for the last sixty years, with the median household income averaging around $20,000 compared to a $35,000 for a white counterpart. The same trend appears in the unemployment rates, where black people in the United States (above sixteen years) are twice as likely to be unemployed as white ones. The life expectancy of black people is significantly lower than that for whites. According to the Census Bureau in the United States, a black male is expected to live for sixty-five years (as of 1995) compared to seventy-eight years for a white man. The most striking fact is that the blacks make up almost 44% of the prison population in the United States, whereas they make up less than 13% of the total population.

These statistics show a pattern of discrimination against people of black color; this is not a coincident. The blacks after spending many years under physical slavery continued to be at a disadvantage in terms of being unable to compete for the means of production and the necessary resources. The most absurd explanation for this trend is to blame the black people for their conditions and miseries. Within the framework of capitalism, it is almost impossible for the weak to catch up and be at equal terms of those who had control of the wealth and the means to acquire them. The data supports this claim in almost every field of life (income, college graduates, unemployment, health status, mortality, school dropouts, incarceration rates, and many others).

Although, for different reasons, the status of Latinos in the United States is not much brighter than those for blacks, like black people, Latinos enjoy high poverty rates and related consequences such as lack of health insurance, high mortality rates, and high imprisonment rates.

Racial and ethnic discrimination constitute one of the

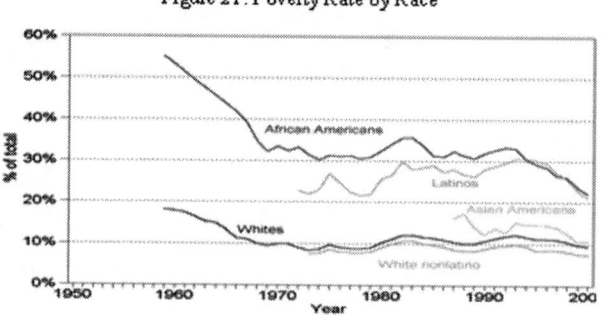

Figure 21: Poverty Rate by Race

most severe assaults on human dignity and integrity in recent history. Race, ethnicity, color, and gender are attributes granted to a human at birth without the least involvement of the person who carries these attributes for the rest of his or her life. When discrimination is carried out on the basis of these attributes, it is a direct assault on the nature of human being as well as on the one who granted these attributes, the Almighty God. Such discrimination cannot and should never be allowed to prevail. With great regret, lament, and sorrow, discrimination on the bases of color, ethnicity, and gender have rigorously marked the twentieth century and the first decade of the twenty-first century.

Another type of assault on human dignity prevails in other parts of the world. This time it is directed at the mental and intellectual makeup of people. Millions of people around the world are persecuted because of an opinion they carry or a political view they express. It is sufficient to browse through one of the annual reports issued by the Human Rights Watch (HRW) organization[93] or Amnesty International[94] to discover massive and dreadful assaults on human life, integrity, and intellectuality. The irony is that many of the tyrants whose records on human rights violations are shamefully atrocious disguise their assaults behind the labels of "democracy." According to HRW 2008 report[93], "democracy has become the sine qua non of legitimacy." Brutal presidents such as Karimov of Uzbekistan, Robert Mugabe of Zimbabwe, Pervez Musharraf of Pakistan, Hosni Mubarak of Egypt, Meles Zenawi of Ethiopia, among others, find utility in holding electoral charades to legitimize their reign. When George Bush had to comment on atrocities committed by Musharraf of Pakistan, he said, "Musharraf is somebody who believes in democracy and that Pakistan was on the road to democracy"[133].

Violations of human rights worldwide come in various forms and span many fields. One of these fields is related to child labor, which is a direct by-product of poverty in many places in the world. The International Labor Organization estimates that 246 million children between the ages of five and seventeen are currently working; that is 15% of the world's children population[95]. The sad part of this story is that more than 200,000 of these children work as soldiers in various rebel or government forces, thus directly endangering their lives. The irony is that child labor further contributes to deepening poverty of the poor nations while increasing the profit of global capitalist corporations due to cheap labor. It is estimated that countries in sub-Saharan Africa, Asia, and Latin America would gain more than $4 trillion a year if child labor were to be eliminated in these countries. Until child labor is completely banned, the $4 trillion will go to the accounts of global capitalist corporations.

Perhaps the most devastating impact of local, regional, and world orders on the plight of humanity is the spread of worldwide genocides. Genocide is defined in part as "acts committed with intent to destroy, in whole or in part, a national, ethical, racial or religious group"[96]. One of the largest genocides in contemporary history occurred against the Native Americans at the hand of European colonial powers in America. The highest estimates for this genocide place the toll at 100 millions deaths![97]. More than 5 million Jews were killed in a brutal genocide by the Nazis during World War II. In Rwanda, more than 1 million civilians vanished at the hands of the Hutu tribes. More than 4 million Palestinians have been displaced out of their lands as refugees and more than a million have been killed by Israeli occupation since 1948. A massive genocide has ravaged Iraq since 1990, where more than 3 million people died as a result of malnutrition and lack of medical care caused by sanctions and blockade. Since the invasion of Iraq in 2003, more than 1.5 million have died[98]. Since the Soviet invasion of Afghanistan in 1979 and then the American invasion in 2001, more than 3 million Afghan lives have vanished.

These are only few examples of the genocides which have taken place under the dominance of capitalism in the world. It requires a publication on its own to account and analyze all acts of genocide and mass killings.

What is even more saddening is the fact that millions of people around the world suffered a great deal of imprisonment and torture whenever they intended to protest against poverty, genocide, and inhuman conditions. Thousands of political prisoners continue to be held with or without trials in many countries around the world. Many are held in secret prisons run and managed by intelligence agencies such as the CIA, the MI6, and their satellite intelligence agencies.

Profiling based on color, religion, nationality, and affiliation has become a standard practice in many countries including well-established democracies such as the USA, Britain, Germany, France, and other countries.

The main point here is that the world under capitalism throughout the past century has suffered from the scarcity of security (food, health, and life) more so than scarcity of resources as preached by the founders of capitalism.

The performance scoreboard of capitalism clearly indicates that capitalism has failed to deliver happiness, security, and well-being to billions of people around the globe. It has cultivated a land that grows sore trees with fruits of poverty, sickness, wars, hunger, and dissatisfaction. It has reduced the role of God to wiping the tears of the hungry and pacifying the anger of the oppressed. And it has raised the role of the individual to a god who provides life and death and accumulates wealth and owns the universe.

The failure of capitalism to deliver justice, security, and satisfaction may not necessarily cause its failure as a system; it may continue to function under the reign of corporations and superrich entities. However, the recent financial crisis and economic downturn provides evidence that the main engine running the system of capitalism may be malfunctioning. The signs of failure of the system itself are the subject of the next section.

5

Capitalism: Signs of Failure

When I arrived for the first time to the land of the largest capitalist nation in the world, I was amazed by the power of capitalist productivity in the United States of America. As a young teenager, less than sixteen years old, I saw huge tractors and combines cultivating hundreds of acres and producing tons of corn and soybean grain, all operated by a single family. I saw the hands of a farmer hardened by the land he cultivated and softened by the money his land generated. I did not see then the invisible hands of the banks financing all that operation. I could not see any signs of failure then.

A year later, my education fate flew me to the other extreme. I arrived at the land of the largest socialist nation in the to spend the next six years studying while observing socialism in the Union of Soviet Socialist Republics (USSR). I recall how often I had to stand in line to buy a grocery product, only to be disappointed an hour later because the item I waited for is no longer available. That system would not last, my instincts told me. I recall having to buy a communist publication as a condition for buying a book of math or computer science. That system would not last for long, I felt it.

I recall having to step over people lying drunk in my morning journey to school and on my way back. I recall scores of students graduating from medical, law, and engineering schools without even attending classes; they were political activists or rich foreign students. I recall people having to go through surgery only to fulfill the quota plan for the surgeon at a given hospital. I recall the primitive radio monitor fixed on the wall of my dorm room, which must have been a two-way radio. Every time I disabled the radio, technicians would show up at my room to fix it; I never asked for the service. I knew that system could not last for long. My gut feelings, my instincts, and simple analysis turned out to be true only ten years after I graduated and left the Soviet Union. Socialism collapsed and the Soviet Union was dismantled by 1991.

The six years I spent in the Soviet Union gave me an experience of a lifetime. For one thing, I could not experience the life under socialism today even if I wanted to. Most importantly, I learned the principles of economy, political economy, and social structure of both socialism and capitalism. The teachings of Karl Marx, Vladimir Lenin, and Friedrich Engels were as important part of the curriculum as the subjects of math, physics, and engineering. The theory of historic materialism developed by Marx and later refined by Lenin suggested that capitalism would fade away only to give rise to socialism. That view was dead beaten in real world when socialism fell first. Marx's theory of the "surplus value" was correct only in the sense that under capitalism the wealth tends to accumulate in the hands of the few. But the other part of the theory that the poorer classes of workers and farmers would revolt for their stolen rights of ownerships never materialized.

When I arrived at the land of capitalism for the second but longer period of time, I observed what I could not have observed during my first trip when I was a young boy. The farm I lived in during my first trip was no longer the same. It was confiscated by the bank which, few years earlier had financed its production, in exchange for the debts which my host family failed to pay. The hardworking farmer lost his land and the seed company he co-owned with his brothers. This system would not last, my instincts told me.

The same monster, the bank, swallowed the machine factory owned by one of my friends in the city of Milwaukee in Wisconsin. I recall how my friend traveled to my home country in attempt to set up a factory to help industrialize a developing country. I recall how the owner (my friend) was enthusiastic about helping people get jobs, supporting education, and how much he detested laying people off their jobs. Just like every other business under capitalism, his was also owned by the bank. Typically, businesses in capitalist countries are indebted to one or more banks. I still recall the words of an investing bank representative to the owner of a small technology company: "You cannot be in businesses without being in debt." My machine factory owner friend lost his machine shop, the one that produces real products right here in the land of capitalism. It was making products and generating profit when it was confiscated by the bank. The banks for some time were going after the life insurance policy of my friend as a guarantee for their supposedly lost wealth! I knew then that this system would not last.

During my tenure at one of the largest corporations in the world (more than 160,000 employees at the time), I witnessed how scores of the best engineers and technicians were escorted out of the building under the auspices of layoff. The first round of layoffs which eliminated more than fifty thousand jobs was done at a time when the company was profitable and making lots of money. The layoffs were necessary to boost the stock prices of the company which have soared over the roof.

I admit that these are just stories, instincts, and guts feelings. So where are the signs of failure if there are any? After all, capitalism has gone through several rounds of recessions, depressions, downturns, low productivity, and corporate failures in the past. It has always emerged as strong or even stronger. Why is it different this time?

As explained earlier, faults or defects do not necessarily generate errors. And errors do not necessarily lead to failure. A fault generates an error only when certain conditions occur and trigger that fault. Only then an error occurs. An error is a deviation from the normal behavior of the system. If the error is observed, detected, isolated, and contained properly, then failure could be avoided. Just like in any physical system, the recovery from an error or a deviation from the normal behavior of the system is not automatic; a correct identification and isolation of the problems and a correct containment is absolute necessity to restore the system and to prevent failure.

The great depression of the 1929 was an erroneous behavior of the economy and the market at large. The stock market collapsed; many people lost their lands, farms, homes, and companies. It took several years of rebuilding the economy and a great war (World War II) to contain the erroneous behavior of the market and to resume a normal functioning of the system. The conditions which led to the depression (i.e., the erroneous behavior of the economy) were related to inflated stock values as reported by the *Economist* magazine on November 2, 1929: "There is warrant for hoping that the deflation of the exaggerated balloon of American stock values will be for the good of the world"[134]. It was reported that the prices of financial market increased during the period between 1925 and 1929 by 120%, while economic growth for the same period has not exceeded 17%. And when the market has collapsed, it lost over 93% of its value, which means that the market returned to its real normal value which was obviously much lower than what the stock market had indicated.

Another market error occurred in 1987 when the market collapsed again. Observers noted that the prices of financial market had inflated significantly compared with the real size of the economy, where the difference between the inflated values and the real ones was more than 200%. It took another war of large magnitude to contain the effects of this erroneous behavior. The Gulf War led by George Bush, the father, helped contain the problem and bring the economy back to its normal behavior.

In 1999, the economy generated another error when the so called "Internet bubble" was deflated and the market lost hundreds of billions of virtual dollars. The economy was heading to a steep dive. The containment procedure was invoked again: a lengthy war! This time the war did not succeed in containing the error or ending the crisis. On the contrary, the wars launched in the name of fighting terrorism against Afghanistan and Iraq fueled up the crisis and deepened the financial problems. By the time the year 2008 arrived, the crisis had reached a serious peak. A massive government intervention with more than $1.5 trillion in the United States alone was rushed to the aid of a failing economy. Scores of scholars rushed to declare an end of an era, the era of liberal capitalism.

Although the root causes of the current crisis are not significantly different from the previous ones, the conditions which led to the current crisis and the environment in which it functioned, as well as the containment procedures, are significantly different. Two major phenomena emerged as prominent signs of the most recent financial crisis, which have the capacity of collapsing the political economy of capitalism. The first is the creation of virtual economy parallel to the real economy. The second one is a massive government buyout of private banks, insurance companies, auto industry, real estate, and more. These two phenomena will be discussed in the next subsections.

5.1 Virtual Economy

Before describing the aspects of the virtual economy, let me draw a parallel concept which exists in computer systems. Analogy helps understand the scope and the significance of the problem.

In the earlier days of computer systems, memory devices were very expensive and their sizes were relatively small. For example, 1 megabyte of memory (RAM) cost more than $10,000! It was almost impossible to build a computer system with say 100 megabytes (memory would cost more than $1 million). The smart architects of computer systems invented the notion of *virtual memory*. The idea was to create the illusion that the memory was virtually large (say 100 gigabytes). The illusion is made possible by using the relatively inexpensive and large storage provided by hard disk space.

The concept of virtual memory works under the assumption that user programs do not need to reside in the main (expensive) real memory all the time. A small portion of the program will reside in main memory, while the rest of the program and its data reside on the cheap but large disk space. Over time, pieces of the program and data will be swapped back and forth between the memory and the disk. The user will never know that the memory is too small to hold her program. For the user, the memory has a virtually large size. She is happy and can execute larger programs using much smaller real memory; it is an illusion, but a nice one. Of course the computer system *may crash* when a *greedy* program begins to use more real memory than the system actually has. This concept is known for computer architects as *thrashing* and they are well aware of it and have come up with different ways to cope with it or prevent it altogether. Now, where is the analogy in the economic system?

The simplest financial economic analogy to the virtual memory concept is the credit card system. Take the example of a family with a monthly income of $3,000. The family pays $2,500 as a minimum payment on their debt balance, which could be $360,000 including the payments on a house, two cars, and holiday shopping. The actual real wealth of the family is $36,000 a year (36 megabytes in computer analogy); this amounts to $360,000 over ten years (similar to 360 megabytes of virtual storage). Instead of using the real wealth of $36,000 a year, the family uses the extended (virtual) wealth of ten years ($360,000). In reality, the $360,000 does not exist at the time when the family begins to use this large virtual money.

The bank supported by the Federal Reserve steps in and allocates the large amount of money in anticipation that this money will actually be generated over time. If all goes well, the family continues to earn $3,000 a month and continues to pay their minimum payments; then everything goes smooth and the difference between what is virtual and what is real will not surface to cause any problem. The family continues to happily live with the illusion of $360,000 virtual wealth.

But when something goes wrong, such as a layoff of the working member of the family, which is not uncommon, or a serious health condition occurs and consumes more money than what the insurance company pays resulting on more healthcare debt, or any other reason, then *thrashing* will take place. The virtual capacity of the family evaporates, and the assets acquired with virtual memory may also vanish. In fact, the collapse of the virtual wealth of the family may affect the absolute real wealth of the family, such as a land owned through inheritance!

This type of scenario occurs all the time, and we all know many real-life examples. One outstanding example, which was reported in the media, is the case of the billionaire Donald Trump. He is used to running projects sizing in billions of dollars, and when he fails to meet the demands of the creditors, he files for bankruptcy[135].

Figure 22 shows the growth of the virtual wealth (proportional to the debt), while the real wealth (proportional to income) remained almost steady for more than thirteen years. Note how the home-related debt has increased from $120,000 to $183,000 per family while the corresponding income remained unchanged over the same period.

At the larger scale of the economy, where corporations, factories, and all types of enterprises interact and function, the concept of virtual wealth is similar to the examples above but much larger in scale. Over the years, the virtual economy under capitalism became the most dominant part of the economy which has almost totally masked the real economy. In fact, the virtual economy has become so prominent that the political leadership warns against the possibility of pushing the economy down from the virtual values to its more real values.

In a statement made to a congressional committee on April 3, 2008, the Fed Reserve chief Bernanke said[99],

> *If Bear Stearns had been allowed to fail, it would have led to a chaotic unwinding of Bear Stearns investments held by individuals and other financial institutions. Moreover, the adverse impact of a default would not have been confined to the financial system but would have been felt broadly in **the real economy** through its effects on **asset values** and **credit availability**.*

Note how Bernanke alludes to the protection of the real economy as the objective cited for protecting Bear Stearns from failing.

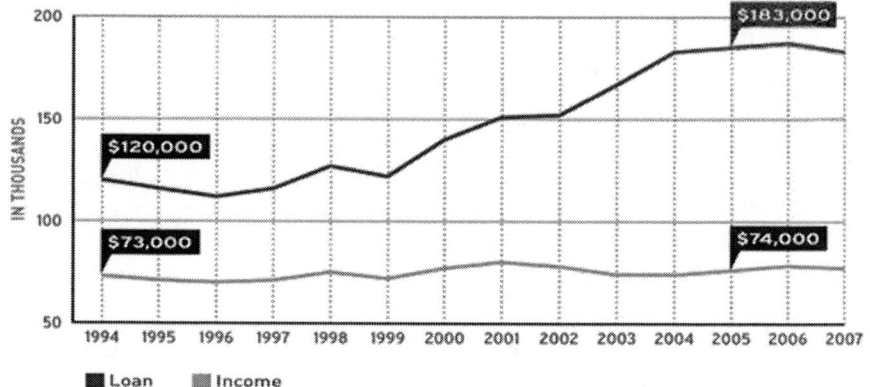

Figure 22:
Increasing Percentage of Income Goes to Housing

In 1994, $73,000 was the annual median income for a loan of $120,000. By 2005, as subprime lending peaked, nearly the same median income could get a $183,000 loan.

*Inflation adjusted. Totals include all first-lien mortgages, not just subprime. Salary and loan numbers reflect the median, or midpoint, of all salary and loan data analyzed.

Source: Analysis performed using federal Home Mortgage Disclosure Act data acquired from the National Institute for Computer-Assisted Reporting.

Source: Analysis performed using federal Home Mortgage Disclosure Act data acquired from the National Institute for Computer-Assisted Reporting.

In an article published by the *Newsweek*, October 11, 2008, Daniel Gross writes[100], "*Back in 2002, Apple's stock was trading far below the level of cash on its books, ascribing a value of zero to its brands and products, compared with several billion at the height of the boom.*" Note how the statement refers to the existence of two views of the economy: a real economy which is reflected by the level of cache on corporate books and an inflated, exaggerated view which is reflected in the current stock values of the market; in this case the virtual value was observed to be below the real value.

Virtual economy (VE) is strongly related to the failure of the financial capitalist system as being witnessed today. VE allows the economy to appear much larger than its real size. As in the case of virtual memory computers, virtual economy is based on the assumption that the real money will not be tapped into, and therefore, it is possible to deal with an assumed larger (virtual) value for the money.

Recall that one of the main principles of capitalism is related to the definition of value of products. Product value under capitalism is a measure of the relative benefit of a given product or its relative exchange value compared to the benefit of other things; in case the exchange value is relative to money, the value is known as the price. Hence, the foundation of capitalism allows the existence of a virtual relative value for products instead of a real value which people can always refer to. As such, in the market economy, it is possible for the value of a given segment of the market, such as oil, to fluctuate between two extremes in a short period of time. The definition of value under capitalism allows for this fluctuation to occur depending on the current conditions. Economic, political, and social conditions would act as a trigger which causes the values of various products and market segments to fluctuate and create turbulence which potentially can cause a total collapse.

Virtual economy organization (similar to virtual memory organization) provides two views of the economy. The first is the real value of commodities and services in a given economy which corresponds to the real economic growth and production. The second view of the economy represents the virtual imaginary value of the market. The virtual values of the market are typically measured by the exchange value which is the monetary value or the price.

A virtual economy system, similar to virtual memory systems, is bound to crash (thrash) when the instant demand for finance at any given time exceeds the real value of the real economy. The current financial crisis in the United States and the world at large is a striking example of virtual economy crashing or (thrashing). Conditions which facilitated the current crash include the overwhelming expenses of multiple wars, the unexpected high cost of hurricanes, and the unexpected high rate of defaults on house loans. The total cost of wars in Iraq and Afghanistan is approaching $1 trillion. Hurricane Katrina added more than $150 billion to the burden of the economy[136]. The cost of defaults on house loans exceeded $1.5 trillion[137]. A combination mix of these conditions caused the bill to exceed the real value of the economy which in turn deflated the virtual economy and caused the collapse.

The phenomenon of virtual economy, where the money in transactions appears much larger than the real money, began to surface at the level of state economies at the end of the nineteenth century when financial markets began to take shape in New York. This phenomenon grew to be an integral part of capitalist economies, especially in the United States and Europe, due to four major factors, namely, the stock markets, interest-based economy, the removal of gold as a basis for the monetary systems, and the detachment of monetary growth from real economic growth. At the political front, the cold war between the capitalist and socialist camps in the second half of the twentieth century further strengthened the virtual economies in the West. These conditions are further analyzed in the next subsections.

Stock Markets and the Virtual Economy

The stock market activities at the start of the twentieth century created a new phenomenon in the economy, where the wealth associated with stock values grew at much higher rate than the wealth associated with the real economy. When the stock market collapsed in New York in October 1929, the economists attributed the crash to the great difference between the inflated values of stocks and the values of the real assets of the economy. Although economists may not agree on the cause of the 1929-1932 stock market crash, they all admit that the utility stocks prices drove up too high.

The *Economist* magazine insisted on November 2, 1929, that the stock prices were too high and wrote[134], "There is warrant for hoping that the deflation of the exaggerated balloon of American stock values will be for the good of the world." In other words, the stock values were highly inflated. To elaborate further on this issue, it was found that the stock values in the financial market increased during the period between 1925 and 1929 by 120%, while the economic growth for the same period has not exceeded 17% (an average of 3.5% per year). In 1932, when the market finally collapsed, it lost over 90% of its value. The market returned to its real value which was obviously much lower than what the stock market indicated (101, 134).

President Herbert Hoover concurred that the prices of the stock market were extraordinarily high and that they were nothing but a speculative bubble caused by the mistakes of the Federal Reserve Board. Hoover explained, "One of these clouds was an American wave of optimism, born of continued progress over the decade, which the Federal Reserve Board transformed into the stock-exchange Mississippi Bubble"[102]. Thus, the common viewpoint was that stock prices were too high.

One similarity between the crash of the 1929 and the current crisis is the rush of economic analysts and politicians to falsely declare the end of the crisis. Leading economists of the first half of the twentieth century such as Irving Fisher and Maynard Keynes declared the end of the 1929 crisis only six months after the crash. Both managed to lose a large portion of their wealth in the subsequent stock market crash.

Aside from all the postanalysis of the 1929 crash, one fact stands straight. That is of the existence of two views of the market: a real one which measures the production rate and the real economic growth; the second is the virtual view which represents the speculative values. In reference to the real economy and its performance, Harold Bierman[102] concludes in his article on the 1929 crash, saying, "There was little hint of a severe weakness in the real economy in the months prior to October 1929." The high productivity rate during the period preceding the 1929 crash was evident and easily observed by economists. The problem is that the virtual value of the stock market grew at a much higher rate than the production market. The virtual view of the market provided a much higher value than the real one. In the case of the 1929 crisis, the virtual value of the market was more than 90% higher than the real one. The crash (thrashing as known in computer systems) brought the market back to the levels indicated by the real economy before the crash.

Much like the force of gravity which pulls every object back to the center of gravity, there will always be a tendency for the market to return to its real value, which represents the center of economic gravity. A continuous and strong force will always be required in order to sustain a much higher value of the market than its real one, in much the same way a force is always required to keep an object elevated against the force of gravity. The market forces which are used to raise the virtual values of the stock market include speculations, public trusts and confidence, among others.

In 1987 the market collapsed again. Observers noted that the prices of stock market had inflated significantly compared to the real size of the economy. Prior to 1987, the stock prices increased at an exponential rate, where the real economy continued to increase at a more normal rate. The Dow Jones Index rose form 776 points in 1982 to 2,722 points in 1987; that is more than 300% increase over five years' period. In the same period, the (real) economic growth rate was about 15%, which is roughly 3% per year. The difference between the virtual and real economies was very large. Overvaluation of the stock market has been cited as one reason for the 1987 crash[103]. The 1987 crash was global. Stock markets around the globe collapsed. The market was pulled back by its own gravity towards the base of the real value of the market.

By the end of the twentieth century, the virtual economy climbed again to reach new peaks which were several times larger than the size of the real market value. The advances in computer technology and Internet led to the creation of what has been known as the "Internet bubble." The Internet bubble is by far the best example which illustrates the disconnect between virtual and real economies. All a company needed to trade on the stock market at an incredibly high price was the prefix *e*—for electronic or the postfix *.com* to indicate its relation to the Internet.

The Internet bubble caused the market to inflate beyond control. Between March 2000 and October 2002, the dot-com bubble crash wiped out $5 trillion in market value of technology companies[104]. The stock value for some companies plunged from above $100 to below $1. One of the drastic examples is InfoSpace, whose stock dived from $1,305 to $22 per share[105].

The most recent crisis which peaked in 2008 was given several labels, the most prominent of which is "economic meltdown." The meltdown term refers to the loss of more than $15 trillion over a very short period of time. The Dow Jones Index reported a loss of more than $500 billion in one single day. John Phelan, chairman of the New York Stock Exchange, called the collapse a near meltdown caused by a confluence of factors: "the market's *inevitable turnaround after its long climb*, heightened anxieties over rising interest rates and future inflation, and the impact of computerized trading"[106]. Bear Stearns Bank lost more than 90% of its value, diving down from $16.7 to $1.7 billions. Lehman Brothers Bank lost more than 93% of its value and ended up filing bankruptcy. Washington Mutual Bank lost more than 60% of its value before being acquired by J.P. Morgan; the list goes on to include large banks, insurance companies, auto industry, and more. When Lehman Brothers collapsed, the British *Guardian* newspaper noted that "a fundamental fissure opened up in capitalism"[106].

The end result of the split view of the economy is a virtual value of the economy provided by the stock market, which does not reflect the production reality of the economy. Lucent Technologies (currently Alcatel-Lucent) delivered world-class telecommunications products and services when its stock traded at more than $100 a share. After its stock price has fallen to almost $0.5, it continued to provide same superb products and services. Productivity and stock values under capitalism have become two distinct animals. The stock value of some company may grow up and increase at the time when its production or profits remain unchanged or in some cases decrease. Similarly, the stock value may remain unchanged or even go down when its production or profit is increased. Amazon.com, for example, traded its stocks at more than $300 a share when the company did not generate any real profits. The cases of Enron and Arthur Andersen are striking examples in this regard. As a result of the massive fraud at Enron, shareholders lost tens of billions of dollars. The Enron scandal[44] was a corporate scandal involving the American energy Enron Corporation based in Houston, Texas, and the accounting, auditing, and consultancy firm Arthur Andersen. The scandal, which was revealed in October 2001, eventually led to the bankruptcy of Enron, at that point, the largest in American history. Arthur Andersen, which at the time was one of the five largest accounting firms in the world, was dissolved.

The value definition under capitalism allows the creation of two faces for the economy: a real face and an imaginary virtual one. The real face is associated with the economic growth and production. This side of economy is the true measure of the strength of the economy; this is the benefit value of the economy. The imaginary or virtual face reflects the image seen and observed by the local and global communities. When the difference between the virtual and real value of the economy remains small, there does not appear to be a serious problem. However, when the difference becomes very large, the consequences can be seriously damaging; the collapse of the markets in 1929, 1987, 2000, and 2008 are real-life examples of such danger.

The collapse of the virtual market and its turnaround after a long climb is almost imminent and inevitable. Analysts can cite all types of reasons and conduct all sorts of analysis to explain the "crash," "collapse," "meltdown," or any other term they choose to use for the same phenomenon. But in all cases, one thing is certain: it is impossible to convert the virtual value of a certain segment of the market into real wealth larger in size than the real value of that segment. The mere thinking that Bill Gates, for example, may convert his huge amount of Microsoft stocks into say $20 billion in cache is insane!

As an example, assume that the real value of some company is equivalent to 10% of its total virtual value; this is not uncommon in the realm of virtual economy world. Practically, the amount that can be turned into real money can be no more than 10% of the total virtual capital given by the stock value of the company; the rest is equal to none.

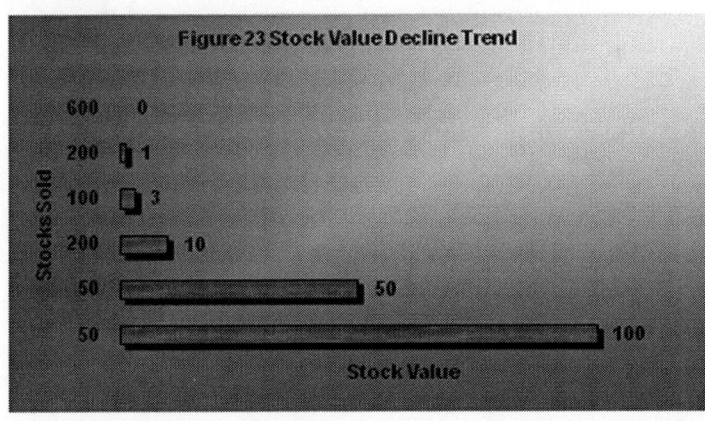

When the owners of the company shares (or stockholders) notice that a major investor begins to sell his possessions (to convert them to real money), a panic among shareholders begin to propagate; they rush to sell their possessions hoping to cache in some real money before their stocks lose value. Then a collapse takes place and brings down the virtual value of the company to its more realistic basic value.

Let's work out the example more thoroughly using simple analysis and calculation so as not to confuse the readers (figure 23). Assume that there are one thousand shares in a company. Also, assume that each share is worth $100. So the virtual stock value of the company is $100,000. For the sake of argument, assume that the real value of the company based on its assets and production is $10,000. In other words, the real value of the company is 10% of its virtual value. Now assume that a major investor sells fifty stock shares at $100 and caches $5,000. If the rest of the shareholders start selling their shares hoping to get real money from the company, they will be able to get no more than $5,000 at best, which is the remaining portion of the real value of the company. This translates to 5,000/950, which is approximately $5.25 per share. Now if one more person was able to act faster than the rest and sell fifty shares at say $50 and caches $2,500, then the rest of the crowd will have to share the remaining nine hundred shares for no more than $2500; that is $2.75 a share if all shares are sold at once. Say that two hundred more stocks were traded at $10 a share which amounts to $2,000. What remains of the company value is $500 distributed over seven hundred shares. The stock value of this company will be dropped down to $0.71. Eventually when all $10,000 are gone, the share will go to zero. The remaining stocks will lose their value completely.

This is how the stock values of Enron, 3Com, Martha Stewart companies collapsed and were tarnished when senior executives began to sell large amount of stocks in attempt to convert their stocks into cache. The first few individuals who manage to sell a large portion of their stocks get lucky and transfer part of their virtual wealth into real one. Those who come late or wait for a short while lose. In the final analysis, a company will never be able to translate its virtual value into real cache equal to its virtual value. Just as in virtual memory computer system, it is impossible to stack all the virtual memory pages into the real RAM memory pages! When a program attempts to do that, the system crashes; the difference is that in the case of computers, they call it thrashing instead of crashing. The result is the same.

Banks, Usury, and the Virtual Economy

Usury is the second major cause for the creation of virtual wealth which causes the economy to appear much larger in size than its real value. Usury is defined in *Merriam-Webster* dictionary as "the lending of money with an interest charge for its use"; this comes from the Medieval Latin *usuria*, which means interest. A modification was made to the meaning of usury to indicate the interest rate charged above a predetermined rate. This modification was made in order to legitimize the charging of interest on money. In the Islamic culture and religion, the word *usury* is mapped to the word *riba*. *Riba* comes from the word *increase*. When applied to the concept of usury, it means the increase of money at the expense of the money of other people. This definition is based on the Quranic verse:

> *That [usury-riba] which you lay out for increase through the money of other people will have no increase with Allah.* (Quran 30:39)

Usury, or the interest rate as most frequently referred to, is a cornerstone of the financial policies under capitalism. It is used by the Federal Reserve to adjust market and economy fluctuations. During a recession, the Federal Reserve Bank reduces the interest rate (usury value) in order to encourage borrowing and increase the demands on goods and services. Conversely, it increases the value of usury to curb inflation during excessive economic growth. The point here is to understand that usury in the capitalist political economy is one of the most important tools used for the control of the ups and downs of the economy. Perhaps the single most unique characteristic of capitalist economy is the widespread use of financial institutions that offer loans to individuals, companies, institutions, and even governments themselves.

In this section, we are interested in the role of riba-usury in the creation of virtual wealth. More on the subject of usury will be addressed in the second part of this book when we discuss the Islamic economic system, which is usury free in contrast with capitalism which is based on usury.

The main usury organ under capitalism is the banking financial institutes. Within this usury-based economy, money flows in two directions. In one direction, the money flows from the investors and customers towards the banks in a form of deposit payments. The other direction of flow is from the banks towards the investors and customers in a form of loan payments or withdrawal from customers' accounts (figure 24). Except for rare cases where the inflation rate is higher than the interest rates during the repayment period, the amount of money going towards the bank is steadily more than the amount of money going towards the investors.

The money which flows from the banks towards investors and customers is related to the real economy of production. It is responsible for the increase of production; it is used to maintain price stability as required by the fiscal policy, and it is responsible for creating the supply-demand balance in the market.

Figure 24: Money Flow from and to the Banks

The amount and rate of money which flows in the direction of investors and customers will certainly be less than the amount and rate of money which flows in the direction of the banks. Over time, the banks accumulate more wealth than the total wealth collected by the market either through loans from the banks or through production of goods and services. The difference between the wealth accumulated by the banks and the wealth sustained by the market provides another reason for the dual views of the economy: the real and the virtual. To further illustrate this phenomenon, consider the following two cases.

Consider the loan case, where the bank provides a loan for an investor. Let's assume that the bank provided a loan of $100 million with 5% usury for one year. Let's assume also that the inflation during this period was 2%; the actual value of the interest rate becomes 3% after inflation adjustment. Assume further that the investor who borrowed the money was able to use the borrowed money to produce goods and services and generate 2% profit at the end of the loan period. Now the total amount of money to be paid back to the bank is $103 million, while the real available money due to the loan, investment, and profit is $102 million. This means that there is $1million in the bank account which does not correspond to any real value on the ground. This surplus is the usury; it represents the pure growth of money which does not correspond to any growth in the economy. The economy grew by $2 million; the money grew by $3 million. Only $2 million of the money growth corresponds to economic real wealth growth. This is what the Quran refers to as money growth at the expense of other people's money: *"That [usury-riba] which you lay out for increase through the money of other people will have no increase with Allah"* (Quran 30:39).

Note that the biggest borrowers in the world are governments which borrow money to pay for their operation and not for profitable production. Consequently, the accumulated pure usury will be much higher than the ratio of (1%) as indicated by the above example. That is why, in a short period of time, usury money grows to several hundreds of billions of dollars and becomes much greater than the size of the real economy. It is worthwhile to know that the real economic growth rate in United States was no more than 3.5% during the last thirty years, while the actual interest rate (after inflation adjustment) was more than 8% per year. On the average, 4.5% of the wealth increase was on the virtual side, which did not correspond to the real economic growth. This means that the virtual money over thirty years was (135%) of the actual value of the economy. So if the real value of the US economy was $5 trillion, then the usury-related excess wealth was $6.75 trillion. The total virtual wealth will appear to be $11.75 trillion instead of $5 trillion.

The second case which leads to an increase in the virtual money is the case when investors invest their money in the banks for a given usury/interest value. Assume that an investor invests in the bank $100 million for a usury of 5% rate averaged over ten years after taking into account inflation. After ten years, the value of the invested money becomes $150 million. For the bank not to lose money, it in turn invests the $100 million. Let's say the bank gets an average 7% return on the reinvestment of the $100 million. The bank now has $170 million; it made $70 million profit over ten years. Let's say that $50 million of the profit generated by the bank (5%) was a result of investment in real production projects; the rest ($20 million) was usury gained through the reinvestment of the money in other banks. The end result is that the initial $100 million have become $170 million. Only $150 million correspond to real growth of the economy; the remaining $20 million represents usurious money which does not map to any real value on the ground. The reality is that most banks do not invest their money in production processes, but rather by reinvesting in other banks and by recycling the loans to other borrowers. As a result, the virtual money increases at a rapid rate repeatedly until its value becomes extremely high.

In either case, the resultant quantity of the money accumulated in the banks is much more than the quantity of the initial real money that represents the base money and the profits due to real production. However, what encourages and motivates the continuation of the increase in the virtual money is the absence of the urgent need to withdraw large amount of funds from many banks at once. When one of these banks gets exposed to pressure from investors and depositors to withdraw an amount of money that exceeds the amount of the real money, the bank may face the possibility of collapse for being unable to meet customer needs; such was the case with the Bank of Boston in the 1980s. If the government does not intervene to save the bank and back it up with guarantees and funds, a collapse of the bank becomes imminent.

When the problem becomes severe and has the potential of affecting several financial institutions, the big countries such as the United States begin to print and pump money that could possibly match the amount of virtual money. This would lead to a massive inflation, decline in prices, and weak production and may lead to huge financial disaster. Perhaps this was the main motive of the massive bailouts for Bear Stearns, Freddie Mac, Fannie Mae, and other financial institutions as clearly expressed by the Fed Reserve chief Bernanke when he said, "If Bear Stearns had been allowed to fail, the adverse impact of a default would not have been confined to the financial system but would have been felt broadly in the real economy through its effects on asset values and credit availability"[47].

Besides the interest/usury money generation in excess of the production-related profit, the banking system under capitalism allows for money printing and pumping by certain banking authorities. The symbol of such banking operation is the Federal Reserve Bank in the United States. The Federal Reserve Act was passed in the United States in 1913. Today the Federal Reserve Bank is a consortium of several private banks which are not part of the United States government. These banks, under certain arrangements with the US government, create paper or digital money; lend the money with interest to the people as well as to the government through the member banks. The profits generated from the interest goes back to the accounts of the banks and their shareholders. The primary members of the Federal Reserve Consortium include Rothschilds of London and Berlin, Lazard Brothers of Paris, Israel Moses Seaf of Italy. Kuhn, Loeb & Co. of Germany and New York, Warburg & Company of Hamburg, Germany, Lehman Brothers of New York (no longer exists after its collapse), Goldman Sachs of New York, and Rockefeller Brothers of New York

It has been recognized early on that giving some banks the power of issuing money and making profit on interest generated from lending this money to people is very detrimental to the economic well-being of any society. Thomas Jefferson believed that "the banking institutions having the issuing power of money are more dangerous to liberty than standing armies." According to Jefferson, "If the American people ever allow private banks to control the issue of their currency, first by inflation, then by deflation, the banks and corporations that will grow up around the banks will deprive the people of all property until their children wake up homeless on the continent their fathers conquered. The issuing power should be taken from the banks and restored to the people, to whom it properly belongs"[108]. Today and after two hundred years, the banks continue to control the money dynamics and the majority of the people own debts to these banks.

President Andrew Jackson also recognized the dangers of banks when they are allowed to control the monetary system of the nation; he even viewed the banks charging people usury on money as vipers and thieves[109].

Abraham Lincoln went even further than his predecessors and ordered the government to issue what was called *greenback notes* in the amount of $450 million to avoid a massive interest bearing loans from banks. The bankers were intending to charge between 24% and 36% interest rates for loans to finance the civil war. Recognizing the power and adverse impact of the banks on the nation, Lincoln stated in 1865 in a statement to Congress, "I have two great enemies, the Southern Army in front of me and the bankers in the rear. Of the two, the one at my rear is my greatest foe"[109].

It was during the presidency of Woodrow Wilson in 1913 when the Federal Reserve Act was passed in the United States. Regretting his approval of the act, Wilson later made the following comments: "I am a most unhappy man. I have unwittingly ruined my country. A great industrial nation is controlled by its system of credit. Our system of credit is concentrated. The growth of the nation, therefore, and all our activities are in the hands of a few men"[110].

In the most recent history, President Kennedy tried to restore power to the US government by issuing a decree enabling the government to issue silver-based money. On June 4, 1963, President Kennedy signed Executive Order 11110, which virtually stripped the Federal Reserve Bank of its power to loan money to the United States government at interest[111]. This order gave the Treasury Department the authority to issue silver certificates against any silver in the treasury. There is no evidence that this order has been revoked or amended by any administration after Kennedy, although the decree has never been activated since the assassination of John F. Kennedy five months after the decree was signed. After the assassination of Kennedy, all US Treasury Department silver-backed notes were withdrawn from the market. Had the Kennedy decree been acted upon since it was created, the national debt of $11.9 trillion would have been nullified. Today, US government pays close to $400 billion in interest every year to the Federal Reserve Bank. This is a recipe for failure.

The Pennsylvania congressman McFadden who served as chairman of the Banking and Currency Committee for more than ten years summed up his view on the Federal Reserve Bank in his remarks to Congress in 1934:

> *Mr. Chairman, we have in this country one of the most corrupt institutions the world has ever known. I refer to the Federal Reserve Board and the Federal Reserve Banks, hereinafter called the Fed. The Fed has cheated the government of these United States and the people of the United States out of enough money to pay the nation's debt. The depredations and iniquities of the Fed has cost enough money to pay the national debt several times over... This evil institution has impoverished and ruined the people of these United States, has bankrupted itself, and has practically bankrupted our government. It has done this through the defects of the law under which it operates, through the maladministration of that law by the Fed, and through the corrupt practices of the moneyed vultures who control it.*

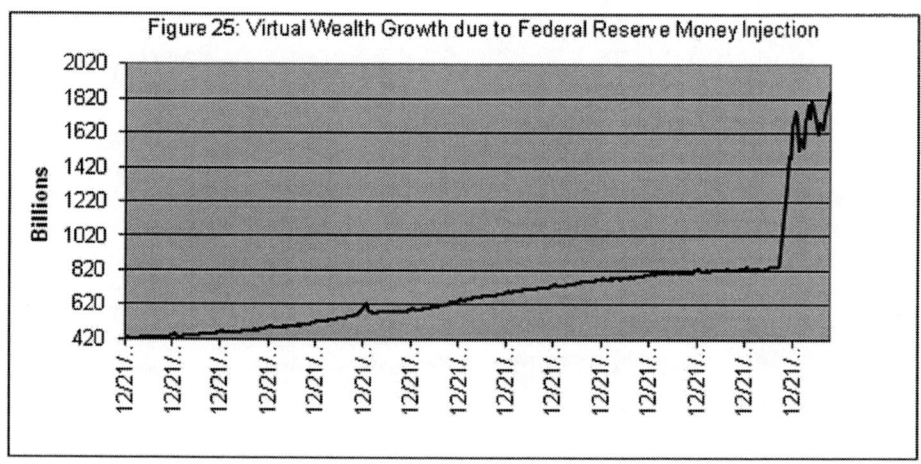

Figure 25 shows how the Federal Reserve Bank pumps money into its own account without consideration to the economic growth on the ground[107]. The data shows how the money reserves multiplied more than four times between 1994 and 2008; the total cache currency and reserves doubled in less than four months after the collapse of the Lehman Brothers Bank. The currency reserves rose from $850 billion on September 10, 2008, to $1,702 billion on December 31, 2008. It is needless to say that during this period (112 days), the economy could not have grown 200%.

The practice of the Federal Reserve contributes to the explosion of virtual wealth instead of working to control it. Instead of containing the phenomenon of virtual wealth growth at the expense of real economy growth, the Fed aggravates it.

Worldwide, the interest baring debt of states and governments is shocking. The total amount of debts for sixty countries exceeded $65 trillion at the end of 2008[112]. The interest paid on this debt exceeds $3 trillion a year; this interest alone is more than the amount of money required to pull the world out of the deep recession it plunged in.

At the world level, the International Monetary Fund (IMF) and the World Bank (WB) practice similar role to the one played by the Federal Reserve in the United States. The IMF and the WB grant loans with interest to almost every country in the world; the IMF and WB impose on many of the recipients of their loans conditions which impact the real economic growth of each country as well as the currency reserves and values. The external debt to IMF of twenty-five poorest countries reached $129.3 billion at the end of 2008.

The stories of IMF wrecking nations' economies are repeated in Argentina, Jamaica, Latvia, Ukraine, Hungary, Ethiopia, and many more. In an article published by the Center for Economic and Policy Research (CEPR)[113], the impact of IMF policies on the economic downturn of Ukraine, Latvia, and Hungary is detailed. These countries turned to IMF to help them cope with economic downturn. In all three countries, there were mistakes in economic policy that increased their vulnerability to external shocks. The governments' responses to the downturn, along with IMF conditions for assistance, have caused harm with procyclical policies. In Hungary, for example, a surge of foreign borrowing caused the country to run large account deficits in 2006 and 2007 (7.5 and 6.4% of GDP, respectively).

Latvia also suffered from a large reversal of capital flows due to a combination of procyclical fiscal and monetary policy—supported by an IMF agreement as well as funds from the European Union. By some estimates, the Latvian economy contracted by as much as 18% in 2009.

The decision by the Latvian government, in conjunction with the European Union and the IMF, to maintain Latvia's pegged exchange rate with the euro, has made recovery much more difficult. With the currency fixed rate, the only way to reduce the country's account imbalance was through shrinking the economy, which reduced imports faster than exports and reduced real wages.

This is similar to the IMF-sponsored policies in the deep Argentine recession of 1998-2002, where a fixed, overvalued currency worsened and prolonged the downturn until the Argentine currency collapsed in 2002.

Despite the ill practices and flawed policies of the IMF, the G8 group leader committed more than half of the allocated financial bailout money to IMF. In April 2009, the G8 leaders allocated $750 billion out of

$1,170 billions (65%) to be spent by IMF on projects presumably aimed at alleviating the poor conditions of poor nations. The previous history of IMF practices raises serious doubts that IMF loans will produce anything positive for the plight of the poorest nations in the world.

The IMF has always placed conditions on loans given to nations, which have deepened the nations' severe economic conditions. It has been noted almost without exception that when poor countries receive IMF loans, the GDP growth rate of these countries decline and the poverty rate increases. Pakistan is a good example of such trend[114], where the government is taking fiscal measures such as increase in general sales tax, increase in efforts in tax collection, removal of subsidies on domestic petroleum products, higher electricity tariffs, and effective measures to solve the issue of circular debt. These measures are ordained by the IMF so that the country may repay the interest charges of the loans it has borrowed from the IMF and its member states.

Ironically, when a nation declines to borrow from the IMF or to adhere to its policies, it risks the consequences of sanctions and political pressure from the main shareholders in the IMF such as the United States, UK, and France.

In summary, the practice of usury and interest accumulation on money investment contributes to the creation of virtual economy far greater in value than the real economy. It drives the wealth of nations accumulated via complex taxation systems towards the ever-growing accounts of local and international banks. The end result is a relatively small handful of people end up in control of a vast amount of wealth, most of which is virtually usury and interest.

Gold/Silver Standard and the Virtual Economy

Gold/silver standard refers to the monetary system where the currency of a nation is backed by a precious metal such as the gold and/or silver. When the currency such as the dollar is backed by gold or silver, it would be almost impossible to grow the finances of the country to such high limits where the country risks the depletion of its gold or silver reserves. The virtual economy, which thrives in the world of capitalism today, could not have become a reality, if main currency (e.g. US dollar) remained linked to the gold standard.

Until World War I, gold ruled as the monetary standard of all the major trading countries in the world. Each country pegged its currency to gold at a constant and unchanging rate. Under the gold standard, the international monetary systems enjoyed a period of unprecedented stability and prosperity.

In essence, the gold standard provided monetary discipline. The amount of currency a country could print was limited by the amount of gold in their reserves, because countries could have faced the requirement to convert their money to gold. Exchange rates between currencies of different nations remain fairly constant in the classical gold system.

The gold standard era was abruptly interrupted in World War I. Warring countries decided to print money without backing it up with gold in order to finance the extremely high costs of the war. An enormous amount of cache was poured into the markets without a solid backup for the money, giving rise to high inflation. This situation continued throughout the war and beyond. Germany had to repay under a reparations plan 132 billion marks and was required to back this amount by gold. Evidently, this requirement could not have been met by Germany; Germany could not spend its gold to pay for war crimes. The Europe allies have borrowed too much money from the United States, which demanded its loans be paid. The inability of Germany to comply with the postwar reparations plan and the failure of the allied countries to fulfill their loan obligations to the United States constituted a pretext for the Second World War.

In the mid-1920s, the gold standard was partially restored. However, the currency exchange rates were scrambled to reflect imbalances between the monetary power of the United States and the relatively weak currencies of European states, both victors (Britain and France) and defeated (Germany and Italy).

The restoration of the gold standard did not last for long. The world began to sink in a deep depression in 1928; and in 1929 the stock market in the United States crashed, leading to a worldwide economic panic. By 1931, major banks in Austria, Germany, and Hungary collapsed; the UK and many other countries decided to take their currencies off the gold standard. The world monetary system faced the same fate of inflation and lack of confidence for the second time since the beginning of the twentieth century.

Major industrial nations convened a "world monetary" conference in London in 1933 to discuss the possibility of restoring the gold standard; the participants failed to formalize any significant agreement. The world economic conditions fell under the pressure of a deep depression, coupled with a floating monetary system detached from gold, and as a result, high inflation, high unemployment, and high poverty rates. A second world war was imminent in 1939. The war and the massive military spending helped in stimulating the global economy and ending the Great Depression.

It is interesting to note that a by-product of the Great Depression was the introduction of the Keynesian brand of capitalism, in reference to

John Maynard Keynes[139]. Keynes argued that during economic crisis, the market laws of the price mechanism, product value, and relative scarcity cannot regulate the market by themselves; the government must intervene to stabilize the market. This marked the first major deviation from the original theories of capitalism, known as laissez-faire capitalism. Another important outcome of the Great Depression and the subsequent world war was the strong desire among the United States and European allies for economic cooperation and international monetary stability. Negotiations, debate, and serious talks resulted in what has become widely known as the Bretton Woods Agreement[115].

Bretton Woods Agreement established clear bases for currency exchange into gold within fluctuation rate not to exceed 1%; it also set the bases on how to convert currencies into gold. Bretton Woods established a system of payments based on the dollar, in which all currencies were defined in relation to the dollar. The dollar itself was designated to be convertible into gold. The US currency was now effectively the world currency, the standard to which every other currency was pegged. As the world's key currency, most international transactions were denominated in US dollars.

In 1944 the United States used its superior power relative to other European states, particularly Britain, to enforce the US dollar as the currency of choice for international trade. Moreover, the United States was given a veto power over the IMF decisions and operations by virtue of its voting power relative to its quota in the IMF which exceeded one-third of the IMF shares. The IMF was given ultimate authority to monitor the currency values of participating members. It made sure that there are sufficient gold reserves or US dollars in support of the local currency reserves.

The gold standard of Bretton Woods provided monetary stability, which prevented any economy from becoming virtually much larger than its real size. Building a virtual economy by any country would cost its stockpile of gold to deplete under the gold standard. There would not be sufficient gold to match the fictitious wealth of the virtual economy.

The aftermath of World War II and the principles put forth by the Bretton Woods Agreement exposed the deteriorating conditions of largely devastated and ravaged countries. Seventy percent of the world gold reserves accumulated in the United States, which became the world's largest creditor. Countries had sold off most of their gold and dollar reserves, as well as their foreign investments, to pay for the war-generated debts mostly to the United States. Practically, this brought the world economy to a standstill. Europe was unable to produce due to finance shortage, while the US products could not be exported due to shortage of dollars and gold at the other end. In order to stimulate the world economy, especially in Europe, the United States introduced the Marshall Plan[2]. In his historic speech at Harvard's graduation ceremony in June 1947, George Marshall announced the US plan to give additional economic aid to Europe for security, humanitarian, and economic reasons[116]. The Marshal Plan confirmed the position of the United States as the world's strongest economy, de facto leader of the Western world, and the legal inheritor of Europe supremacy and dominance.

The Marshal Plan, US international aid, and massive investment on cold war expenses provided dollar liquidity, eliminated its shortage, and fueled world economy. By the end of 1950s, most of the Western European currencies were convertible to dollar and then to gold. The dollar-gold exchange standard, based on fixed exchange rates overseen by the IMF, could finally be realized.

The increase in liquidity enabled the international economy to grow at a record rate. The 1950s and 1960s experienced a rapid growth of world economy fueled by US dollars. This required a constantly expanding supply of monetary reserves to increase total liquidity. Gold, the primary reserve asset, could not be mined fast enough to meet this demand. A subsequent result would be high inflation in the world's largest economy in the United States and a depletion of gold reserves. An immediate solution to this problem could have been to reduce the liquidity rate in an attempt to preserve the gold reserve. Of course this could have led to a crisis in which most of the world wiuld have plunged into economic stagnation and would have suffered from declining trade.

Henry H. Fowler, US secretary of the treasury under Johnson (1965-1968), warned that it was too much of a burden for the United States to supply the world with currency reserve and gold. The dilemma that the United States and world economy faced was one of two options. One was to cut down on the flow of US dollars to Europe and the third world through loans, aid, and spending on cold war expenses. This of course would slow the economy which was prospering at a high rate and force the world economy to stay within the boundaries of the gold reserves. The other option was to continue to pump US dollars in the world economy. When the central banks in Europe seek to convert their dollar reserves into gold, that request should be denied; in essence the United States should terminate the convertibility of dollar into gold. Abort Bretton Woods Agreement.

---

[2] George Marshal was the secretary of State (1947-1948) during Truman administration

The choice was in the hands of US financial policy makers between two forms of economy. A real economy backed by gold-based currencies, which grows slowly but surely. Or a virtual economy characterized by pure-paper (and later digital) currencies without any backup from any precious metal, gold or silver. The virtual economy option allows for a virtually large liquidity, allows for an unprecedented wealth growth, allows unparalleled superiority over the Soviet Socialists camp, and allows the preservation of the US gold reserves. As attractive as this option could be, it became the first brick in the grave of the capitalist economy.

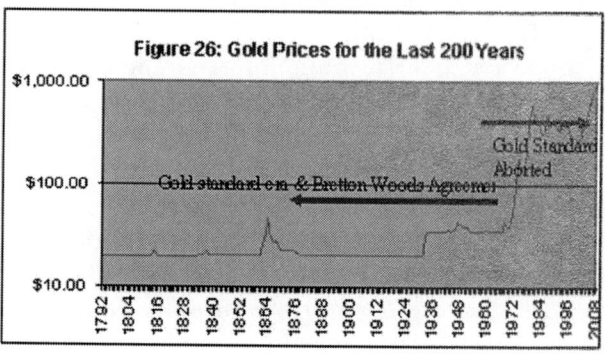

The cold war and the fierce struggle with the Soviet socialism provided the suitable environment for this option to flourish and provided the shield which prevented policy makers from carefully evaluating the dangers of such option. The greed of the financial institutions which were responsible for providing the liquidity, in particular the US Federal Reserve Consortium pushed this option forward with great avidity and eagerness. The path was thus paved for the revocation of Bretton Woods Act.

The dollar-gold convertibility crisis was evident by the amount of dollars held in the central banks of Europe. By 1966, Europe held in its central banks more than $14 billion. The United States had only $13.2 billion in gold reserves, of which $10 billion were needed to support US internal market needs. If governments and foreign central banks tried to convert even a quarter of their holdings at one time, the United States would not be able to honor its obligations. The relatively low price of gold at $35 an ounce as determined by Bretton Woods tempted speculators, gold merchants, and rich entities to purchase and hoard gold, thus increasing the rate of gold depletion in the world markets.

In 1971, the central banks in Europe began to redeem gold for their large stockpile of dollars. The US gold supplies were at the risk of vanishing. On August 15, 1971, the United States stunned the world by declaring that it would no longer redeem dollars for gold from its reserves. Essentially, the United States unilaterally aborted Bretton Woods Agreement. The dollar's link to gold was severed. A quarter century of economic stability had finally collapsed, and a new era of unbounded financial growth began. By 1973, other countries in the world abandoned the gold standard. For the first time in history, the gold officially became just a commodity, whose price is subject to market rules and regulations. Figure 26 shows the rise of gold prices and their fluctuation based on the London Spot Gold Prices[117]. The gold prices remained almost stable until 1972 when the United States relinquished the gold standard. After the financial crisis in 2008, the price of gold exceeded $1,200 per ounce.

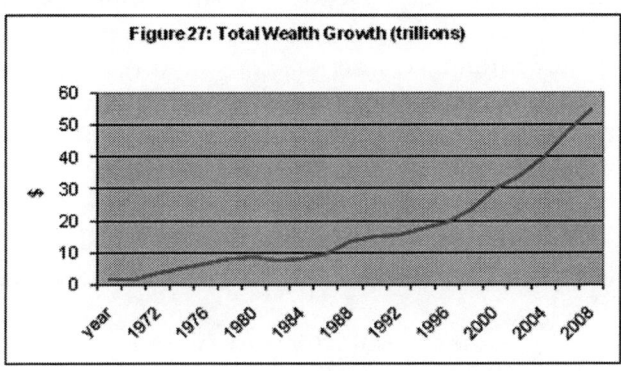

Since the breakdown of Bretton Woods in 1971 and the end of the gold standard, the dollar has become the default international reserve currency. The twenty years prior to 1970, international dollar reserves increased only about 55%, at a rate of 2.7% a year. Between 1971 and 2001, with the adoption of the dollar instead of gold standard, reserves have increased over 2,000%, at a rate of more than 66% a year[118]. Figure 27 shows the growth of the world wealth since 1972. Such growth could not have been possible under the gold standard. But when United States turned against Bretton Woods Agreement and broke the link between the dollar and the gold, it freed the dollar from the rein of the gold and unleashed its potential for virtual growth.

After the death of Bretton Woods Agreement, the gold could no longer set boundaries to the growth rate of the dollar based economy; yet there was another string attached to the dollar, which kept it from skyrocketing at exponential rates as noted in figure 27. The string was a set of regulations and restrictions which were placed against financial institutions after the great 1929 Depression. Restrictions were introduced in the 1930s by political leaders to prevent another depression in the future. In essence, the restrictions limited the ability of the financial institutions to grow their wealth by giving more and more loans and generating more and more interest on the loans. Borrowers were required by the regulations to put a significant amount of money down when they borrowed to finance a house purchase. That left the interest-bearing portion of the loan relatively smaller.

In 1982, the Reagan administration decided that the government regulations were impeding the progress of the economy. The government lifted those regulations and removed the restrictions as Regan signed the Garn-St. Germain Depository Institutions Act in 1982 (140, 141). As a result, the US banks embarked on a credit and loan spree with almost no government restrictions, or sound fiscal prudence. Before the Reagan deregulation, the average American household debt was 60%. By 2007, this figure had doubled to 119%[119]. This was made possible by relaxing the standards placed on borrowing and lending.

The two main constraints placed against the free rise of the dollar wealth were removed by the early 1980s. The gold standard was revoked in 1971 and a decade later the regulations on the financial industry were lifted.

In the final result, the economy in the largest capitalist country has been split into two almost independent branches: a real branch responsible for the production of goods and services and a virtual branch responsible for the production of money. Each branch grows or shrinks at its own pace, and possibly in opposing directions. The real economy might shrink, while the virtual money continues to grow. The growth of virtual money is driven mainly by the stock market value and the interest/usury generated through an extensive credit and loan system. The virtual part of the economy reigned over the rest of the economy.

Virtual economy and the unbounded growth of wealth acted in a way like the *Achilles' heel*. It provided a sense of power, a feeling of strength, a tool of prosperity, and enormous wealth. The danger of the virtual economy is that it creates a state of delusion in the economy, which can deceive senior economists and politicians, and drives them to overtake projects larger than their real wealth. There could be a temporary positive effect for this delusion, especially when competing with others for large projects. America has benefited greatly while in a conflict with the Soviet Union during the cold war era, where the Soviet Union used real money to finance its projects and America used virtual economy for its own projects. But when a state is exposed to a financial or political crisis larger than the size of its real economy, the illusion may push the state to a losing gamble. The current wars in Iraq, Afghanistan, Somalia, and the devastating effects of hurricanes in the United States are just examples of external conditions which contribute to the implosion of virtual economy. More seriously is the case when foreign countries intentionally create real crisis for other countries that depend on the virtual economy in an attempt to push them to the limits of their real economy.

It is interesting to note that the delusion created by virtual economy blindfolds policy makers and prevents them from avoiding imminent catastrophes until the virtual economy reaches the point of thrashing. This has occurred in 1929, 1987, 1999-2000, and 2008. And it is not over yet. The consumer credit is just about to explode in yet another devastating cycle of the virtual economy thrashing.

The irony is that the current state of the economy and the enduring crisis is not entirely due to the grave mistakes by the Nixon and Reagan administrations in the 1970s and the 1980s. The policies undertaken by both could have naturally evolved out of the foundations of capitalism. The regulations which Reagan had removed were in violation of the principles of capitalism to start with, as recognized by Reagan and his administration. The gold standard could have been revoked by any capitalist leader for more than one reason. On one side it puts a limit on how much the wealth can grow which conflicts with the principles of private ownership. Also, it prevents the treatment of gold and/or silver as a commodity whose price should be subject to supply and demand. So what really appeared to be a grave mistake of politicians is in fact a grave defect of the ideology itself.

Similarly, the creation of virtual wealth in contrast to the real economy stems from the definition of value under capitalism which treats the value of objects as a relative one. This concept allows the existence of stock markets where the prices (exchange value) of stocks can be traded independently of the production market.

The same concept of "value" under capitalism allows the money itself to be a commodity which can be produced by money rather than by the production of goods and services. In other words, money can be produced by money, in the same manner vegetables can be produced by labor paid for by money. Capitalism does not place any special constraints on the money. When World Wars I and II revealed that uncontrolled production of money can be catastrophic to the political and economic stability of the world, the Capitalist countries had to unanimously agree on placing special constraints on the production of money. They adopted the gold standard not as a means of implementing an ideological principle but in defiance of the ideological principles of free trade, value definition, and price mechanism. When the effects of World War II drove away and the need emerged to produce more wealth and create more liquidity, the US government did not find it totally uncapitalistic to abort the gold standard.

When the financial crisis shocked and swayed the world in 2008, several world leaders including the prime minister of Britain and prominent French leaders called for the reconstruction of Bretton Woods Agreement[120].

However, none of the economists have argued that a gold standard should be restored on the premise that it belongs to the principles of capitalism.

5.2 State and Public Ownership: Conflict with Capitalism

At the root of the definition of *capitalism* is "private ownership." In *Merriam-Webster* dictionary, *capitalism* is defined as "an economic system characterized by private or corporate ownership of capital goods." Milton Friedman, a Nobel Prize winner in economics, characterized capitalism as a working model of a society organized through voluntary exchange and free private enterprise exchange economy[121]. According to novelist and philosopher Ayn Rand, all property is privately owned under capitalism[121]. By the same token, economist George Reisman confirms the fact that capitalism is a social system based on private ownership[122]. *Encyclopedia Britannica* has the following definition: "capitalism, also called free market economy, or free enterprise economy: economic system, dominant in the Western world since the breakup of feudalism, in which most of the means of production are privately owned and production is guided and income distributed largely through the operation of markets."

Public or state ownership of the means of production such as auto industry or financial institutions is in direct conflict of the foundation of capitalism. The *Chambers 21st Century Dictionary* explicitly rejects state ownership in its definition of capitalism as "an economic system based on private, rather than state, ownership of businesses, factories, and transport services, etc., with free competition and profit-making."

The role of the state in a capitalist society is more applicable to regulations of industry than owning it. The fact that government intervention to own part of the industry may lead to the stabilization of a turbulent economy does not make this intervention a valid move from the perspective of capitalism. On the contrary, this reveals a notable defect in the theory of capitalism which allows only one form of ownership, that is, the private ownership.

When financial and economic crisis reaches a point where the state interferes and takes over some of the failing institutions to prevent a wide-scale collapse of the economy, then the plight of capitalism as a system is questionable. The following dilemma emerges. If capitalism is left to operate under its own theories and principles of free market, free enterprise, and self-maintenance, then a collapse of the financial institutions followed by a failure of the entire economic system may become inevitable. If the government interferes and transfers the private ownership to state and public ownership, then the foundation of the system of capitalism is in jeopardy.

Federal Reserve chief Bernanke clearly identified the dilemma of capitalism when he said, *"If Bear Stearns had been allowed to fail, the adverse impact of a default would not have been confined to the financial system but would have been felt broadly in the real economy through its effects on asset values and credit availability"*[47].

In the most recent financial crisis, the US government took over the ownership of several industries and financial institutions. It took over control of giant mortgage companies Fannie Mae and Freddie Mac. The takeover action has been described as "one of the most sweeping government interventions in private financial markets in decades,"[124] and one that "could turn into the biggest and costliest government bailout ever of private companies"[125]. With over $5 trillion outstanding mortgage backed securities, the failure of these companies would have been disastrous for the housing economy, the American economy, and the world economy[126].

The US government seized control of American International Group Inc (AIG), one of the world's biggest insurers, in an $85 billion deal that signaled the intensity of its concerns about the danger a collapse could pose to the financial system[123]. This takeover puts the government in control of a private company, which marks a historic development in the world of capitalism.

The government extended its property ownership to the auto industry. After negotiating the fate of the failing auto industry in bankruptcy courts, the US government acquired 60% of GM shares and almost 10% of Chrysler. The pretext for the takeover of the auto industry is the same as the pretext for acquiring financial institutions: avoid disaster to the American economy and the world economy.

If the financial crisis had proved anything of significance, it proved that private ownership of individuals and enterprises cannot sustain the economic stability by itself. Private ownership alone creates a unipolar economic structure which is bound to fail as a result of its own weight. This becomes more evident as the economy grows to virtually large sizes and its weight becomes too heavy to survive on a single pole. In order to prevent a total collapse, the governments rush to support the structure with two additional poles: state and public ownership. Capitalism, essentially, is a unipolar economic structure (a structure with a single pole). The irony is that capitalism creates an environment where the size of the economy grows at a very rapid rate. As a result, the crisis of capitalism continues to explode, threatening the capitalist economies to implode from within.

The sporadic augmentation of private ownership with state and public ownership can prove effective only for a short period of time. This will not prevent a total collapse. The reason is that state ownership is added to the system under the pressure of the crisis and not as a result of a well-thought strategy which reveals the necessity and importance of state and public ownership of certain segments of the economy. Under the pressure of the crisis, the state is forced to partially or completely own a segment of the economy without the least theoretical or ideological justification of the move. The nationalization of a particular segment of the economy pushes the economic system away from its regular course without defining a new path or course for the economy to pursue. The end result is an economy without a well-defined character: neither capitalism nor socialism. It is not Islamic either, as will be explained in the next part of this book.

For the sake of historical reference, it is interesting to note that Soviet socialism experienced similar deviation from its normal course when private ownership was introduced to the collective farms within the agricultural industry. This was introduced during the late Stalin and Khrushchev eras to increase the productivity of farmers and avoid a serious shortage of food supplies. More reforms in this direction were introduced under the Gorbachev *perestroika* plans. The argument here is not whether these modifications and reforms are useful or not; the main argument is that this constitutes a major deviation from the original course of the economic system. Such modifications cause the system to lose its main characteristic. Socialism as a system failed altogether in the old Soviet Union and the Eastern Europe countries. One major reason for the failure was the deviation from its normal course of action.

By the same token, capitalism today suffers from the urgent need to change its route and modify its course of action by introducing state and public ownership to the system, although in a nonsystematic manner. The rules of the free market are no longer the only rules that control the flow of wealth and the production of goods and services. The principles of relative scarcity and the price mechanism tend to blur and become vague in the wake of government sporadic intervention in the economy. The long-lived characteristics of capitalist economy, especially growth and predictability, can no longer be sustained due to the inclusion of new subjective factors in the formulas governing free market economy. Today, free market rules point to one direction in the real estate industry, while the government ownership of major mortgage companies force the prices in the real estate to point in another direction.

In summary, the two major signs of failure of the capitalist economy are the creation of virtual economy on top of the real economy and the deviation from the rules of free market by introducing state and public ownership alongside the private ownership. Virtual economy creates an illusion in the economy which allows the total wealth to appear much larger than its real worth. This illusion was made possible by the stock market trades, which exploit the relative values of things, by allowing money to grow through interest/usury, by detaching money from the gold base, and by disassociating the money from the economic strength of a country. The virtual economy is bound to crash and return to the normal values of the economy.

The introduction of state ownership leads to the confusion of the free market rules and to a serious deviation from the original course of capitalism.

I.6 What Is Next?

The economic meltdown, the financial crisis, the government takeover of privately owned enterprise, and the implosion of the virtual economy render the entire politico-economic model of free enterprise and rugged individualism a broken one. There is almost unanimous agreement that a fundamental change to the current politico-economic model is urgently needed. This change appeared in the media in various forms and slogans. One of these slogans was borrowed from Obama's words, "remaking America," which was repeated in the front pages of the *New York Times*, the *Washington Post*, *USA Today*, *LA Times*, and many more[127].

This tone has revoked the belief that capitalism in its purest free market form was the ultimate and highest point of historic economic evolution, a belief which climaxed as the Soviet brand of socialism collapsed in 1991. Francis Fukayama, who advocated the notion of free market superiority in his book *End of History and the Last Man*,[33] revoked that belief in 2008 when he wrote, "The Fall of America, Inc." The article which appeared in the *Newsweek* edition on October 4, 2008, declared that the current version of capitalism has failed; in Fukayama's words, "a certain vision of capitalism has collapsed." A new vision is required.

"A New Form of capitalism Can Remake Broken Country" is the title of another article which appeared in the *Independent Daily* newspaper on January 22, 2009,[127]. The article suggests a new evolution of capitalism that could serve as model for broader collaboration between government and private enterprise.

The names that have been suggested for a new form of capitalism show how the image of capitalism has been tarnished in the eyes of the public. One of the publications[128] presents the following alternative names for new forms of capitalism: "Bubble Capitalism," "Ponzi Capitalism," "Crony Capitalism," and "Geonomic Capitalism."

James Arthur Ray, *New York Times* best-selling author, wrote "A New Form of Capitalism: Dealing with the Cause Versus the Effect," which appeared in the *HuffPost Social News*[129]. In this article, James Arthur argues that socialism and/or communism cannot be a viable alternative to capitalism because socialism itself has failed. He concludes, saying, "I submit capitalism is the only viable option. Yet a new type of capitalism must be adopted, a type that I call Conscious Capitalism." Conscious capitalism addressed the moral factor behind the failure of current free market capitalism.

In the Davos Annual Meeting 2008, Bill Gates addressed the need for a new form of capitalism, which he called "Creative Capitalism"[130]. Bill Gates stated that the world today needs more "system innovation than technology innovation." Creative capitalism, according to Bill Gates, should harness the productivity generated by the pursue of self-interest, while at the same time it benefits the ones who do not have access to the profit. In essence, Bill Gates calls for a mechanism for wealth distribution other than the price mechanism and the forces of the market.

Richard M. Ebeling, president of the Foundation for Economic Education, argues that there is no such thing as "capitalism." Rather there are different types of capitalism from which governments and societies may choose[131]. According to Ebeling, the socialist or fascist brands of capitalism are dismissed only because of the linguistic and ideological connotation associated with these words.

The real issue here is not how to rename capitalism. If this was the issue, a world contest could be organized with a nice prize to choose from a wide range of names or to come up with a totally new name. To list a few of the names that have been tossed around in one or another publications, here is a short list: Liberal Capitalism, Social Capitalism, Fascist Capitalism, National Capitalism, Creative Capitalism, Collective Capitalism, Competing Capitalism, Conscious Capitalism, Bubble Capitalism, Ponzi Capitalism, Crony Capitalism, Geonomic Capitalism, and What-Have-You capitalism.

The discussions on the brand of capitalism, the future of capitalism, the renaming of capitalism, the evolution of capitalism, and the failure of capitalism reveal three major fundamental factors which must be taken into consideration when considering a restructuring of the economic system. The first and foremost has to do with the moral aspect of the system. It is almost unanimously agreed across the board that the collapse of the free market politico-economic model was preceded by a collapse of the moral structure that supports it. Recognizing this factor, James Arthur proposed what he called the "Conscious Capitalism." The new system, no matter what name it bears, must incorporate a moral model. The moral model must be tightly coupled with and inseparable from the system. The moral model cannot be an option, or an extra added value; it has to be an integral part of the system.

The second factor has to do with wealth distribution such that the least privileged and the poorest in a society may have the chance to benefit from the large sums of profits generated by the power of self-interest pursuit. It is simply unacceptable to live in a world with accumulative wealth exceeding $100 trillion and 20% of its population (more than one billion) lives under $1 a day. The new system, no matter what name it bears, must incorporate a distribution mechanism which recognizes the fact that the produced wealth may not reach a segment of the population for all types of reasons. The distribution mechanism must be an integral part of the system and not an option that can be added or removed by politicians based on local or world conditions. The distribution mechanism must be explicit to the extent that the judicial system and political system can enforce it with the power of law.

The third factor has to do with the need for state and public ownership to coexist with private ownership. This necessity has been recognized by scores of economists and politicians and had been known as Keynesian brand of capitalism (in reference to John Maynard Keynes of Great Britain). Keynes argued that the government must intervene to stabilize the market. This necessity has been further asserted through the most recent practices in the United States and score of other European countries, where governments moved to acquire the ownerships of banks, insurance companies, auto industries, and others.

But state ownership cannot be applied on a need only basis and under the slogan of "too big to fail." State ownership should be more fundamentally defined; it should be an integral part of the system which defines the scope of private ownership, the state ownership, and the public common ownership. Who owns what should not be left to the political and economic conditions to dictate. It should not be left until crisis hit home and then force politicians to decide on which property to own and which property to dissolve. "Too big to fail" is too vague of a principle to apply.

The US government moved to own a significant portion of General Motors, Chrysler, Freddie Mac, Fannie Mae, and Bear Stearns using the principle of "too big to fail." Now the government has an overwhelming power of deciding what cars will be produced and what mortgages will be available for home buyers. Would the government move to own part of Wal-Mart if it ever experiences hardship and be deemed as too big to fail? And the government would decide on what type of clothes the people would wear? This is how the Soviet Union operated during the socialist era. It is true that state property should be part of the economic system, but it should be well defined based on integral principals of the system. It cannot be an option or an added value to the system. State and public property should be protected by law in the same manner private property is protected. Private property should never be transferred into state or public property; by the same token, state and public property should never be subject for privatization. The limits and boundaries of each must be clearly defined by the system and not left for the conditions and politicians to set these limits.

These three factors: the moral model, the wealth distribution mechanism, and the property ownership boundary limits, are the essence of the crisis within capitalism. The solution to this crisis is not simply a renaming of capitalism. Neither can a solution be obtained by augmenting the system with some modifications. When the three factors are integrated into the system, the fundamentals of capitalism would have changed in a manner that the future generations would not recognize capitalism at all. Fundamental changes to the principals of a system are not a matter of evolution.

When the socialists finally realized that there were major defects within socialism, they decided to move on; they replaced the system altogether. There was no sense in mending it, adding new features, or evolving it into a capitalist socialism, liberal socialism, modern socialism, national socialism, conscious socialism, creative socialism, or what-have-you socialism. The perestroika of Gorbachev abolished socialism altogether. The alternative for the Russians at the time was capitalism. They moved to capitalism with full force.

What is the alternative to capitalism today? Of course socialism is not an option. Socialism failed after it has been tested for more than seventy years. In the next part of this book, I argue that Islam provides a viable alternative. It provides a system that integrates a well-defined property ownership with clear distinction between private, state, and public; it incorporates a wealth distribution mechanism which eliminates poverty while it boosts productivity and wealth generation, and it provides a sound and practical moral model.

My argument in this book is that Islam provides a comprehensive view of the politico-economic model. It addresses the basic principles upon which any economic system must stand. It systematically details the concept of property ownership; it systematically addresses the wealth distribution such that wealth does not flow in the direction of the rich only;

it provides a moral foundation which systematically calls for the removal of greed and selfishness from the process of production and consumption.

The presentation of the Islamic model in this book is meant to broaden the discussion and analysis of economic systems from the current dual character (capitalism and socialism) to a tri-character (capitalism, socialism, and Islam). My objective is not to persuade the reader with the details of the Islamic system. The main objective, however, is to conclude that yet there is one more system in the world capable of organizing the affairs of people, managing the financial and economic transactions, and conducting the relations between people. This system is the Islamic system. After introducing this system in the next part (part 2), I will then move to part 3 to address the ever-burning question to the non-Muslim reader: is Islam a threat to the world community or a benefit?

REFERENCES (PART 1)

1. G8 Leaders Declaration: Responsible Leadership for a Sustainable Future, http://www.g8italia2009.it
2. Francis Fukayama *"The Fall of America, Inc.,"* Newsweek, October 4, 2008
3. http://www.capitalismhitsthefan.com/
4. Noah Feldman, *"The Fall and Rise of the Islamic State,"* Princeton University Press, 2008, ISBN: 978-0-691-12045-4
5. Patrick Buchanan, *"An Idea Whose Time Has Come,"* www.townhall.com, June 2006
6. Samuel Huntington, *"Clash of Civilization and the Making of World Order,"* First Touchstone Edition 1997, ISBN: 0-684-81164-2
7. Martin Wolf, *"This Crisis is a Moment, but is it a Defining One?"* The Financial Times, http://www.ft.com/indepth/capitalism-future, May 19, 2009
8. Leszek Balcerowicz, *"This has not Been a Pure Failure of Markets,"* The Financial Times, www.ft.com/capitalismblog, May 13, 2009
9. Edmund Phelps, *"Uncertainty bedevils the best system,"* The Financial Times, www.ft.com/capitalismblog, April 14, 2009.
10. Sir Martin Sorrell, *"The pendulum will swing back,* The Financial Times, www.ft.com/capitalismblog, April 8, 2009.
11. Zbigniew Brzezinski, *"Second Chance: Three Presidents and the American Superpower,"* Basic Books, 2007; ISBN: 13:978-0-465-00252-8; pp. 41-42; 182.
12. Jimmy Carter, *"Our Endangered Values: America's Moral Crisis,"* New York, NY: Simon & Schuster, 2005.
13. Barack Obama, "Renewing the American Economy," transcript of speech at Cooper Union, *New York Times*, March 27, 2008.
14. Rick Klein, "McCain Blames Greed for Wall Street Mess," *ABC News*, September 16, 2008.

15. Jo Becker, Sheryl Gay Stolberg, and Stephen Labaton, "White House Philosophy Stoked Mortgage Bonfire," *New York Times*, December 20, 2008, p. A1.
16. Oskari Juurikkala, "*Greed Hurts: Causes of the Global Financial Crisis,*" http://www.acton.org/commentary/425_greed_hurts.php.
17. John Steele Gordon, "*Greed, Stupidity, Delusion—and Some More Greed*" September 22, 2008.
18. http://knowledge.wharton.upenn.edu/article.cfm?articleid=2204, April 14, 2009.
19. http://www.timesonline.co.uk/tol/comment/faith/article4950733.ece.
20. Financial Downfall a Moral Not Financial Crisis, Inner Projection, May 23, 2009.
21. Jeffery Kuhner, "Our moral crisis," Washington Times, October 5, 2009, http://www.washingtontimes.com/news/2008/oct/05/our-moral-crisis/.
22. Moral Crisis More Critical than Financial Crisis, NDTV, April 6, 2009.
23. Timothy Woods, "Moral Crisis & Problems With Modern capitalism," November 20, 2008, http://www.suite101.com/.
24. Theodore Roosevelt Malloch, "The Deeper Roots of Our Financial Crisis" The American Spectator, February 11, 09.
25. http://www.upi.com/Top_News/2008/09/16/Nader-Financial-crisis-pure-greed/UPI-43731221599036/.
26. Charles Tripp, "Islam and the Moral Economy: The Challenge of capitalism," Cambridge University Press, (ISBN-13: 9780521682442).
27. James Joyner, "Islamic Banks Surge, Thanks to Financial Crisis," Atlantic Council, December 24, 2008, http://www.acus.org/new_atlanticist/islamic-banks-surge-thanks-financial-crisis.
28. Washington Post "*Islamic Banking: Steady In Shady Times,*" Friday, October 31, 2008, http://www.washingtonpost.com.
29. M. Umer Charpa presented a paper under the title "The Global Financial Crisis: Can Islamic Financi Help Minimize the Severity and Frequency of Such a Crisis in the Future?"
30. Ossi V. Lindqvist, "*Islamic World and Western World: Is There Mutual Understanding?*"; Ubiquitous ICT For Sustainable Education and Cultural Literacy, October 6-7, 2008.
31. http://www.ameinfo.com/177501.html.
32. Karl Marx, "*A Contribution to the Critique of Political Economy" (1859)*.
33. Francis Fukayama, "*The End of History and the Last Man,*" Penguin, 1992.
34. Adam Smith, "*The Wealth of Nations*" (1776).
35. David Ricardo, "*The Principles of Political Economy and Taxation*" (1817)
36. Thomas Jefferson "*Jefferson's Letter to the Danbury Baptists.*" U.S. Library of Congress. http://www.loc.gov/loc/lcib/9806/danpre.html. Retrieved 2006-11-31.

37. Milton Friedman, *"The Social Responsibility of Business is to Increase its Profits,"* The New York Times Magazine, September 13, 1970.
38. Von Friedrich Wieser,; *Der natürliche Werth* [*Natural Value*] (1889), Bk I Ch V "Marginal Utility."
39. Sorin Cucerai, "The Fear of capitalism and One of its Sources," *Idei in Dialog*, May 2009.
40. Nouriel Roubini, "Laissez-Faire capitalism Has Failed," Forbes.com, Feb 19, 2009.
41. Taqiuddin al-Nabhani, "The Economic System in Islam," 1953.
42. Mohammad Baqir Al-Sadr, "Our Economy—Iqtisaduna."
43. Equal Pay Act of 1963 *(Pub. L. 88-38) (EPA), volume 29 of the United States Code, at section 206(d)*.
44. Robert Bryce, *Pipe Dreams: Greed, Ego, and the Death of Enron*. Public Affairs. ISBN 1-586-48201-7, December, 2008.
45. Emperors of Avarice: CEOs and Corporate Greed, film 2002.
46. Lionel Robbins, *"An Essay on the Nature and Significance of Economic Science,"* London: Macmillan and Co., Limited, 1945.
47. Bernanke Defends Bear Stearns Rescue, http://newsok.com/bernanke-defends-bear-stearns-rescue/article/3224837.
48. Carly Fiorina, http://www.hp.com/hpinfo/execteam/speeches/fiorina/minnesota01.htm.
49. Ayn Rand, *"capitalism: The Unknown Ideal,"* 1967.
50. Ayn Rand, *"The Virtue of Selfishness,"* 1964.
51. World Food Summit at of the Food and Agriculture Organization (FAO), Rome 1996.
52. Bureau of Economic Analysis, National Economic Accounts, http://www.bea.gov/national/nipaweb.
53. World Bank Group, *http://iresearch.worldbank.org/PovcalNet/povDuplic.html*.
54. CPI Inflation Calculator, Bureau of Labor Statistics, http://www.bls.gov/data/inflation_calculator.htm.
55. Hadeeth # 1000, "Al-Muntaqa Min Al-Targheeb Wal Tarheeb," Sheikh Shakir.
56. The Physician Task Force on Hunger in America, Harvard School of Public Health, http://hunger.tufts.edu/pub/hungeramerica.shtml.
57. Ardis Armstrong Young, *"Eliminating Hunger in America,"* http://ageconsearch.umn.edu/bitstream/17653/1/ar880107.pdf.
58. http://www.starvation.net/.
59. FAO Millennium Development Goals Report 2009, United Nations.
60. The World Health Report 2004, www.who.com.
61. UNESCO (2006, 2007). *Strong foundations: early childhood care and education.* EFA (Education for All) Global Monitoring Report 2007. Paris: UNESCO.

62 http://www.ips.org/institutional/.
63 John Madeley, Hungry for Trade (London & New York: Zed Books, 2000), 54-55, 75.
64 Friedmann, "The political economy of food: the rise and fall of the postwar international food order," American Journal of Sociology, 88S (1982): 248-86.
65 http://www.ed.gov/index.jhtml.
66 http://www.nifl.gov/.
67 Book of Hadeeth, Sahih Termizi, Hadeeth Number 2346.
68 http://americanhealthcrisis.com/
69 Pentagon Spending Request—Discretionary, http://www.armscontrolcenter.org.
70 http://www.globalissues.org/article/75/world-military-spending.
71 http://abcnews.go.com/Primetime/Health/story?id=1406691.
72 Chu, M. C. and J. Rhoades, The Uninsured in America, 1996-2007: Estimates for the U.S. Civilian Noninstitutionalized Population Under Age 65, Medical Expenditure Panel Survey, *AHRQ*, Statistical Brief #214, July 2008.
73 Gilmer, T. P. and R. G. Kronick, Hard Times And Health Insurance: How Many Americans Will Be Uninsured By 2010?, *Health Affairs* Web Exclusive, May 28, 2009.
74 The Henry J. Kaiser Family Foundation. *Employee Health Benefits: 2008 Annual Survey*. September 2008. http://www.kff.org/insurance/7672/index.cfm.
75 Schwartz, K., Spotlight on Uninsured Parents: How Lack of Coverage Affects Parents and Their Families, Kaiser Commission on Medicaid and the Uninsured, 2008.
76 Kaiser Family Foundation. HIV/AIDS Policy Fact Sheet: African Americans and HIV/AIDS. February 2005.
77 WHO REPORT 2007, Global Tuberculosis Control, Surveillance, Planning, Financing; http://www.who.int/tb/publications/global_report/2007/pdf/full.pdf.
78 Walsh J. Establishing health priorities in the developing world. New York: United Nations Development Programme, 1988.
79 http://apps.who.int/tb/surveillanceworkshop/tb_in_who_regions/afr/default.htm.
80 World War I casualties. *Twentieth Century Atlas*. http://users.erols.com/mwhite28/warstat1.htm. Retrieved 2008-12-21
81 World War II: Combatants and Casualties (1937-1945)." http://web.jjay.cuny.edu/~jobrien/reference/ob62.html. Retrieved 2007-04-20.
82 Lappe, Frances Moore, Joseph Collins, and Peter Rosset; "World hunger: Twelve Myths," New York: Grove Press. Second Edition 1998.
83 Brzezinski, Zbigniew. *Power and Principle: Memoirs of the National Security Adviser, 1977-1981*. New York: Farrar, Strauss, Giroux, 1983. ISBN 0-374-23663-1. pg. 44.

[84] *Public Papers of the Presidents of the United States. George Bush 1990*, vol. 2. Washington, D.C.: U.S. Government Printing Office, 1991.
[85] Thomas L. Friedman, Special to The New York Times, Wednesday, November 14, 1990.
[86] Blaine Harden, *"Africa's Diamond Wars"* The New York Times 2000.
[87] Amnesty International, 2007.
[88] Hersh, Seymour M. *Chain of Command: The Road from 9/11 to Abu Ghraib*. New York: HarperCollins, 2004. ISBN 0060195916.
[89] UN Press release, February 16, 2006.
[90] Tuskegee University, Alabama USA.
[91] www.whitehouse.gov/news/releases/2003/07.
[92] www.census.gov/hhes/income/histinc/index.html.
[93] http://www.hrw.org/en/reports/2008/01/30/world-report-2008.
[94] http://www.amnesty.org/en/library/asset/MDE23/009/2009/en/692d9e42-b009-462a-8a16-7336ea4dfc3c/mde230092009en.pdf.
[95] http://www.ilo.org/global/lang—en/index.htm.
[96] http://en.wikipedia.org/wiki/CPPCG.
[97] *David Stannard, American Holocaust: The Conquest of the New World* (Oxford University Press, 1992).
[98] http://www.antiwar.com/casualties/.
[99] Bernanke Defends Bear Stearns Rescue, http://newsok.com/bernanke-defends-bear-stearns-rescue/article/3224837.
[100] Daniel Gross, *NEWSWEEK; Oct 11, 2008*.
[101] Harold Bierman, Jr., *"The 1929 Stock Market Crash"* Cornell University, http://eh.net/encyclopedia/article/Bierman.crash.
[102] Hoover, Herbert. The Memoirs of Herbert Hoover. New York, Macmillan, 1952.
[103] John Paul Koning, Explaining the 1987 Stock Market Crash and Potential Implications, http://www.lope.ca/markets/1987crash/1987crash.pdf.
[104] Will dotcom bubble burst again? / QCTimes.com.
[105] http://seattletimes.nwsource.com/art/news/business/infospace/infospaceTimelineDay1_2_intro.swf.
[106] http://www.washingtonpost.com/wpsrv/business/longterm/blackm/87oct.htm.
[107] Martin Weiss, Ph.D., "Bernanke gone berserk! Bank reserves explode!" Money and Market, October 19, 2009.
[108] http://www.quotationspage.com/quote/37700.html.
[109] http://www.libertyforlife.com/banking/federal_reserve_bank.html.
[110] http://people.ucsc.edu/~jgaldo/politics.html.
[111] http://www.john-f-kennedy.net/thefederalreserve.htm.
[112] http://web.worldbank.org/.
[113] Antonio Cordero, "The IMF's Stand-by Arrangements and the Economic Downturn in Eastern Europe," The Center for Economic Policy and Research, 2009.

114. Saira Yousaf, "IMF Loans to Pakistan: History and Current Prospects," http://www.economistan.com/articles/10064.html, 2009.
115. http://www.imf.org/external/np/exr/center/mm/eng/cc_sub_4.htm.
116. Marshal Plan, "National Archives & Records Administration," http://www.archives.gov/exhibits/featured_documents/marshall_plan/.
117. http://www.onlygold.com/TutorialPages/prices200yrsfs.htm.
118. Richard Duncan, *"The Dollar Crisis: Causes, Consequences, Cures," Wiley 2003.*
119. Paul Krugman, "Reagan Did It," New York Times, May 31, 2009.
120. *ReportonBusiness.com Oct. 14-2008.*
121. http://en.wikiquote.org/wiki/Milton_Friedman.
122. *George Reisman, "capitalism: A Treatise on Economics" 1996.*
123. Wall Street Journal, September 17, 2008.
124. Goldfarb, Zachary A.; David Cho and Binyamin Appelbaum (2008-09-07). *"Treasury to Rescue Fannie and Freddie: Regulators Seek to Keep Firms' Troubles From Setting Off Wave of Bank Failures." Washington Post*: pp. A01, Sep. 7, 2008.
125. Duhigg, Charles; Labaton, Stephen and Sorkin, Andrew Ross (2008-09-07). *"As Crisis Grew, One Option Remained," New York Times, Sep. 8,* 2008.
126. Charles Duhigg, "Questions Remain After Fannie Mae, Freddie Mac Takeover," The Online News Hour, PBS, Sep. 8, 2008
127. "A new form of capitalism can remake broken country," Independent.ie, January 22, 2009.
128. Scott Baker, "A new form of capitalism is needed: Geonomics," One OpEdNews.com, March 28, 2009.
129. http://www.huffingtonpost.com/james-arthur-ray/a-new-form-of-capitalism_b_302170.html.
130. *Bill Gates, "Creative capitalism," Davos Annual Meeting, 2008.*
131. *Richard Ebeling, "Competing capitalism and the New Rationales for Economic Collectivism," The Future of Freedom Foundation, www.fff.org, December 1992.*
132. William Doyle, *An American Insurrection: The Battle of Oxford, Mississippi* (Doubleday, 2001).
133. ABC News' Charles Gibson Interviews The Bushes at Camp David, Nov. 20, 2007.
134. Reactions of the Wall Street slump, the "Economist archive," Nov 23rd 1929.
135. "Trump Trips Up." Time. 1991-05-06.
136. Burton, Mark L.; Hicks, Michael J. "Hurricane Katrina: Preliminary Estimates of Commercial and Public Sector Damages." Marshall University: *Center for Business and Economic Research.* September, 2005.
137. *http://en.wikipedia.org/wiki/Subprime_mortgage_crisis#Financial_market_impacts.2C_2007.*

138. Edward Wolff, "The Wealth Divide: The Growing Gap in the United States Between the Rich and the Rest," *The Multinational Monitor*, vol 24, number 5, 2003
139. *http://www.investorwords.com/2693/Keynesian_Economics.html*
140. Reagan, Ronald. *"Remarks on Signing the Garn-St Germain Depository Institutions Act of 1982"* (1982-10-15).
141. Cornett, Marcia Millon; Tehranian, Hassan (1990). "An Examination of the Impact of the Garn-St. Germain Depository Institutions Act of 1982 on Commercial Banks and Savings and Loans". *Journal of Finance* **45** (1): 95-111. Table of ContentsPart

PART 2

The Rise of Islam

But seek the abode of the Hereafter in that wealth which Allah has given you and neglect not portion of this world, and be kind as Allah has been kind to you and seek not corruption in the earth.

—Quran 28:77

By the grace of God, this religion (Islam) will rise such that a man would be able to cross the desert fearing nothing for his life or cattle.

—Prophet Mohammad

Islam gives hope to the slave, brotherhood to mankind, and recognition of the fundamental facts of human nature.

—Cannon Taylor, 1887

Islam has still the power to reconcile apparently irreconcilable elements of race and tradition.

—H. A. R. Gibb, 1932

In the contemporary world there is a crying need for the propagation of the Islamic virtue.

—A. J. Toynbee, 1948

But today, tens of millions of Muslims appear to be . . . returning to their roots in a more pure Islam.

—Patrick Buchanan, 2005

The trend is with them. In Muslim countries running the geographical span from Morocco to Indonesia, substantial majorities say that the Shari'ah should be the source of law for their states.

—Noah Feldman, 2008

1

Introduction

The discussion of Islam could not have been more controversial at any time in history than the way it stands today. At the time Islam is being sought for a genuine advice on the financial predicaments of the world, it is also pursued as a suspect when terrorism strikes. The debate on how much Islam is responsible for the acts of terrorism in the world today continues to make headlines of major media platforms. In the meantime, the debate on how much Islam can contribute to the construction of a more sound financial system is growing day after day. Yet the prospects of Islam as a system and a way of life are not less dramatic. Scores of Muslim and non-Muslim scholars, academics, and thinkers continue to contemplate on the rise of Islam to the ruling reign of nations and the potential outcome and consequences of such sovereignty.

The rise of Islam, as presented in this book, does not only refer to the rise of the Islamic state of khilafah or to a mechanical implementation of the Islamic code, otherwise referred to as *Shari'ah*. Neither is it the resumption of holy wars, otherwise called *jihad*. Nor is it the transfer of the court and judicial system to Islamic courthouses. Although in the fullest extent, Shari'ah, jihad, and the courthouses are integral part of Islam. The rise of Islam in the context of this book refers to the resumption of an Islamic way of life in which materialism falls to the backseat while piety moves to the driver seat. It is a life in which matter becomes the tool for satisfying the objectives of the human life, rather than it being the objective which drives the human momentum

It is a well-known fact that for thirteen years of Prophet Mohammad's twenty-three years as a messenger, the code of Shari'ah, the jihad, and the courthouses were not a dominant part of the culture of Islam. Although a large portion of the Quran was revealed during these thirteen years. The main focus during this period was the intellectual foundation of the religion and ideology as well as the nonviolent ideological and political struggle led by Prophet Mohammad (PBUH) and his companions.

The remaining ten years of his life as a messenger, Prophet Mohammad constructed a state and built a society. The Islamic code of Shari'ah was gradually introduced into the society until it was completed before Mohammad (PBUH) departed this life for his final destiny. It can be argued that the first thirteen years of his life, Prophet Mohammad, supported by revelation of the Quran from the Almighty God, established a foundation upon which the state and society was implemented. Without this foundation, the code could not have produced the envisioned systems of political, economic, and social life. Without this foundation, the systems could only have survived while the Prophet was alive only to disappear after his death. The truth of the matter is that the systems of Islam lived for 1,300 years and won the praise of the followers, the friends and the foes alike. Bernard Shaw, Irish writer and Nobel Prize winner in 1925, made the following comments on Mohammad and his leadership: "I believe that if a man like Mohammad were to assume the dictatorship of the modern world he would succeed in solving its problems in a way that would bring it the much needed peace and happiness."[1]

When we talk about the rise of Islam, we have to address both the foundation and the structure of Islam. This is what gives Islam its ideological framework. And this is exactly what makes Islam relevant when we discuss the ideologies of capitalism or socialism, especially when these ideologies face a serious challenge.

When the world order experiences a crisis stemming from the ideology which dominates its economic and financial system, the image of an alternative ideology rises and tackles the very minds of the people. When socialism began to fail in the old Soviet Union, the local public in the Soviet Union and the global public in the world began to search for an alternative ideology. Capitalism was ready to engage the minds of the ideology seekers and to fill the vacuum created by the collapse of socialism. That was a natural process.

Today, capitalism as an ideology is experiencing a crisis which threatens a collapse of the ideological framework in the world at large. It is only natural for people to search and investigate alternative ideologies. The dilemma that faces the world is that the other two potential ideologies are not immediately available to replace the current one. Socialism has collapsed more than twenty years ago, and there is no serious attempt to revive it. Islam has fallen as an ideology more than eighty years ago, although there are serious and vigorous attempts to resume its full implementation.[2] Had the ideology of Islam been practiced and implemented in some country in the world, then it would have been natural for Islam to fill the vacuum which could result after the collapse of capitalism. More so, Islam would have competed with capitalism to fill the vacuum after the collapse of Soviet socialism at the end of the twentieth century.

The irony is that the ideological framework of Islam (the foundation plus the structure) was practically removed from the world at the start of the twentieth century. Hence, for Islam to be applicable as a viable alternative to current ideologies, it must *rise again* in its capacity as an ideology. The process of rising has indeed started, and it will not be too long before the world begins to experience the ideology of Islam in practice. Patrick Buchanan described this process as an idea whose time has come, and that no army in the world could stop this rise.[3] This process will be further analyzed and discussed in the subsequent sections.

Hence, the term *rise of Islam* in this book refers to the rise of the ideology of Islam. This should relax the concern that some may have regarding the fact that Islam as a religion has never fallen and continues to be an ever-growing religion in terms of the number of followers.[4] It should also remove the confusion stemming from the fact that the sources of Islam, in particular the Quran and the statements of Prophet Mohammad, have been preserved and documented with utmost accuracy; so the term fall and rise of Islam does not apply to this part of Islam either. In effect, the term *rise of Islam* refers specifically to the revival of the ideology of Islam in its capacity as an intellectual foundation, a structure built upon that foundation, and a methodology for implementing the ideology.

The next section will explore the details of Islam as an ideology; this should clarify exactly what we mean by the ideological framework of Islam and what are the major components of this ideology.

2

The Ideology of Islam

Among the many existing definitions,[5] an *ideology* can be defined as a set of aims and ideas that directs one's goals, expectations, and actions; an ideology can be thought of as a comprehensive vision, as a way of looking at things. The word *ideology* itself does not carry any positive or negative semantics or connotation. According to Destutt de Tracy,[6] the word *ideology* is assembled from two parts, *idea* and *logy*. In other words, ideology describes the logic which derives the set of goals, aims, rules, and systems from a basic and comprehensive idea. From this perspective, an ideology is just an ideology; it is neither positive nor negative, neither good nor bad, neither acceptable nor rejected. It provides a systematic way of describing ideas, concepts, systems, regulations, and methods. In this regard, the ideology of socialism cannot be criticized simply because it comprises an ideology. Socialism can be criticized based on the ideas and beliefs it carries; it is the content of the ideology that could be subject for scrutiny and criticism. By the same token, capitalism cannot be rejected or accepted simply because it stands as an ideology. It is the principles of capitalism and the impact of its application that should be subject for criticism and scrutiny. The same applies to Islam. We cannot accept or reject the notion of Islam on the basis that it formulates an ideology.

David F. Forte, professor of law at Cleveland State University, in an article published by the Heritage Foundation,[7] takes the extreme point when he equates ideology to terrorism and killing and insists that Islam should be viewed only as a religion capable of providing charity. In his own words, "Our policy ought to be that all peoples, of all religions, who fulfill their religion with devotion, charity, equality and concern for others will be celebrated and protected, but that any person—whether in the name of religion or socialism or history—who seeks to take over a state and turn that belief into an ideology, an ideology which terrorizes and kills innocent people, is our enemy and the enemy of all religion." Where it should be clear that terrorism cannot and should not be tolerated under any circumstances, it should also be clear that terrorism is not equivalent to "ideology."

What is at stake here is not the names or terminology used to describe Islam. What is more important than terms or names are the ideas and concepts underlying the definitions and terms. The term *ideology* is certainly more neutral than the term *Islamism, fundamentalism, Extremism, phonetic-ism*, or the like. To avoid any confusion, I will try to use the plain word *Islam* in lieu of the term *ideology of Islam* where applicable.

The Foundation of Islam: Historical Perspective

Around the year 610 CE, Prophet Mohammad (PBUH) began to receive Quran in the form of revelation from Allah, god the Creator.[8] Mohammad was living in Mecca. Mecca was famous for hosting the Sacred Mosque built around the place called the *Ka'aba*. The Sacred Mosque is believed to have been built by Prophet Ibraheem and his son Ismail. The religion propagated by Ibraheem in Mecca and its surrounding preached the oneness of god and the supreme values which were carried out by subsequent religions of Judaism, Christianity, and Islam. Over time, the Arabs in Mecca and its surrounding managed to distort the religion of Ibraheem and introduce polytheistic religion with multiple gods. The Arabs in Mecca and Arabia grew accustomed to worshiping stone idols as material representatives of Gods. Since the Ka'aba was considered a holy place by Arabs in the area, the tribes of Mecca worked out their way to become the hosts and custodians of all gods worshiped by Arabs in Mecca and elsewhere. This status has secured for Quraish, the main tribe of Mecca, a special status and prestige, and won them the title of the custodians of the holy place (*Al-Haram*). Besides the prestige, honor, and status, Quraish was in a position to gain financially and economically from their position as custodians of Al-Haram. The Quran later reminded Quraish of this special status in a Surah named "Quraish."[9]

Before the declaration of Islam by Prophet Mohammad, the religion in Mecca was reduced to traditions and mythical stories and representations of god. The role of god as a source of legislation and commands was bestowed upon the influential and wealthy leaders in Mecca.[10, 11] Eventually, the supreme values of the religion of Ibraheem were brought to null in Mecca and the Arab communities. The most sacred ritual of the old religion was the circulation around the Ka'aba in anticipation of god's mercy and forgiveness. The Arabs under the influence of Quraish evolved that practice into a bizarre when they allowed the circulation to be conducted by nude men and women.[12] This practice was officially and practically aborted after the conquest of Mecca by Prophet Mohammad twenty years after the revelation of Islam.

Slavery in Mecca and the rest of the Arab land was a practice, which enabled the rich and powerful to enslave the weak and poor. Slavery was coupled with male and female prostitution. The rich and powerful men were allowed to sleep with the wives of the less fortunate in order to improve their offsprings. The ill practices of Mecca included money lending for a percentage of usury. In case the indebted fails to pay the interest, the creditor had the right to enslave the indebted or any member of his family.

Those were some of the conditions which prevailed at the time when Mohammad was designated as a prophet. The mind-set of the Arabs had become so engraved with corruption, mythology, abuse, oppression, disorder, discrimination, self-proclaimed supremacy, and much more. The mind-set required a comprehensive change before any change on the ground could take place. Changing this environment and creating a new system to replace the corrupted one in Arabia could not have succeeded without a strong new foundation.

For thirteen years after its initiation, the message of Islam as revealed in the Quran and practiced by Mohammad focused entirely on an intellectual foundation aimed at creating a new mind-set. This was deemed necessary to create an environment for change as well as to create a base upon which the systems of Islam could be built.

During this period, Islam addressed a myriad of fundamental questions, such as who is god? Is there a god? What is the purpose of believing in a god? Who could carry a message from god? What is the impact of believing in a god on society and the individuals? What is the relationship, if any, between people and god? Although the questions seemed simple and innocent, the elites of Mecca understood that the answers to these questions could undermine their leadership, reduce their influence, and collide with their interests.

The first revelation ever to be received by Prophet Mohammad was a *Surah* (chapter) called *Iqra'a* (Read). It started with the following words:

"Read in the name of your Lord; the one who created all the creation; He created man ..."[13] For the first time in Mecca since the dismissal of the religion of Ibraheem, the notion of lord was attributed to the Creator. This notion did not resonate well with the chiefs of Mecca, who assumed the position of lord in their capacity as custodians of the sacred holy mosque. It is not coincidence that the same Surah ended with a declaration of disobedience to the chieftains of Mecca *"Nay; you are not to obey him (the Chieftain); instead prostrate to Allah and come nearer to Him."*[14] This declaration was vigorously confirmed in Islam to the extent that it constituted the first step to enter into the new religion. The declaration of Islam by any individual begins with the statement *"There shall be no god except Allah."* In essence, this declaration negates all forms of gods, which were numerous in Mecca, and confirms only god the creator, Allah.

The Quran through subsequent revelations created a platform to debate all issues related to god. This can be traced in many verses and places. It is beyond the scope of this book to go into great details into the arguments, debates, and discussion brought forward by the Quran and Mohammad. However, I will provide some examples to demonstrate the significance of the intellectual foundation in the Islamic culture.

In a sequence of verses in Surah Al-Toor (chapter 52), which was revealed in Mecca before the migration to the state in Medina, the Quran invokes the following debate with the polytheists of Mecca in an attempt to provoke their thoughts:

> *Were they created of nothing, or were they themselves the creators? Or did they create the heavens and the earth? Nay, they have no firm belief of that. Or are the Treasures of thy Lord with them, or are they the managers of world affairs? Or have they a ladder, by which they can climb up to heaven and listen to its secrets? Then let such a listener produce a manifest proof ... Or have they a God other than Allah? (52: 35-43)*

Occasionally, the Quran provided an argument for the correctness and soundness of the ideas it presents. Here is an example from Surah Al-Mumenun (chapter 23):

> *No son did Allah beget, nor is there any God along with Him: if there were many Gods other than Allah, then each God would have taken away what he had created, and some would have lorded it over others (23:91).*

Along with the concept of one and only one god, Islam promoted certain concepts to help create a society with particular character. One of these concepts has to do with wealth and ownership. Islam promoted the idea that all wealth and resources in the world belong to Allah in the first place. And it is Allah who enables people to acquire part of this wealth while they are living on this earth. Once this belief is established, it becomes much easier to request the rich to share part of their wealth with the poorer ones. The idea here is that the one who acquires more wealth than others has more responsibility in terms of redistributing part of the wealth to the less-fortunate ones.

This concept is best illustrated in the Quran through the story of *Qarun*, a wealthy man and a follower of Prophet Moses (PBUH).[15] The story reports that *"Qarun was one of the people of Moses"* and he was so rich that the keys of the treasures of his wealth were too heavy to be lifted by strong men. His fellow men requested of him to spend part of his wealth to help the poor and the needy. Qarun refused and claimed that he acquired wealth using his own knowledge and skills. His fellow men reminded him that because of greed and arrogance, god had destroyed the wealth of people who *"were superior to him in strength and greater in the amount of wealth they had collected."* Qarun ignored the warnings and paraded with great pride and arrogance in front of all people. Soon after, god *"caused the earth to swallow up him and his wealth."* The story of Qarun aims at creating the notion that individuals who end up with great wealth should remember that the source of their wealth is god, and they should be open enough to the concept of spending part of this wealth on the needy ones. This concept will become handy when the society is reformed according to the Islamic principles.

The Quran and Prophet Mohammad provided serious critique of some of the practices of the society of Mecca, while building new concepts and ideas. In Surah Al-Mutafifeen (chapter 83),[16] the Quran condemns those who deal in fraud and use different scales, one for sale and one for purchase. At the time of purchase, they use a scale that allows them to receive more goods than they paid for; at the time of sale, they use another scale which allows them to give fewer goods than the price paid for the goods. This practice was common in Mecca at the time when Islam was launched.

More explicit criticism came in Surah Al-Fajr (chapter 89),[17] where it was pointed out that the rich people in Mecca had no mercy for the orphanage, no sympathy for the poor and needy, and were full of greed and excessive love for wealth accumulation. The practice of usury received serious defamation as well. In Surah Al-Rum (chapter 30)[18] the Quran derides usury as a means of growing wealth at the expense of the wealth of other people.

The approbation and appreciation of justice is demonstrated in more than forty verses in the Quran. By the same token, oppression received serious scolding and admonishment in more than 170 locations in the Quran. The reference to oppressors was occasionally explicit by referring to specific tyrants in Mecca.[19]

Evidently, the custodians of the holy places in Mecca, the merchants, the chiefs, and the wealthy felt that they were targeted and threatened by the new message of Islam. A message that calls for the ban of usury did not resonate well with those who increased their wealth by making profit simply by lending money and receiving usury. The message which called for the worship of only one god seemed antagonistic to the custodians of numerous stone gods in Mecca. The message that stated that all children of Adam are equally human irrespective of their color, race, wealth, gender, or any other consideration was detested by the ones who preyed on slavery and discrimination.

Soon, a tedious struggle arose in Mecca. On one part, Mohammad and his followers assert that the only one who deserves to be called a god is the one who created all creation, the one who provides the wealth and the capacity to multiply it, the one who will hold people accountable for their deeds in this life and in the hereafter. On the opposite side stood the powerful men of Mecca in defense of their sovereignty, their numerous gods, their culture, their usurious financial wealth, and their tribal supremacy. While Mohammad used only intellectual and verbal means to lead his part of the struggle, the elites of Mecca chose methods of suppression, torture, and execution.[20]

Throughout the first thirteen years of the rise of Islam in Mecca, very few rules and regulations of Islam were revealed. Only prayer among the rituals of Islam was ordained and organized in Mecca, albeit towards the end of the Meccan period. The other rituals of fasting, pilgrimage, and *Zakah-charity* were revealed in Medina after the migration from Mecca. The period of Mecca was dominated by the intellectual ideological foundation and moral and ethical values. Islam had the privilege of criticizing existing practices while it had no practices of its own to be scrutinized. The model of Islam was mostly theoretical during the thirteen years in Mecca. Islam only provided an intellectual and ideological creed base and claimed that any system built upon this creed will be a just and fair system.

By the end of the thirteen years' period in Mecca, Prophet Mohammad had achieved three subobjectives. The first is a solid intellectual foundation fully argued and tested against many of the contemporary ideas. The foundation confirmed the oneness of god and the absolute sovereignty of god as a source of directions, guidance, regulations, and rules. It established the Quran and *Sunnah* (Prophet Mohammad statements and actions) as a reference for god's revelation to people. It established the accountability principle for all acts by all people; no one could stand above the laws of god.

The second subobjective was the creation of a group of people, historically known as the companions of the Prophet, who firmly believed in the foundation and demonstrated readiness to sacrifice the best of their belongings in support of their belief. The third was the establishment of a nucleus for statehood in the city of Medina (210 miles north of Mecca).

The Structure of Islam: Historical Perspective

Around the year 623 CE, thirteen years after the initiation of Islam, Prophet Mohammad and his companions migrated from Mecca to the city of Medina (called Yathrib until the day of migration). That same year marked the beginning of the Islamic calendar. Muslims chose this year to mark the calendar instead of the year Islam physically began thirteen years earlier. The significance of this year is that it marked the transfer of Islam from being a theoretical model into a practical one.

Prophet Mohammad added to his role as a messenger who receives god's revelations, the role of a statesman who applies the rules upon people. His leadership position in Medina was unanimously approved without the least challenge, not even from Jewish tribes living in the vicinity of Medina or the group which did not thoroughly accept Islam.

Right after the migration to Medina and the creation of the nucleus Islamic state, the revelation of the Quran took a new direction. The emphasis now is more focused on the rules, regulations, structure, organization, and relationships between people. The people in Medina, who were under the rule of Islam, were requested to bring their issues, problems, disputes to Mohammad for ruling and judgments.

Prophet Mohammad did not spare any time before he began to organize the relationships in the new society. He established a matching system, by which he matched individuals who migrated from Mecca to counterparts from Medina. This matching or coupling schema allowed the new immigrants to make smooth transition into a new place and locality after they have left all their wealth and belongings back in Mecca. Wealth sharing was the most visible result of the matching program. Prophet Mohammad also drafted a treaty governing the relationship between the Jewish tribes and the Muslims in Medina. The treaty defined the mutual responsibility for the safety and protection of Medina and its surrounding.

The rules of marriage, divorce, inheritance, maternity, and fatherhood were soon revealed. One of the largest chapters, Surah Al-Nisa[21] (chapter

4, "The Women"), contains numerous rules which govern the relations between husbands and wives. Rules of war and peace were reveled over an extended period of time following war and peace incidents.[22] Rules of trade were also revealed over extended period of time and can be found in many chapters, especially Surah Al-Baqara (chapter 2).[23]

In the meantime, many of the day-to-day activities were addressed and resolved by Prophet Mohammad as people brought forward their daily issues. Occasionally, people brought issues of pure technical merit thinking that these issues also should be addressed by the Messenger of Allah. In one incident the Prophet advised the people of Medina on palm tree pollination; his advice was counterproductive, although the people took his advice as binding. He then told the crowd, *"You know the technical issues of your life better than I do."*[24]

In a short period of time, the Islamic state in Medina under the leadership of Prophet Mohammad grew to a stable position with coherency among constituents of diverse tribes and ethnicity.[25] The two main tribes of Medina, the once-rivals Aws and Khazraj, became grateful of the new bond of brotherhood. The Quran drew their attention to their state of affairs before the arrival of Mohammad and his companions and how it has changed.[26]

After several encounters with Mecca and the Jewish tribes around Medina, the Islamic state spread its dominance to the whole of the Arabian Peninsula. Soon after, the new Islamic state engaged the Roman and Persian empires on the north and east of the Arabian Peninsula. The shape and character of the structure of Islam became more distinct. The laws and regulations are derived from revealed sources. The sovereignty does not fall on the shoulders of individuals, but rather on the intellectual foundation. New laws for trade, property ownership, investment, and spending are in place. The morals and ethics of piety replaced the ethics of tribalism and tribal pride. The relationships among components of the society are constructed and characterized by Islamic character.

By the end of the tenth year after migration, Prophet Mohammad (PBUH) passed away, leaving behind a well-defined state and coherent society. But he did not name a successor who could assume the position of the political leadership. What he left behind is a complete religion embedded within the realm of the Quran and Sunnah. Before burying the dead body of the Prophet, the prominent companions held a meeting and elected Abu Bakr Al-Siddiq as a successor for the Prophet. They called him the caliph (khalifah), which literally means *the successor*. Abu Bakr was appointed to the post of caliph through a process called the *bai'ah* (pledge of allegiance). It was immediately recognized that Abu Bakr assumes the political leadership only and has no prophecy role of any kind. The Islamic state came to be known since then as the state of the caliphate (khilafah). The state continued to function in the same manner: rules and regulations derived from the texts of the Quran and the Sunnah.

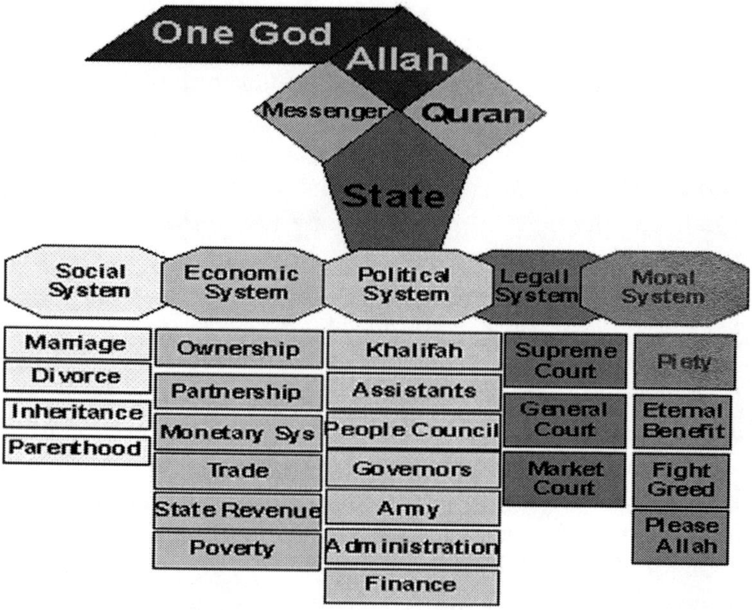

With the appointment of Abu Bakr as the first successor of the Prophet, the shape and the context of the Islamic structure has taken its distinct character and shape. The structure included a state with the *khalifah* as the head of the state. The khalifah assumes the post of the head of state through a process of election followed by a process of *bai'ah*. A council representing the people is charged with the process of appointing the khalifah. The khalifah appoints assistants to help him carry the governing responsibilities. Disputes within the state are handled by judicial personnel. Remote areas within the state are governed by governors appointed by the khalifah. Over time, these organs of the state became more stable and better defined. The state of the khilafah collectively became responsible for the implementation of the systems of Islam. Through a large set of rules derived from the Quran and the Sunnah, it can be shown that the structure of Islam comprised economic, social, political, and judicial systems. Of particular interest to this publication is the economic system, which will be discussed in greater details in subsequent sections.

The ideological structure of Islam is summarized in figure 28. The intellectual foundation consists of the basic creed which in turn contains the belief in Allah as the one and only god, in Mohammad as the last

Figure 28: Structure of Islamic Ideology

messenger of Allah to all people, and in the Quran as the final divine revelation to mankind. The method of implementing the ideology is the Islamic state, which is responsible for the implementation of the various systems.

The systems of Islam include the social, economic, political, legal, and moral systems. The social system treats the issues that emerge out of man woman relationships such as marriage, divorce, inheritance, and parenthood.

The economic system deals with issues related to ownership definitions, partnerships and corporations, monetary system, internal and external trade, sources of revenues for the state, and poverty resolution mechanism.

The political system defines the structure of the state and governance organs. It includes the post of the khalifah, the assistants to the khalifah, the people council structure as well as its composition and responsibilities, the governors of state, the army structure and its responsibilities, the administration departments, and the financial department.

The legal system defines three court systems: the supreme court, the regular court, and the market court. It defines the scope and code for each court type. The moral system defines the basic traits and qualities of the people in the Islamic society, a society that stands on piety more so than law. The moral system aims at creating people who would rather provide their scarce food to the ones who are in more need for the food.[27]

3

The Rise and Decline of Islam

The Expansion of Islam

The mission of Islam which began in Mecca and flourished in Medina had all what it takes to grow into a global one. The Quran explicitly stated that Mohammad was a messenger not only for the Arabs but for all mankind.[28] It also stated that one of the objectives of this mission is to take over other religions and systems. In essence it laid down the foundation for the spread of Islam and the expansion of its state. Indeed, the moment the Prophet (PBUH) departed this world, the armies of the Islamic state were on the borders of both the Roman and the Persian empires.

Less than one hundred years after the creation of the Islamic state in Medina, Islam had spread from Spain (Andalusia) to Sumatra. The Muslim ships dominated the Mediterranean Sea and the India Ocean. During its expansion, very little resistance came from either the Roman Byzantine or the Persian troops. Both empires have suffered from internal chaos, corruption, and decline of morale. Islam provided to the newly conquered nations a religion with rational and simple creed as well as a system characterized with justice and fairness. Many people favored monotheism and found the Byzantine trinity and Persian dualism distasteful. Islam was more to their liking, and they not only converted to Islam, but helped to spread it further.

Islam removed much of the financial burden and taxation which was imposed upon the people of the conquered lands. It removed the boundaries between nations and treated all nations and peoples by the same standard. There was no national or ethnic supremacy. The Muslims practiced to the fullest extent the principle declared by the Quran: "*Honor is measured by piety rather than by national identity.*"[29] Lynn Nylson in *Medieval History*,[30] says that "Muslims practiced religious toleration, and the social and economic doctrines of Islam were far more humane than those of the other peoples of the time." She concludes that the Quran gave the peoples of the Roman and Persian empires a common set of laws and values.

Together with the spread of Islam and the expansion of its state, a new civilization emerged. This civilization translated the theoretical model which was constructed over an extended period of time into a practical one. It was able to transform nomad warrior Arabs into a civilized group of people capable of looking after the affairs of others in return only for the pleasure of the Almighty Allah. The civilization created a new imagery of the rulers of the land: never above the law or above the people. It is reported that when an envoy of the Persian king came to Medina looking for the caliph Omar Bin Al-Khattab, he was astonished to find him lying asleep under a tree. He did not find a palace like that of his own king or guards like those he was used to. His comments elegantly characterized the traits of the leaders of the new civilization: "Rule with justice and rest with a sense of security."[31]

The rapid and smooth expansion of Islam was documented in the book *World Civilization: The Global Experience*,[32] in which the authors state,

> *In the seventh century C.E. the Arab followers of Muhammad surged from the Arabian Peninsula to create the first global civilization. They quickly conquered an empire incorporating elements of the classical civilizations of Greece, Egypt, and Persia. Islamic merchants, mystics, and warriors continued its expansion in Europe, Asia, and Africa. The process provided links for exchange among civilized centers and forged a truly global civilization.*

Being a technologist myself, I found most intriguing the comments of former CEO of Hewlett Packard (HP) in a speech delivered to a conference held under the theme "Technology, Business and Our Way of Life: What Is Next."[33] She noted that the Islamic civilization which dominated the world for more than eight hundred years was one driven by invention. The Islamic military allowed a degree of peace and prosperity that "had never been known." In recognition of the Islamic civilization contribution, she notes that today's technology "would not exist without the contributions of Arab mathematicians." On the philosophical front, Muslim philosophers like Rumi "challenged our notions of self and truth." In the domain of tolerance and civic code, leaders like Suleiman "contributed to our notions of tolerance and civic leadership." What makes Fiorina's observations distinct and unique is that they came two weeks after the 9/11 acts of terrorism which rendered Islam unjustly scrutinized for notions of terrorism and savage behavior.

On the economic side, the Islamic civilization was characterized by prosperity at the societal level and poverty elimination at the individual level. Ira Marvin Lapidus notes in her book *The History of Islamic Society* that the civilization in North Africa and Spain was fostered by "extraordinary economic prosperity."[34] Historians like Ibn Katheer and Al-Tabari report that within the first sixty years of its rise, Islam managed to remove poverty at all levels. The main charity institution in Islam, *Zakah*, experienced a positive overflow of money when recipients of this form of charity virtually disappeared due to prosperity and financial stability.

Historians, politicians, writers, and critiques agree that Islam spread and expanded at a breathtaking speed. They describe different aspects of the civilization and some have provided some sort of explanation for that phenomenon. Noah Feldman in his book *The Fall and the Rise of Islamic State* attributed the rise and spread of the first Islamic state to the implementation of the *Shari'ah* (the Islamic legal code) coupled with a check-and-balance mechanism maintained by self-proclaimed scholars. French historian Lamartine[35] attributed the phenomenon to a momentum generated by the extraordinary character of Prophet Mohammad (PBUH). Similar observations were made by Sir Bernard Shaw.

It is true that the personality and character of Mohammad had a great impact on the rise and spread of Islam. But for that impact to last many centuries ahead requires more elaborate discussion. Similarly, the implementation of the rules of Islam in the form of Shari'ah was instrumental to the sustainability of the Islamic state and civilization. But for that Shari'ah to remain relevant for such a long period of time requires more analysis.

The leadership and methodology provided by Prophet Mohammad remained relevant and influential for one simple reason. Mohammad was perceived by Muslims as one who receives revelation from Allah. The belief in Mohammad as a messenger from Allah was tantamount to the belief in Allah as a god. So when the Muslims set out to document Mohammad's life, they knew that they were compiling another source for the revelation in addition to the Quran. It is not a coincidence that early Muslims formulated a whole new methodology for compiling the statements, the actions, and behavior of the Prophet (PBUH).

Muslim scholars invented what amounts to a profiling knowledge database in which they collected all possible details about each and every one who has been in direct or indirect contact with the Prophet. This was deemed necessary to authenticate any piece that was attributed to the Prophet. In the process, the Muslim scholars like *Bukhari, Muslim, Nisa'i, Tirmidhi, and Abu Dawoud* managed to filter out thousands of references falsely attributed to Prophet Mohammad (PBUH). To the Muslims, the life and products of Prophet Mohammad were part of the creed. The Quran confirmed this fact in several places. In one location, it made a direct link between loving Allah and following Mohammad.[36] In another place, the Quran asked the Muslims to take and accept everything that the Messenger of Allah provided to them.[37]

In pursuing the prevalence of his mission, Prophet Mohammad assumed strategies, tactics, and plans which are both tangible and practical. He never relied on superstitious or supernatural forces in sketching or implementing the plans. At the time when he preached that victory is ultimately provided by god, he insisted that all preparations and precautions need to be carried out by the people. In other words, he made it clear that the success or failure of the mission depends on the degree of commitment, devotion, and sacrifice of the people who carry the mission. The fact that the ideas, concepts, rules, regulations, and values are just, fair, and supreme do not suffice for the message of Islam to rise and prosper. The existence of a group of people who believe in the ideas and its systems is as essential as the correctness of the ideas themselves.

The Quran carefully drew the line between the personality of the Prophet and the divine revelation. The emphasis was on the divine revelation. In numerous locations, the Quran warned the Prophet himself to keep a strict observation of the revealed code.[38] In Surah Al-Maidah (chapter 5, verse 49), the Quran makes the following restriction *"And so judge (O Muhammad) among them by what Allah has revealed and follow not their vain desires, but beware of them lest they turn you far away from some of that which Allah has sent down to you."* The point is that the Islamic creed left no doubt that the Prophet was but a man who receives revelation from Allah, and that the Muslims will only be worshiping god when they follow the Messenger. Then as long as the creed remains alive in the minds and hearts of the believers, the impact of Prophet Mohammad remains alive and active.

By the same token, when the Quran revealed code of conduct, it did so in conjunction with the creed itself. The Quran did not simply ask the believers to do a good deed or to refrain from doing an evil deed. Rather it emphasized the link between the action and the divine source that stands behind the command of the action. For example, when the Quran revealed a rule regarding the prohibition of alcoholic drink, it wrapped the rule within a set of other supreme values. In Surah Al-Maidah (chapter 5, verse 90) it says, *"O you who believe! Intoxicants (all kinds of alcoholic drinks), and gambling, and Al-Ansâb, and Al-Azlâm (forms of lottery) are an abomination of Shaitân's (Satan) handiwork. So avoid (strictly all) that (abomination) in order that you may be successful."* Note how the verse begins with an address "O you who believe!" reminding the audience of their belief, which is important for their compliance with the command. Then it links the prohibited acts, e.g., alcoholic drinks, to the acts of the devil (Shaitan). When this verse was revealed, the Muslims dumped all the wine they had previously stored to the extent that the streets of Medina were flooded with wine.

When the Quran requested of the believers to give money to those who are in need, it did so in a style conducive to generosity and munificence. In Surah Al-Baqara (chapter 2, verse 245), the Quran motivates the believers to lend their money to their fellow men saying that this act is equivalent to giving Allah a loan.[39] In other places it repeats the fact that Allah requests the believers to expend the wealth that has been provided to them by Allah. This notion is most clear in Surah Al-Hadeed (chapter 29, verse 7), which states, *"Believe in Allah and His Messenger and spend of that whereof He has made you trustees. And such of you as believe and spend (in Allah's Way), theirs will be a great reward."* This style is consistent throughout the Quran, whether the rules are related to wealth, trade, food habits, marriage, divorce, war, peace, family relations, morals, ethics, or any other issue.

The point is that Islam was very keen about maintaining the ultimate sovereignty to Allah the creator rather than to the laws and regulations that come from him. The adherence to the laws and code of conduct is eventually a proof for the sincerity of one's belief in the creed of Islam. In Surah Al-Nisa'a (chapter 4, verse 65), the Quran confirms this conclusion: *"But no, by your Lord, they can have no Faith, until they make you (O Muhammad) rule in all disputes between them, and find in themselves no resistance against your decisions, and accept (them) with full submission."* This brings back into play the fact that Prophet Mohammad spent more than 65% of his life span as a prophet building and strengthening the creed as a foundation of faith and the ideology.

The spread of Islam, the expansion of the Islamic state, and the dominance of its civilization were a natural consequence of the adherence and devotion of the Muslim community at large (the Muslim *Ummah*) to the intellectual foundations of the faith. What Noah Feldman observed through his research and analysis is the manifestation of this observance to the creed through the implementation of the Shari'ah. The role of the scholars was merely to sustain the links between the code of Shari'ah itself and the source of the code, i.e., Allah the supreme. When people requested an Islamic opinion on any issue, the scholars (*ulama*) did not simply provide an abstract Islamic opinion on the particular issue (e.g., allowed, obligated, recommended, banned, or discouraged). Rather, they would derive the rule from given texts in the Quran or the Sunnah (Prophet's statements and acts). They would pass on the rule together with the evidences used to derive that rule. This way, they kept the audience connected to the divine revelation which gives power to the rule and provides the audience with the reason to adhere to the rule.

This practice was thoroughly documented in the literature of the prominent scholars around whom the main schools of thought were organized. The famous books of the major scholars Abu Hanifah, Ja'afar, Al-Shafi'i, Ahmad Bin Hanbal, and Malik Bin Anas provide an outstanding proof to this effect. Within each school hundreds of books were composed. Each and every one of these books provides a collection of rules with all relevant texts from the Quran and Sunnah and the logic used to derive the rules from these texts.

The Decline of Islam

The state of khilafah established by Prophet Mohammad in the year 623 came to a complete halt on March 3, 1924. After thirteen hundred years of growth, expansion, and dominance, Islam lost the instrument responsible for its realization in the economic, political, and social lives of people. The decision to abolish the state of khilafah was taken by the National Assembly in Istanbul under the direction of Mustafa Kemal Atatürk. The termination of the state was not the beginning of the decline; in fact it was a result of a long process of decline which began at a much earlier stage in history.

Noah Feldman, in his book *The Fall and Rise of the Islamic State*, attributes the decline to the diminishing role of the scholars in maintaining a check against the rulers' obligations to implement the Shari'ah of Islam. This process began more than one hundred years before the final collapse took place. There is no doubt that the role of the scholars is instrumental to the sustainability of the Shari'ah. Their role, however, is to continuously rejuvenate the energy of the creed in the minds and hearts of the people and the rulers alike. When the rules of the state were compiled and coded in a book called the *Majillah*, they were given as abstract rules stripped off the divine source that gave them power in the first place. The rules were correctly derived from Islamic sources. No one could argue against their legitimacy from an Islamic perspective. Due to the separation between the rules of the Shari'ah and the divine code behind these rules, the public almost lost the connection of their creed to their daily life affairs, except maybe for the daily rituals. When the decision to abort the khilafah came in 1924, the general public did not feel that the base of their Islam and the foundation of their faith were being uprooted.

Taqiuddin al-Nabhani, the founder of *Hizb ut-Tahrir*,[3] makes a compelling argument regarding the decline of the Islamic ideology in his book *Concepts of Hizb ut-Tahrir*.[40] He argues that the main cause for the decline of the Islamic Ummah is the "weakening of the Muslim minds which rendered them unable to clearly understand Islam." This weakening was manifested in the people's inability to understand the link between the laws implemented by the state and the origin of belief, i.e., the creed. In other words, he attributes the physical decline of the state and the ideology to an intellectual and mental decline. The cause of the mental decline as argued by Nabhani dates back to the second century of Islam when the Muslims began to translate and incorporate the philosophies of Greece, Egypt, India, and Persia. While it was all right to read and translate the philosophies according to Nabhani, it was dangerous and of grave consequences to subject Islam and the Islamic ideas to the norms and standards of those philosophies. Such practice diminished the significance of the divine nature of the Islamic ideas which was the main power that gave the legitimacy, the energy, and the reason of being.

Another reason for the weakened understanding of Islam provided by Nabhani was the reduced role of the Arabic language at the start of the seventh century (Islamic calendar). The Arabic language is vital for *Ijtihad*, defined as the process of deriving the rules from the texts of the Quran and the Sunnah, which are documented in Arabic. The weakening of Ijtihad eventually leads to the reuse of previously derived rules and their application to newly encountered cases, without the need for repeating the process of derivation. As a result, the citation of the divine revelation which supports the correctness of the rules will no longer be necessary. While the confidence in the correctness of the rules remained in tact, the spiritual power which stands behind the rules starts to fade.

Being a political leader and a founder of a political party, Nabhani did not ignore the role of Western expeditions into the heart of the Muslim lands in the nineteenth century in diluting the minds of Muslims and creating an atmosphere of vagueness and doubts around the principles

---

[3] Hizb ut-Tahrir is a party founded in 1953 for the objective of reviving Islam through the establishment of the Khilafah state.

of Islam. The expeditions helped instigate the feelings of nationalism and tribalism within the Muslim Ummah. The rise of the notions of nationalism as a major cause of the decline was cited by Abdul Qadeem Zallum in his book *How the Khilafah Was Destroyed*.[41] Zallum noted that the rise of Arab, Turkish, and Balkan forms of nationalism were responsible for the eventual collapse of the Islamic state. How could Mustafa Kemal of Turkey abolish the state of khilafah by a draw of a pen? Zallum answers this question saying that the Muslim Ummah had already reached a stage where Muslims could no longer clearly see the need to sacrifice their lives in order to preserve the existence of the state of Islam.

Whether it is the rise of nationalism, the impact of Western expedition and colonialism, the fading of Ijtihad, or the diminished role of scholars, the end result is the same. A growing distance began to emerge between the Muslims' minds and the divine source of revelation. By the time the distance between the minds and the divine revelation reached a dividing threshold in the Islamic society, the creed has lost its driving force within the minds and hearts of the Muslims. At this stage, neither the scholars nor the rulers could have moved the masses to preserve what Prophet Mohammad has created thirteen hundreds years earlier. The concept of Allah being the only god was degenerated to the ritual practices only, while the gods of the market, trade, economy, politics, peace, and war returned numerous as was the case in Mecca before the start of Islam. The adherence to the rules of Islam became more of a mechanical process rather than an act of worship and obedience to god.

The point here is that the collapse of the Islamic state in 1924 culminated a long process of decline. The removal of the state was a declaration of an end of a civilization that lasted for more than thirteen centuries. The collapse of the Islamic state, the removal of its ideology, and the end of its civilization had devastating impact on the world of Islam and the world at large. The majority of the Islamic lands fell under the colonial occupation of European powers. Within these states, chaos has replaced order, ignorance and backwardness replaced knowledge and progress, corruption and greed replaced the Islamic morals and ethics. Despite the tremendous wealth of oil and natural resources in the lands of Islam, the number of poor people within the Muslim world exceeds 50% of the total number of poor in the world. Internal and external wars since the decline of Islam have devastated the land, killed millions, forced millions into exile, and caused millions to be considered refugees within the land that once before was their land as well.

At the world level, the removal of the Islamic state and its civilization left the world to be dominated by two materialistic ideologies: socialism and capitalism. For the first time in history dating back to the rise of Christ (PBUH) and later Mohammad (PBUH), the world has been vacated of godly-based systems. Socialism thrived for seventy years and dominated a large part of the world while totally rejecting the notion of a god behind this world. The impact of socialism on the lives of the people had been more than devastating, atrocious, and grievous. Now that is history, and historians continue to document the era of socialism. As I stated earlier, socialism will not be thoroughly investigated in this book.

On the other side of the fence, capitalism ruled and thrived under the notion that god has to stay out of the domain of money, politics, and social lives of the people. The record of capitalism has been notoriously disdained in the domains of poverty, child mortality, education, health, and security. Immoral values of greed, selfishness, egoism, arrogance, mockery, and derision have become the norms of both political and economic domains under capitalism. Part 1 of this book has argued the decline of capitalism and its imminent collapse.

The Second Rise of Islam

It should be immediately stated that the decline of Islam and the removal of its state and civilization from the world was not due to internal faults and defects in the foundation of Islam as was the case with socialism and capitalism. On the contrary, it was the departure from the foundation of Islam which led to the decline rather than the compliance with its principles. The close observance of the divine revelation and the strict compliance of its ordinance and rules caused and facilitated the first rise, expansion, and spread of Islam, its state and civilization. It is the same cause and reason that is driving the second rise today.

It can be argued the rise of Islam today is caused by necessity as well as ordinance and obligation. Since the collapse of the Islamic state and the removal of the Shari'ah, the Muslims in Muslim-majority countries have experienced some of the worst conditions ever. The geopolitical distribution of the Muslim lands shows a great disparity and irregularity. This is evident in the composition of small states with less than a half million population but with extremely large wealth and very large states with more than one hundred million extremely poor people. Kuwait, for example, has less than one million Kuwaiti nationals with more than $140 billion GDP. Egypt, on the other hand, has a population of more than eighty-four millions and a GDP of $165 billion. This huge disparity in wealth created unbearable conditions which have promoted serious calls for the integration of Muslim lands and the unification of Muslims under one state. Initially, the unification calls were prompted by Arab pan nationalism.[42] After several setbacks experienced by Arab nationalists, the call for the integration of Arab lands and states was carried forward by Islamic advocates.[43]

The industrial revolution which was a distinctive feature of the twentieth century seemed to have missed the majority of the lands of Islam and Muslims. The Ottoman Islamic state before its collapse was shouldering Europe in manufacturing capabilities and industrial infrastructure. After its collapse in 1924, the wheel of inventions, industrial growth, and manufacturing came to a terminal halt. Not far a way from where I live close to the point where the river Yarmouk and river Jordan meet, there is an astonishing sign of the freeze experienced after the collapse of the Islamic Ottoman state. A railroad bridge which was built at the end of the nineteenth century by the Ottomans and then destroyed by the British during World War I has never been repaired; it stands as a witness on how the industrial infrastructure froze for the past one hundred years. Aside from light transformational and oil-gas production industries, the majority of Muslim countries are almost vacant of any significant heavy industry.

After centuries of rule of law and high ethical standards for government, the Muslim states became among the most corrupt states worldwide. Figure 29 shows the corruption ranking of Arab and Muslim states.[4] The corruption perception index (CPI) measures the "abuse of entrusted

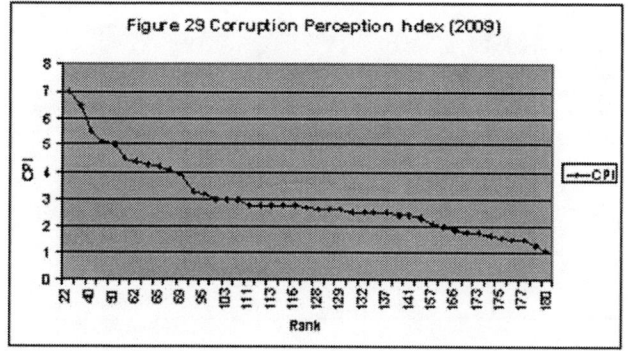

power for private gain."[44] Except for four states, the Arab and Muslim states scored less than 5 on a scale from 1 to 10, indicating a high level of corruption. The 37.5% of the states worldwide which had score less than

---

[4] Source: Transparency International http://www.transparency.org/about_us.

or equal to 3 are either Arab or Muslim states. Corruption conditions have impacted all aspects of life in these countries and have become a driving force for regime and system changes.

Before the decline, Islamic schools and universities in Andalusia, Baghdad, and Cairo ranked top in the world and were the source of knowledge and enlightenment. British historian Sir John Davenport reports on a letter sent by King George II of Britain to the caliph in Andalusia asking him to enroll a delegation from England into Islamic universities.[45] Since the decline of the Islamic civilizations, the universities in the Islamic world have fallen behind. Figure 30 shows the ranking of universities around the world.[5] There is only one Arab university within the top 200 universities in the world, two among the 500 top universities, and only four among the top 1,000 universities. Based on a calculated higher education scoreboard, all Muslim and Arab countries lag behind in their higher education score with Saudi Arabia, the oil-rich country leading the score with 38%! In the wider scope of the Muslim world, Turkey has one university among the top 500 and Iran has one in the top 1,000 schools in the world. Given these devastating and demoralizing figures in higher education, it is only natural to expect a parallel decline in the industrial sector as discussed earlier.

Perhaps the most shocking outcome of the decline at the political level was the occupation of Palestine by Israeli Jewish people following thirty years of colonial rule by the British. In 1948, armies of Egypt, Jordan, Syria, and Lebanon were unable to take control of Palestine after the withdrawal

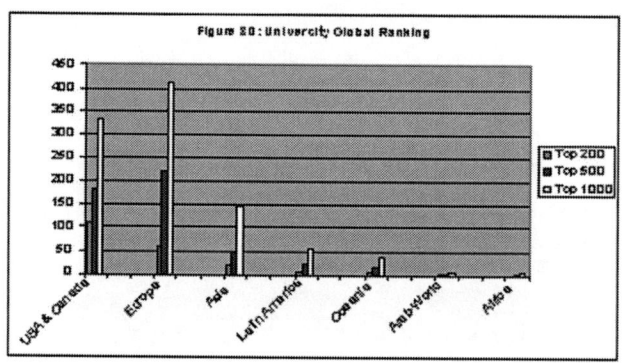

of British soldiers. This was a result of total collapse of the geopolitical system of the Muslim world after the removal of the Islamic state and

---

[5] Source: Ranking Web of World Universities, 2009
http://www.webometrics.info/Distribution_by_Country.asp.

its systems. Less than twenty years later (in 1967), the same countries suffered another defeat by the Israeli forces and lost more land in the war. Whether it is in the diplomatic, political, or military fronts, the Arab and Muslim countries could not achieve any reasonable success in resolving the conflict in Palestine. Other geopolitical problems surged in Kashmir, Eritrea, Bosnia, Kosovo, and Azerbaijan.

Internal wars between Muslim countries, despite the strong prohibition of fight among Muslims, have consumed millions of lives. Among the most overwhelming and shocking was the war between Iran and Iraq, which lasted for almost ten years (1980-1989) and consumed more than one million casualties on both sides. Yemen, Saudi Arabia, and Egypt fought a bloody civil war in the early 1960s. Pakistan and Bangladesh fought several wars before Bangladesh broke away from Pakistan. Iraq invaded Kuwait in 1991, and the consequences of the war ensued until Iraq itself became a victim of occupation by the USA. Along the boarders of Turkey, Iraq, and Iran, a war has been going on for decades between Muslim Kurds and Muslims from Turkey and Iraq. The toll of the decline on the unity, integrity, and security of Muslims has been more than shocking.

Political corruption, wide disparity of wealth distribution, lack of industrial infrastructure, education backwardness, steep poverty, occupation, and low health standards created a deep polarization between the general public and the political leadership. Almost without exception, the political leadership in the Muslim world maintains a grip on power and authority using brutal police force supported by foreign intelligence and backup. The relationship between the general population and the authorities had been remarkably hostile. This can be seen from the annual human rights reports, which reveal horrible stories about torture, imprisonment, sanctions, detention without charges, and in some cases mass murder of political prisoners.[46]

Repulsive and repugnant conditions which prevailed in the Muslim world at the start of the twentieth century created an atmosphere conducive for revolutions and change. Two parallel movements began to formulate almost simultaneously in many of the Muslim states. One movement was characterized by nationalism, while the other one was more geared towards Islam. But since Islam has just been evicted out of the political scene in a most humiliating manner, the Islamically characterized movement was too soft and reluctant in voicing its objectives and ambitions. The nationalist movements were more vocal, violent, and forceful. Nationalist movements were able to organize the national liberation movements which led to an official liberation of the majority of the countries from the rule of colonialists. To a large extent, the nationalist movements were also able to draw the support of the Islamic movements which existed at the time. In the Indian subcontinent, the nationalist movement of Muhammad Ali Jinnah was able to recruit the support of the Jamaat-e-Islami (the Islamic Group) led by Syed Abul A'ala Maududi. In Egypt, the nationalist movement led by Gamal Abdel Nasser was also able to enlist the support of the *Muslim Brotherhood.*

By the middle of the twentieth century most of the Muslim and Arab countries had gained their "official" independence from British and French colonial powers. Nationalist movements of Nasser and the *Bath* parties in the Arab world, Ali Junah of India and Pakistan, and the Kemalists in Turkey have enjoyed triumph and support. On the other hand, Islamically oriented movements were overshadowed by sentiments of nationalism and patriotism.

The role of Islam in challenging the new conditions which emerged after the collapse of the Islamic state was minimal during the first half of the twentieth century. The general theme which clouded the Muslim world during that period was that Islam as an ideology was to blame for the decline and backwardness. In plain words, the general public of Muslims lost confidence in the ability of Islam to lead them out of the deep decline they plunged in. Consequently, scholars like Muhammad Abduh, Jamal al-Din al-Afghani and Rashid Ridha focused their writings and scholarly work to convince the general Muslim public of the validity of Islam as a religion with a rational creed.[47, 48] Their main concern was to create a positive image of Islam in the minds of people.

The first two major Islamic movements were created almost at the same time in both Egypt and the Indian subcontinent. The Muslim Brotherhood was created by Imam Hassan al-Banna of Egypt in 1928, five years after the khilafah was abolished. The movement's main concern at the time was to restore the image of Islam and to restore confidence in Islam as a way of life. It was not until the 1950s when one of the prominent thinkers and leaders of the group, Sayyid Qutb explicitly wrote about the necessity to resume the life under the dominance of Islam.[49, 50] Sayyid Qutb was executed by Egyptian government in 1966.

Maududi established Jamaat-e-Islami movement in India in 1941, which paralleled the brotherhood in Egypt.[51] The Islamic group in India contributed to the separation of Pakistan from India and the creation of Pakistan. Maududi proposed an Islamic constitution for the newly created country. Despite the involvement of the group in the creation and stability of Pakistan, the country ended up to be one more secular state in the land of Muslims.

In 1953, another movement (*Hizb ut-Tahrir*) was created in Jerusalem (*Al-Quds*) by Taqiuddin al-Nabhani. This time, Nabhani focused on the necessity to reestablish the state of khilafah which was demolished in 1924. He realized, though, that the collapse of the Khilafah was a result of the Islamic decline and not the cause of it. Therefore, he incorporated in his movement ideas, thoughts, and procedures deemed necessary for a revival of the Muslim mind-set before the state can be reinstated.

The governments in the Muslim world took very strong steps to prevent any of the Islamic movements from realizing their objectives. Members and supporters of the movements faced persecution, imprisonment, exile, denial of rights for passports or work, and execution in some Muslim countries.[52] The earlier Islamic movements led a nonviolent approach in pursuit of their goals. Nabhani maintained that the first rise of the Islamic state was accomplished by Prophet Mohammad (PBUH) using only political and ideological methodology and that militancy was prohibited at the stage of building the state. The Muslim Brotherhood and the Jamaat-e-Islami also supported this approach and moved to make use of the democratic processes, whenever they were made available to them.

Throughout the 1950s, '60s and '70s, the major Islamic movements led a strong but nonviolent struggle and managed to confirm Islam as a main ideology seeking to shape the life of the people and to run their economic, political, and social affair. While the focus of attention was on countries in the Middle East and Pakistan, another movement was shaping up and ready to produce fruits in Iran. Ayatollah Khomeini had already started his own movement and was preparing his followers for a revolution in one of the fiercest police states in the area. In 1979, Khomeini succeeded in his revolution and was able to topple the regime of the shah of Iran using nonviolent means of revolution. The Islamic revolution in Iran proved to the masses of Muslims across the entire Muslim world that Islam has the capacity to challenge existing governments and deploy some form of Islamic rule. The revolution in Iran boosted the efforts of other movements which were making very slow progress at that time. In the meantime, the regimes in other Muslim countries increased their pressure against the movements and forced some of them to become more violent and aggressive.

The pressure and oppression practiced by various governments and their police and intelligence services created an atmosphere of violence and counter violence in the Muslim world at large. This had led to the creation of a new phenomenon within the Islamic movement, which promoted militancy as a means for retaliation against oppression as well as a means to take over the state by force. Within these conditions, the movement of *Al-Jihad* emerged in Egypt; the majority of its members have been previously imprisoned and tortured in Egyptian prisons. At the same time, a *jihad* war broke out in Afghanistan against the Soviet occupation.

This war drew fighters from all over the Muslim world; it also drew and enjoyed the support of the United States and Western Europe. Muslims who were looking for the Islamic triumph, as well as those who have been demoralized and persecuted in their own countries, found the proper place for them along the borders of Afghanistan.

By the time the war ended in Afghanistan and the Soviets were forced to pull out, an army of trained militant Muslims was in tact. Having received extraordinary training in Afghanistan, *Al-Qaeda* emerged with strong emotions of victory and strong convictions to replicate their experience in other parts of the Muslim world.

The collapse of the Soviet Union and Eastern Europe delivered to the Muslim world new states, which previously were not considered part of the Islamic world due to the dominance of socialism. The newly created states were soon engulfed by the dynamics of the Islamic movements.

By the end of the twentieth century, the status of Islam and the Muslim world can be summarized as follows. The Muslim populations worldwide continued to exhibit several signs of the decline which characterized their lives almost one hundred years earlier. Political oppression was still in effect. Occupied lands have not been liberated. Poverty was still on the rise. Human rights continued to be violated by regimes and governments supported by western powers, officially condemning human rights violations, but practically endorsing the violators. Globalization had deepened the local economic problems. Politically, nationalism had failed to change any of the conditions of the people. Political leaders linked to the Western powers proved to be among the most corrupt worldwide. Furthermore, world ideologies are not measuring up to their slogans and promises. Socialism had failed its own people and had collapsed altogether. Capitalism had failed the majority of the people in the world and had left more poor than rich, more oppressed than free. All pointers and indexes point into the direction of Islam as a potential and viable solution and savior.

The dynamics of the local, regional and international conditions singled the Islamic movements as the most influential and most capable of shaping the future. The public opinion has shifted almost entirely towards the Islamic rise and the reestablishment of its state and civilization. In the eyes of many observers, the rise of Islam to the driver seat of the political leadership is no longer a debatable issue. It has become a matter of time, which is becoming nearer by the day. Towards the end of the first decade of the twenty-first century, the Islamic movements which have been facilitating the next phase of the rise of Islam fall into one of three categories.[53]

First: The militant groups, which emerged after the Afghan jihad war as well as the result of excessive persecution practiced by governments against Islamic activists. The militant groups usually confuse the concepts of jihad in Islam with the methodology for Islamic revival. Example of these groups are the former jihad group of Egypt, the Front of the Islamic Salvation (FIS) of Algeria, the Islamic courts of Somalia, Taliban of Pakistan and Afghanistan, and Al-Qaeda. Quite often, we see all of these movements referred to as Al-Qaeda, which is not necessarily true.

Second: The evolutionary groups. These groups existed throughout the twentieth century; they believe that the resumption of the Islamic way of life will be accomplished gradually and over an extended period of time. These groups use the local elections and political processes to gain power and influence. Through elections, the groups hope to influence the laws and regulations and tilt them towards Islam. They also hope to gain access to the common public opinion platforms and official media. Examples of these groups include the Muslim Brotherhood in Egypt, Jordan, Iraq, and Kuwait; the Jamaat-e-Islami of Pakistan and Bangladesh; the Islamic Justice and Development Party of Turkey; and others.

Third: The revolutionary groups. These groups believe that Islam as an ideology should be installed as one installment in the same manner Prophet Mohammad created the state when he arrived at Medina. They do not believe in militant approach for massing a revolutionary change. Rather, they rely on the support of the public opinion as well as the support of the stronghold elements in the society. Examples of this group include the Khomeini movement, Hizb ut-Tahrir (global organization), and *Tanzeem e Islami* of Pakistan.

All the Islamic movements, irrespective of their philosophies and methods, insist that the revival of Islam and the reestablishment of its state are both a necessity and an obligation. It is a necessity because of the conditions which engulf the Muslim world as well as the rest of the world. It is an obligation because Prophet Mohammad established a state which became responsible for the implementation of Islam and was continued after the death of the Prophet by his companions. These two factors (the necessity and the obligation) have significantly contributed to the recent trend of the rising Islam.

The grounds for this trend were cultivated by a lengthy ideological struggle between the ideas of Islam and those of nationalism, socialism, capitalism, democracy, fascism, and all ideas which do not incorporate god at the root of their systems. Similar to the thirteen years period of Prophet Mohammad's mission, the struggle of the Islamic movements was faced with serious repression within their local societies and states. The oppression was as cruel as the one launched by the society of Mecca against Prophet Mohammad and his companions. The difference is that this one was more sophisticated and equipped with technology and more repressive means.

There is a wide sense of agreement worldwide that the triumph of the Islamic movement is imminent and inevitable. The time and conditions are more suitable than ever to reinstall Islam as a comprehensive ideology which will resume its role in the local, regional, and world orders. Besides the work of the Islamic scholars, activists, and movements, several historic events contributed to the phenomenon, where Islam is ready to assume a position on the stage of world ideologies. These events and conditions are summarized below.

First: nationalism, being the strongest opponent of Islam especially in the Arab world, had suffered serious defeat. The Arab Israeli wars revealed serious failure and inability of nationalistic movements to resolve a long standing occupation of Palestine. The last stronghold of Arab nationalism was defeated in Iraq when the *Ba'ath* party failed to prevent a humiliating fall of Baghdad. In Palestine itself, the nationalistic Palestinian movement could not stand in the face of the rising Islamic militant groups. The election polls uncovered this phenomenon in the majority of the Muslim lands. Wherever elections were allowed to be conducted in a rather open and transparent manner, members of the Islamic movements easily surpassed members of the nationalist movements. This was evident in the Algerian elections in 1992, when members of the Islamic Salvation Front won most of the parliament seats leaving behind the Nationalist Liberation Front. The first free parliament election in Jordan in 1991 revealed a majority for members of the Muslim Brotherhood movement. Even in Iraq where elections took place for the first time after the removal of Saddam and the Ba'ath party, members of the Islamic movements from both Sunni and Shi'a sects won the majority of the seats. The same was repeated in Turkey, and to a lesser extent in Pakistan.

Second: The collapse of socialism and the Soviet Union. Socialism as an ideology was the main instrument used by nationalist parties in the Muslim world to claim justice and promote wealth distribution. This tactic was used mainly to quell and suppress the Islamic movement by depriving them of an appealing platform through which they can influence the masses. The impact of socialism and the Soviet Union began to slow after the invasion of Afghanistan by the Soviets in 1979. When the Soviet Union was ultimately dismantled in 1991 and socialism was demolished, Islam and its uprising movement enjoyed a tremendous success. Muslim republics who came out of the Soviet Union added extra power to the already-powerful Islamic uprising.

Third: The Iraqi occupation of Kuwait and the subsequent war. The war launched by the US and UN coalition forces to evict Iraq from Kuwait dramatically changed the dynamics in the whole region. For the first time in many decades, a voice of serious opposition rose from Saudi Arabia. Until 1991, the Saudi monarchy maintained a close grip on its population and operated with almost zero internal opposition. After the end of the war, the Jordanian intelligence released thousands of activists from prisons and reinstated parliamentary elections which brought members of the Muslim brotherhood to the parliament. Egypt relaxed its harsh treatment of the Muslim brotherhood and allowed their members to run for elections.

Four: The Islamic revolution in Iran. As stated earlier, the revolution proved to the Muslim masses that Islam has the capacity of staging a revolution, building a state and society, and challenging most repressive regimes like that of the shah of Iran. Besides, Iran began to provide direct and indirect aid to various Islamic groups such as Hezbollah, Hamas, and Jihad.

Semi-Islamic Models

When Prophet Mohammad (PBUH) migrated to Medina in the year 632, he built an Islamic state and an Islamic society, with a structure, foundation, and pillars derived from the pure divine revelation. He was warned time and again in the Quran to keep a straight path as ordered by his Lord. In Surah Al-Shura (chapter 42, verse 15), the Quran directs this call to Mohammad, *"So unto this religion of Islam invite people; and stand firm on all that is ordained by Allah as you are commanded; and follow not their desires but say: I believe in whatsoever Book Allah has sent down, and I am commanded to do justice among you."* With this type of order, the Prophet could not have built a state with nationalistic or cannibalistic flavor. He could not have built a society with specific favors to Arabs, or rich men, or special elites. The only characteristic of the sate and the society he built was Islamic. The only sovereignty that existed in his state was that of Islam. This character gave that initial state enough power and energy to survive for nanny centuries. Even when the seeds of decline hit the state, it took hundreds of years before it collapsed.

It is interesting to note that in one of the prophecies of Prophet Mohammad (PBUH) he described the stages of the Islamic reign.[54] He described the first stage to be the stage of prophethood and mercy, which historians agree that it was the period during which the Prophet was the ruler and then followed by the four guided caliphs. Then he describes a stage of dynasties reigning over the Islamic state. The third stage is the state of dictatorship, where the rules of Islam are abrogated by force and the rulers gain their positions by force as well. Then the Prophet described a final stage where Islam rises again and he describes this stage as "Khilafah following the model of prophethood."

Having said that, it is not difficult to see that the Islamic models which have emerged in the last few decades are but semi-models compared to what the Prophet had described. The first of these models was the Islamic Republic of Iran. Although the Iranians succeeded in staging a massive revolution, they ended up building an Islamic state with sectarian Shi'a and nationalist Iranian characteristics. The local rules and laws are mostly Islamic, but the overall character of the society and the state remains particular to Iran and to the Shi'a school of thought.

In the Sudan, the government experimented with another model in the 1980s. They converted some of the laws in the country into Islamic laws. Not all laws were converted into Islamic ones. The laws of the economy, foreign affairs, and political structure continued to be secular. The Islamization of the laws in Sudan was finally terminated.

The Taliban in Afghanistan was another mode of a semi-Islamic model. Unlike the revolutionary approach of Iran, the Taliban gained power as a result of a civil war they launched against the regime in Afghanistan. The Taliban model of the Islamic state, although short-lived, did not match to the model implemented and promoted by Prophet Mohammad. On one side, it was a state for Afghanistan and the Afghan people; on the other side it applied a certain vision of Islam adopted by the ruling faction. More importantly, the Taliban model did not deploy the Islamic systems of economy, financial affairs, and foreign policy.

The Saudi model is yet another semi-model of the Islamic state. The local laws and regulations and the court system in Saudi Arabia are mostly Islamic. But the economic system, the financial system, the foreign affairs, the government structure are not modeled according to Islam.

The limited success in implementing semi-models of Islam shows how far the Muslims have drifted away from a true model of Islam. After centuries on the path of decline and almost hundred years after the collapse of the Islamic state, it is not surprising that the Muslims have lost a clear vision of the comprehensive Islamic model. The political system of Islam is quite often mixed with the democratic ones due to similarities in some practices, like election and accountability. The economic system for a long time was confused with socialism, and lately it had been mixed with some forms of capitalism. This is due to the weak understanding of Islam, which resulted in the decline in the first place.

For Islam to resume its ability to disseminate justice and gain the appreciation of Muslims and non-Muslims alike, the complete set of coherent systems of Islam should be recreated. Today, Muslims and non-Muslims alike see only one or few aspects of Islam whenever Islam is discussed. The image of the Islamic state has been linked more to the image of Taliban in Afghanistan than to the state that Prophet Mohammad created and was carried out by caliphs Abu Bakr, Omar, Othman, and Ali. The image of Islamic economy is more linked to the Islamic banking in Kuwait and Saudi Arabia than to a more comprehensive one like the one which prevailed for many centuries. The image of Islamic politics is more associated with the politics of Iran than those advanced by Prophet Mohammad and his successors.

Today, more than any time in the past, there is an urgent need to sketch a more practical and comprehensive image of the Islamic model of governance and finance. This is necessary for Muslims who have been marching a long marathon towards the reestablishment of Islam. It is essential for them to know precisely what is it that they are trying to build, lest they build another system and label it with Islam. It is also necessary for people in the world at large, so they may know what kind of ideology will rival the ideology of capitalism.

A thorough description of the ideology of Islam in terms of its foundation, pillars, and structures is long due. There are numerous publications which describe one or more aspects of Islam. However, very few have addressed in great details the ideology in terms of its intellectual foundation, systems, and methodology. This description is beyond the scope of this book. It will be the subject of another publication. The focus of this book will be on the economic part of the ideology since this is the most relevant part to the current global economic crisis. Furthermore, the economic system in Islam is probably the least understood part of the Islamic systems by Muslims and non-Muslims alike. A particular emphasis will be given to the derivation of the economic principles from the divine sources of Islam. The economic system in Islam will be the subject of the next section.

4

The Economic System in Islam

The economic system in Islam is an integral part of the Islamic ideology. The rules related to the economy and finances are intertwined with other rules pertaining to marriage, family relations, politics, morals, rituals, beliefs, and others. *Zakah*, one of the components of the Islamic economy, is revealed in the Quran together with the ritual of prayer in more than fourteen verses in the form "establish the prayer and pay the Zakah." In Surah Al-Mujadilah (chapter 48, verse 4), one of the options to recover from a marriage-related sin was to feed sixty poor people.[55] What this really means is that the Quran and the Sunnah of Prophet Mohammad contain scattered texts which include rules related to finances and economy as well as to other topics. Prophet Mohammad was not an economist with a degree in economics. He was a prophet and a messenger of God who received revelation on various issues including economics. A derivation process, therefore, becomes necessary to obtain and systematize the economic structure.

This further implies that the economic structure is part of a bigger schema of Islam and should not be separated either from its siblings (other systems) or root (the foundation of Islam). The economic system of Islam can and will produce the expected outcome of justice and fairness only when taken together with the rest of Islam. This will be evident when we discuss the development of the economic and financial system in Islam in the next section.

This chapter presents three main topics. The first one is the gradual development of the economic and financial system of Islam. The second topic is the political economy in Islam. The last topic is the financial system in Islam.

4.1 The Development of the Economic System in Islam

If you open the Quran and browse its chapters looking for a Surah on the Islamic economy, you will not be able to find any. The closest you will get is Surah Al-Anfal (chapter 8), which was named and revealed in relation to the proceeds of war and contains few rules on the distribution of the proceeds. Similarly, Prophet Mohammad did not issue specific statements, deliver speeches, or make public announcements totally dedicated to what we can call today an economic structure. The texts which include references to economic and financial issues were revealed over the course of twenty-three years (the life span of Mohammad as a prophet). Quite often a reference of economic substance may be made in relation to an incident that required a rule or judgment of some sort. One example is the rule related to the ownership of conquered land, which was revealed in conjunction with the battle of Khaibar.[56] So the full picture of the economic system needs to be constructed from verses in the Quran, statements of the Prophet, and judgments on specific cases. The following subsections present and address four major principles deemed essential to the development of the economic system in Islam.

Rizq (Wealth) and Its Role in the Islamic Economy

Essential to the development of the economic system in Islam is the concept of wealth known as *Rizq* in Islamic terms. What is wealth? And who is the provider of wealth? Islam maintains that the amount of wealth acquired by any human throughout his life is determined by Allah. People strive in this life to acquire exactly what Allah has prescribed to them. In his endeavor to acquire wealth, man has no knowledge of what could be allocated to him by god. But once he acquires any amount of wealth, it is essential that he believes that this wealth had been allocated to him by Allah.

It was important to engrave this concept in the minds of Muslims for several reasons. For one, Islam wanted to maintain a good level of humility in the society especially among those who would become rich and wealthy. Knowing that the wealth has been granted to them by Allah removes that sense of arrogance and self-centered feelings. Second, Islam was building generosity within the society, which would be deemed necessary for dealing with the poor. Third, Muslims will be required to spend voluntarily beyond what was required of them by the laws of the state. Fourth, the Islamic state was going to face multiple wars at its infancy, which required the financial support of its constituents.

In the Quran, there are more than one hundred references to the fact that Rizq (wealth) is provided by Allah. Following are few examples of these references. In Surah Al-Rum, there is a direct reference to the fact that Allah is the one who provides wealth.[57] *"Allah is He Who created you, then **provided wealth** for you, then will cause you to die, then (again) He will give you life (on the Day of Resurrection)."* (Quran 30:40). In another place[58] it states, *"O mankind! Remember the Grace of Allah upon you! Is there any creator other than Allah who provides wealth for you from the sky and the earth? None has the right to be worshiped but Him."* (Quran 35:3)

Whenever the believers are asked to spend part of their wealth on the poor and needy ones, the Quran reminded them with the fact that this wealth was provided by Allah in the first place. The importance of this concept is evident by confirming it right at the beginning of the Quran. In Surah Al-Baqara (chapter 2), which is essentially the first and largest chapter after the opening chapter, it reads, *"That is the Book (the Quran), whereof there is no doubt, a guidance to those who are pious and aware of Allah; Who believe in the unseen world and perform prayer, and spend out of the wealth We have provided for them."* So part of the belief foundation of a Muslim is to believe that the wealth he has gotten is granted by Allah, and thus when requested to spend that wealth under the command of Allah, he would comply without reluctance.

The Quran argues that one of the reasons that the disbelievers abstain from feeding the poor is that they do not accept the fact that the wealth they earn is given and provided by Allah. In Surah Yaseen (chapter 36, verse 47), which was revealed in Mecca before the establishment of the Islamic State, the Quran exposes the reason behind the Kuffar (disbelievers) refusal to contribute towards the poor and needy. It says, *"And when it is said to them: Spend of that wealth which Allah has provided you, those who disbelieve say to those who believe: Shall we feed those whom, if Allah willed, He (Himself) would have fed? You are only in a plain error."* Evidently, the people of Mecca who have rejected the religion of Mohammad do not share the idea that the wealth they own is the providence of Allah. They argue, if it is Allah who provides the wealth, then he might as well provide the poor directly rather than asking us to do so.

At first glance, the argument of the disbelievers seems to be logical, except that it does not account for the fact that Islam seeks the purification of the human soul and its cleansing from greed, self-indulgence, and miserly behavior. In Surah Al-Tawbah (chapter 9, verse 103), the Quran says, *"Take Sadaqah (alms) from their wealth in order to purify them and sanctify them with it."* The concept of Rizq in Islam and the subsequent motivation for spending in compliance with the commands of Allah lays down the foundation for a moral system in support of the financial and economic systems. Without a solid moral system, the economic system, no matter how sophisticated, is bound to fail. We have seen a clear example in the system of capitalism, which due to lack of a moral system is heading to a collapse.

While building a set of moral values, deemed necessary for the economic structure, the Quran exposed the antimoral values which characterized the behavior of the Meccan society. The most clear reference to moral defects in the financial behavior of Mecca came in Surah Al-Fajr (chapter 89, verses 17-20): *"Nay! But you treat not the orphans with kindness and generosity. And urge not one another on the feeding of Al-Miskeen (the poor)! And you devour wealth all with greed. And you passion wealth with much love."* The implication is that Islam seeks to build a new society and systems, where greed will not be tolerated, orphans and poor will not be ignored, and wealth will not be accumulated for the sake of accumulation only.

Islam was preparing the stage for an economic system that does not allow interest or usury (called *riba* in Quran) to be gained as part of loans transactions. Before the rules of sanctioning usury were completely revealed, the Quran insisted that the usury should not be used as a means for increasing wealth. It further pointed out that usury allows the wealth of one to grow on the expense of the wealth of other people. In essence, usury leads to money growth without a corresponding growth of products. In Surah Al-Rum (chapter 30), the Quran reminds the people that it is Allah who provides the wealth in the first place, and that Allah wants those who have more wealth to spend and help the less fortunate. Then the Quran criticizes the usurious acts and praises the practice of charity giving.[59]

Without usury, it is feared that the loans may dry out and people refrain from giving loans. The Quran, in an attempt to motivate the people to continue giving loans to other fellow members of the society, charged that a loan given in goodwill without the expected usurious return is considered as a loan to Allah. Allah will multiply the rewards for those who give loans in pure goodwill and as a gesture of help and support to others. Verse 11 in Surah Al-Hadeed (chapter 57) says, *"Who is he that will lend to Allah a goodly loan (without interest): then Allah will increase it manifold to his credit, and he will be rewarded a good reward."*

The belief that whatever wealth a person owns must have been provided by the will of Allah is a cornerstone concept in the economy and finances of Islam. More wealth in the hands of a person should not lead to arrogance and haughtiness of the rich. In the meantime, it should not create a feeling of envy and jealousy in the hearts of the poor towards the rich ones. This is essential for preventing the development of a class system with the rich and wealthy forming one class and the poor and needy forming the other one.

Furthermore, the concept of Rizq leads to the conclusion that the current wealth status of any one in the society is not permanent. A poor is not destined to remain poor, and a rich is not guaranteed to remain rich. Thus, the poor will never cease striving to acquire wealth, and the rich will never stop thinking about preserving his status. This type of thinking is critical and vital for continuous productivity.

Abundance of Resources

Contrary to the "scarcity of resources" principle advocated by capitalism, Islam advances the principle of "abundance of resources." In numerous locations in the Quran, the idea that Allah has created abundance of resources and created in them benefit for the people is repeated time and again. Islam wants to propagate the belief that the core resources in the world are not scarce, and that god has created more than enough for all the people to enjoy. Islam wants to create a mind-set which appreciates the abundance of resources and remembers at all times that these resources had been provided by god, the creator, in a manner that people can utilize them and make something good out of them.

In Surah Al-Nahl (chapter 16), the Quran enumerates many of the wealth resources and reminds of the fact that these resources were originally created by Allah. In verses 5-8, it says,

> *And the cattle, He has created them for you; in them there is warmth (warm clothing), and numerous benefits, and of them you eat. And wherein is beauty for you, when you bring them home in the evening, and as you lead them forth to pasture in the morning. And they carry your loads to a land that you could not reach except with great trouble to yourselves. Truly, your Lord is full of Kindness, Most Merciful. And He has created horses, mules and donkeys, for you to ride and as an adornment. And He creates other things of which you have no knowledge*

In the midst of the production cycle, people tend to forget that the very animals they raise (cattle, sheep, horses, camels) had existed in this world independent of man, and they have been created in a manner that man can tame these animals and utilize the benefits in them. In order to appreciate the inherent benefits of these animals, one can compare them with other animals in the wild, which cannot be utilized for food or transportation, for example, the lions, tigers, wolves, hyenas, and others.

The Quran continues the list of resources and the benefits created within them. In verses 10-13 in the same chapter (Al-Nahl 16), the Quran turns to water as a major resource used for irrigation, plantation, and drinking. The verses read thus:

> *He (Allah) Who sends down rain from the sky; from it you drink and from it (grows) the vegetation on which you send your cattle to pasture. With it He causes to grow for you the crops, the olives, the date-palms, the grapes, and every kind of fruit. Verily! In this is indeed an evident proof and a manifest sign for people who think. And He has subjected to you the night and the day, and the sun and the moon; and the stars are subjected by His Command. Surely, in this are proofs for people who understand. And whatsoever He has created for you on the earth of varying colors and qualities from vegetation and fruits (botanical life) and from animal (zoological life) Verily! In this is a sign for people who remember.*

Along the same lines, the Quran reminds of the abundance of resources created in the seas, oceans, and rivers. These resources include the fish, the precious stones, and the ability to sail ships in the seawater. In verse 14, chapter 16, the Quran says,

> *And He it is who has subjected the sea (to you), that you eat thereof fresh tender meat (i.e. fish), and that you bring forth out of it ornaments to wear. And you see the ships sailing through it, that you may seek (thus) of His Bounty (by transporting the goods from place to place) and that you may be grateful*

In a reference to the fact these and other resources are abundant and will not be in shortage at any point in time, the Quran says in verse 18 of the same chapter,

> *And if you would count the favors of Allah, never could you be able to count them. Truly! Allah is Oft-Forgiving, Most Merciful.*

The idea here is that Islam was preparing to create a new society with certain values and attitudes. The people in the society are required to maintain humility and humbleness no matter how rich they become. Thus, it is important to remind them that the origin of the wealth they possess is created by god in the first place. Also, people are required to realize that no matter how much resources they consume or own, there will be more than enough resources for all; consequently, rich societies should not feel threatened if other societies grow to the same level of wealth and richness. This concept becomes very useful when compared to Engel's law which tries to explain the reason behind soaring food crisis.[60] Engel's law, formulated by German statistician Ernst Engel, states that as people from developing countries make more money, they begin to buy more expensive food such as meat. This rise in affluence also results in more people consuming meat throughout the world. This creates a higher demand for grain and subsequent raise in their prices.

This analysis goes back to the scarcity of resources principle. When food is considered to be scarce or may become scarce, the prices should go up in order to limit the consumption of food by certain segments of the population. When the poor segment becomes wealthier and attempts to consume more of the already-scarce food, the market should increase the cost of food, eventually preventing the previously poor segment of the population from accessing the food resources.

The Islamic focus and emphasis on the abundance of the resources and the fact that resources are originally provided by Allah leads to a more relaxed view by all segments of the society and less competition for the consumption of food. While competition remains high for production, the competition for consumption may in fact decrease in an Islamic society. In this regard, Islam promotes the value of altruism, where Muslims are encouraged to leave part of their needs unsatisfied for the purpose of satisfying the needs of others.[61]

The concept of the resources being the creation of Allah has another dimension in the economic system of Islam, besides the preparation of people to be more giving, more thankful, and more appreciative of the wealth they acquire. This dimension is more philosophical in nature, which renders its expected results to be produced over a longer period of time. Islam maintains that god had created the universe (including the sun, the stars, the moon, the earth, and others) and had subjected its laws such that man can benefit from this universe. In contemporary civilizations, where religion is separated from life, the relationship between man and nature is described at best as one of defiance and insubordination, a relationship in which man struggles to overcome obstacles posed by the nature. It is common to talk about man defeating the laws of gravity when he was able to fly out into the open space.

The Islamic perspective on this issue is that god created the universe in a manner which allows man to be able to utilize its inherent benefits and powers. The word used in the Quran is *Sakh'ar*, which literally means "subjected or subordinated the universe to the commands and actions of man." What this really means is that the laws and systems under which the universe operates are made in a manner that they can be discovered, and they can be utilized such that man can produce and extract the benefits in the universe. References to this concept in the Quran are numerous. For example, in Surah Al-Jathia (chapter 45, verses 12-13), the Quran says,

> *Allah is He Who has subjected to you the sea, so that ships may sail through it by His Command, and that you may seek of His Bounty, and that you may be thankful. And has subjected to you all that is in the heavens and all that is in the earth; it is all as a favor and kindness from Him. Verily, in it are signs for a people who think deeply.*

The fact that we can build ships that can sail in the seas is due to the way seas have been created in terms of water density, wave dynamics, wind speed, the depth of the sea levels, and other factors. Evidently, man is not the one who specified the requirements and specifications of the seas, oceans, and rivers; man discovered these specifications and found out how they can be used for ship sailing.

The point here is that Islam wants the people to believe and realize that all that is in the universe has been created in a manner to serve the better life of the people. Eventually, we the people are not at war with the so called "Mother Nature" or the universe. On the contrary, we are at peace; we are in a state of collaboration and cooperation. The universe and all the inherent laws within it are created in a manner to serve us the humans. This view is bound to promote the people to continuously seek further utilization of the available resources provided in the larger sphere of the universe. This concept is essential for continued discovery and innovation. When the Muslims understood these issues, and their civilization was intact, discovery and innovation were always on the rise.

The abundance of resources principle and the subjecting of the universal resources to the human use form the second cornerstone in the economic system in Islam. In essence, this principle allows the economic system in Islam to promote production and enhance productivity, while it relaxes consumption. In other words, it is a society that competes for more production (to utilize what Allah had made usable) and for less consumption (to spare more for the poor and needy).[62]

Poverty

The Islamic view on poverty is best summarized by the statement "If poverty were a man, I would kill it." This statement was made by Umar Bin Al-Khattab, the second caliph in Islam, and repeated by Ali Bin Abi Talib, the fourth caliph. Islam, over the course of its revelation, developed a categorical intolerance to poverty and hunger. Abu Dhar Al-Ghafari, one of the companions of the Prophet, is reported to have said, "I am most shocked by a poor man who cannot find food at home and does not come out with his sword in his hands." The statements of Umar Bin Al-Khattab, Ali Bin Abi Talib, and Abu Dhar signify the level of intolerance for poverty and hunger in Islam. This view stems sequence from the fundamental thought established by Prophet Mohammad (PBUH) and the Quran.

Prophet Mohammad, in a direct reference to poverty and hunger, rejected the slightest possibility that one person would go hungry while the neighborhood he lives in has plenty. In the words of the Prophet, *"Allah and his Messenger will disown a community which allows one of its members to sleep hungry."*[63] This strong resentment of hunger and poverty was demonstrated in another statement by the Prophet, where he said, *"He who resorts to his bed with full stomach while his neighbor is hungry is not a true believer."*[64] Note how the Prophet skillfully links the rejection of poverty to one's faith and belief. He does not simply make an administrative rule asking to provide food for the poor people in the neighborhood. Rather, he relies on the intellectual foundation of belief which he spent more than thirteen years putting together, one brick at a time. Then, he turns to this intellectual faith foundation and utilizes it by saying, if you truly believe in Islam as you claim, then you cannot allow your neighbor to go hungry. So the faith foundation is used to build this sense of responsibility among the members of the society.

Statements like these coming from the Prophet, the leader of a movement, and the head of state assert an important fact: poverty is not to be allowed in the Islamic society. The successors of the Prophet, the caliphs, took the same stand and continued to emphasize the need to sustain a poverty-free society. Note that the emphasis of the Prophet and his companions, when dealing with poverty and hunger, was focused on the specific individuals rather than on the community as a whole. The fact that a community is doing well in terms of economic status makes its members more responsible for the well-being of every member of the community. Under capitalism, the economic well-being of the community is measured by the economic growth; an increase in the GDP is interpreted as a sign of a healthy economy. Alarms begin to sound in a capitalist society when the economic growth slows down or halts for an extended period of time. In Islam, the alarm sound goes off when hunger persists within a community despite the fact that the community as a whole may have abundance of food and goods. Islam does not allow the community to rest as long as there is at least one hungry man or woman or child.

The Quran refers to two categories of poverty. One category is called the "Miskeen." This is the category of hungry people who are unable to feed themselves or those who depend on them. The second category is the "Faqueer." This is the category of poor people who do have some income but their income is not sufficient to take care of their daily normal expenses such as housing, health, education, transportation, and the like. Over the course of its development, Islam recognized other categories of people who might be in need for financial help and support, albeit their need can be temporary. In Surah Al-Tawbah (chapter 9), the Quran defined eight categories of people eligible to receive funds collected from the main charity institution in the Islamic state, the charity of the Zakah.[65] (These categories will be discussed later in this book).

The act of feeding the hungry Miskeen received a great attention in the Quran, to the extent that it was raised to the highest status and equated it to the most sanctified rituals. If a Muslim becomes too ill to go through fasting during the month of Ramadan, Islam permits the Muslim to feed a Miskeen (hungry person) in lieu of each missed day.[66] When a Muslim violates certain rules, Islam required of him to feed poor hungry people to make up for the violations. If a Muslim breaks his fast during Ramadan without a valid reason, he has to pay retribution for this violation by fasting two consecutive months or feeding sixty hungry people for each violated day.[67] If a Muslim swears by Allah that he will perform a certain task but he fails to fulfill his promise, then he is required to make up for this violation by feeding ten Miskeens.[68] One of the ill practices before Islam was to allow the man to abandon his wife without officially divorcing her. Islam prohibited this act. One of the options placed by Islam to make up for this violation is to feed sixty poor and hungry people.

These types of practices ordained by Islam are meant in the first place to show how important it is to fight hunger in the society. Islam clearly sent a signal that hunger should be dealt with by all means. In the meantime, Islam recognizes that in a complex society where people have variant capacities and capabilities, and with all the dynamics of war and peace, the diversity of economic prosperity and downturn, it is possible for some people to fall behind and become unable to afford the basic needs. Thus, Islam wanted to bring this issue of caring for the poor and needy to the daily rituals and practices of the people.

To further signify the importance of dealing with hunger, Islam declared that the poor and needy have certain right to the wealth of the wealthy. In two locations in the Quran, the Quran makes the following statement: *"Give to the kindred his due and to the Miskeen."*[69] In other words, the wealth that should be paid to the poor by the rich is not a form of taxation; rather it is an obligation upon the rich and a right for the poor as affirmed by Allah. This concept is further explained in Surah Al-Ma'arij (chapter 70, verses 24-25), where it says, *"And those in whose wealth there is a known right for the ones who are deprived of it."* The "known right" is a reference to the annual rate (2.5%) of one's wealth to be given to the poor and needy.

In Surah Al-Haqqa (chapter 69), the Quran vigorously deplores and deprecates anyone who does not take the necessary steps to facilitate the feeding of the poor and hungry. The Quran equates this deplorable behavior with the act of disbelieving in Allah the great.[70] In its struggle with the polytheists of Mecca, Islam exploited the greedy nature of the society of Mecca and denounced their ill treatment of the poor and deprived people.[71] Islam continued to pound on the issue of hunger in Mecca, which presumably was prevalent during the time when Islam was still rising. In a direct hit, the Quran addressed one of the elites in Mecca challenging him to spend his wealth to better the lives of his relative orphans, or the lives of the desperate poor.[72] In Surah Al-Maoon (chapter 107, verses 1-3), the following criticism was made against Abu Jahl, one of the chiefs of Mecca at the time: *"Have you seen him who rejects the religion of Islam? That is he who repulses the orphan (harshly); and urges not on the feeding of Al-Miskeen."*

In contrast, the Quran highly praised the ones who generously spend in order to feed and provide for the needy and hungry. It gives high value for those who give food, in spite of their love of it, to the Miskeen, the orphans, and the captives. And they do so not anticipating any worldly return, except the pleasure of Allah.[73]

The point Islam wanted to make early on is that poverty of each individual in the society is considered a problem of highest priority. It is ranked above and beyond the rituals and must be resolved if the faith and belief in Islam was to prevail. In his book *The Perfect Political Economy*, Al-Maliki concludes that the main problem addressed by the Islamic economic system is the poverty of the individuals in the society.[74] Before instituting laws, regulations, and mechanisms to resolve the poverty of people, Islam raised the level of awareness among its constituents regarding poverty and hunger. Further, Islam highly valued the trait of giving and spending for providing food and commodities for those who could not afford them. By heavily criticizing the anti-Islamic society in Mecca and denouncing its practices as being unfavorable to the poor, needy, and orphans, Islam placed a burden upon the Muslims to rid their society of similar practices. No wonder, then, that the caliphs of Islam vowed to kill poverty!

The Value Definition in Islam

Within the framework of capitalism, the material value is the only value that has weight and significance. And the materialistic value of a product is defined in terms of the benefit it carries to people and in terms of its exchangeability with other products or things. When the value of a product is measured in terms of money, then the value of the product is called the price.

Islam has a totally different approach for value definition. First, Islam recognized two broad categories of values, one category is related to the actions taken by people, and the other is related to the things and commodities. Within the first category, Islam recognizes four types of values which should be attained when the human performs an action. These values are the spiritual, moral, human, and the materialistic values. The value in this respect refers to the objective sought by performing the action.

Spiritual values are associated with acts whose only purpose it to please god, the creator. For example, the acts of prayer, fasting, and pilgrimage are ordained upon the Muslim and should be carried out in a certain order. These actions have no value except to please Allah, and consequently to satisfy the instinct of worshiping embedded within the human self. A Muslim does not perform prayer in order to exercise his back, although prayer may benefit the back muscles. Rather, a Muslim performs prayer for the sole objective of pleasing his god. The Quran says, "Establish the prayer for my remembrance.[75]" Similarly, a Muslim does not fast during the month of Ramadan in order to lose weight, although he may lose weight while fasting. But he performs fasting only to win the pleasure and satisfaction of Allah. It is reported that Prophet Mohammad had said, *"Allah says: all your actions belong to you, except fasting. It is mine; and I am the one who provides the rewards for fasting."* The Quran confirms that fasting had been prescribed upon people so that they may have piety for Allah.[76]

The second category of values is related to moral values. Islam defines certain acts whose sole objective is to achieve a moral value. This is an attempt to create in the society the tendency to perform actions for the purpose of achieving moral objectives. For example, Islam urges a Muslim to develop kind character, honesty, trustworthiness, truthfulness, and generosity. Islam also urges a Muslim to get rid of certain morals such as being mean, miser, jealous, envious, and greedy. These moral values stand on their own merit and considered viable objectives which should be sought and achieved on their own. The value of kindness is extended to include animals. It is reported that Prophet Mohammad had told of a woman who brought on herself the anger of Allah because she locked up a cat without feeding her. He also spoke of a man who deserved the reward from Allah because he went out of his way to get some water for a thirsty dog. When he was asked whether a Muslim can be rewarded if he is kind to an animal, he replied by saying, *"If you are kind to any living being, you will be rewarded."*

When a Muslim says the truth, or returns the trust to whom it belongs, or stands up for what is right, or rejects the oppression, he does so for the very reason that these values are good values and he has to maintain them. Why would a Muslim comply with these moral objectives and try to achieve them? Of course this goes back to the main intellectual foundation, which tells the Muslim that these objectives are defined by Allah, and therefore by complying with them, a Muslim in essence is obeying Allah.

The third category of the values is the human value. By this, we mean the value related to helping and supporting humans in general. Examples include saving the life of a human who happened to be caught in fire, or drowning in water, or wounded in an accident, or any similar incident. It also includes honor, dignity, and integrity values. Human values are essential for creating collaboration and support within the society. The Quran talks about the act of feeding the poor, or the captive, or the orphan without expecting anything in return. Islam prohibits hiding knowledge, since knowledge is for the benefit of all humans. The Quran highly praises the believers for the fact that they repress anger and they pardon the mistakes of fellow men.[77] In a reference to the significance of a human value, the Quran speaks of the dignity and honor bestowed upon the children of Adam.[78] The human value is sought on its own, irrespective of any other value.

The fourth category is the materialistic value. This is the most commonly known value and shared by all people and ideologies. In their trade, work, investments, farming, hunting, and similar acts, people seek to attain the materiel benefit returned by such acts. Islam recognizes profit seeking and the benefits of material acts. Since the pursue of material benefit is the most natural behavior of humans, Islam did not need to overemphasize this type of value; on the contrary, it needed to reduce the human zeal and aggressive behavior in his endeavor to achieve the materialistic values.

In a general reference to man's natural love of material benefits, the Quran states in Surah Al-Imran (chapter 3, verse 14), *"Beautified for men is the love of things they covet; women, children, much of gold and silver, branded beautiful horses, cattle and well-tilled land. This is the pleasure of the present world's life; but Allah has the excellent return (Paradise with flowing rivers) with Him."* Recognizing the need to pursue the materialistic benefit besides the spiritual values, the Quran states in Surah Al-Qassass (chapter 28, verse 77), *"But seek, with that (wealth) which Allah has bestowed on you, the home of the Hereafter, and forget not your portion of lawful enjoyment in this world."*

The point is that Islam moves to create a society with multiple dimensions. The society does not flourish and prosper with the materialistic aspect only. Capitalism provided an excellent example where material progress by itself, no matter how big the progress is, does not provide the peace and tranquility yearned for by the people in the society. The rates of divorce, suicide, poverty and hunger, and crime soar high when the materialistic values dominate the society at the expense of human, moral, and spiritual values. Islam realizes that humans by the very instincts created within them would naturally pursue the satisfaction of their instincts. For example, a father and a mother need not be reminded vigorously of the need to love and care for their children. They do that in a very natural way, except during family crisis. Children, on the other hand, need to be reminded and encouraged to maintain their love to their parents and to care for them, especially when they are old. The children's roles towards their parents are not as natural as it is for parents towards the children. Recognizing these variations in the roles, the Quran places extremely high value on taking care and looking after parents. Being nice and obedient to parents comes next to worshiping Allah, as stated in the Quran.[79] On the other side, the Quran warn the parents not to lose their good faith while attending to the needs of their children.

The value of a thing, a product, or a commodity is the benefit inherent in this thing. This benefit according to Islam is not a measure of the human labor invested in the product as proclaimed by Marx. Neither is it a measure of the demand by the consumer or the supply by the producer or both.

Islam maintains that the reason behind the benefit in a given matter is the set of properties and characteristics of that matter. For example, the benefits of the iron are due to the properties of the iron which are determined by its atomic structure. This structure is what makes iron behave differently from gold or copper. Without this atomic structure which defines the basic properties, matters could not have produced the benefits which give the matter its value. It is true that the human needs to exert effort and labor to produce the final product which is deemed useful by the consumer. But it is also true that there are some material objects which do not require any human labor to be beneficial; water, forests, meadows, air, sunlight and heat, and wind are just examples of material objects which provide value without any need for human labor or effort.

So the real cause and reason for any material benefit is the original property of the object. This property is initially created by Allah. And the value of any product is directly related to the original properties of the components of the product, and without these properties, the product cannot provide any value. In this regard, the value of any material object is real and not relative. And this value is a measure of the benefit inherent in the object. This measure is determined at the time when the benefit is being evaluated by people.

The fact that different people may demand or value the benefit of an object differently at different times and under different conditions does not change the value or the benefit of the product. For example, the value of a telephone device is that it enables the communication between two people in two different locations. This benefit is the same whether the communication is needed for an emergency, or for a chat, or even for cheating.

The level of demand, urgency, or scarcity of the product has an impact on how much the human is willing to give in exchange for the product. This is what the economists correctly identify as the price. And the price of the product is not the value of the product, and is not a measure of the benefit of the product. The fact that the price can be negotiated for the same product, and can fluctuate over time or even at the same time (in auctions), or for different people, shows that the price is not and cannot be a measure of the benefit of the product. It is true that capitalists have recognized this difference, but only when they divided the value into two categories (benefit and the price). So price should not have been confused with the value in the first place.

The main difference between the Islamic view of value and that of capitalism or socialism is that Islam believes that the origin of value benefit is the creation made by Allah. Hence, no matter what the final shape of the material object or product is, Islam continues to recognize and admit that this product is sourced by Allah. Therefore, when Allah allows or prohibits the use of the product in a certain setting, a Muslim submits because the product could not have been produced without its initial properties which are created by Allah. Similarly, a Muslim submits when Allah asks him to give part of the products to other people named by Allah. With this understanding, a Muslim would not say, "Why should I spend and feed the poor; after all, I made the wealth with my own knowledge and skills," as was proclaimed by Qarun.[80]

The Islamic view of values, whether the value of actions or value of things, provides a comprehensive view by which a balanced society can be created. The spiritual, moral, and human values supplement the materialistic value in the sense that the economic growth in the society would not lead to wide disparities, greed, arrogance, poverty, high crime rates, suicide, and moral bankruptcy. The value definition in the Islamic ideology constitutes the fourth cornerstone in the Islamic political economy and economic system

The political economy of Islam will be the subject of the next section. It should be noted that this political economy would not be productive or even practical without the four principles discussed in this section, namely, that the Rizq (wealth) of individuals is provided by Allah, that the resources used to increase the wealth are abundant and created by Allah, that poverty must be swiftly dealt with, and the existence of spiritual, moral, and human values alongside the materialistic values.

4.2. The Political Economy in Islam

Before proceeding in the discussion of the Islamic political economy, I should note that the term *political economy* is used in the context which refers to the processes of production, consumption, and distribution of wealth as related to the economies of states. In this respect, political economy addresses the strategies and methods which directly impact the economy of states and the ability to achieve the economic objectives set forth by the economic system. Hence, the term *political economy* can be used within the framework of ideologies such as Islam, capitalism, or socialism. Therefore, the reader should not expect to see the term "political economy" being used in some verses in the Quran or statements of the Prophet. However, the subjects studied under the umbrella of political economy will be extracted and evaluated from original texts of the Quran and the Sunnah as well as from the consensus of the companions of the Prophet and the causal reasoning derived from the original texts.

The political economy addresses a myriad of subjects related to the sources of wealth, the nature of wealth, the methods of increasing wealth, and the methods of distributing wealth. In particular, the political economy deals with property ownership, currency, exchange rates, gold standard, Riba (usury), hoarding, trade and commerce, corporations, human labor, and satisfaction of human basic needs. Next we discuss the Islamic perspective on each of these issues and show how Islam manages the various economic resources to enhance production, regulate consumption, and eliminate poverty.

Before I proceed to describe the components of the Islamic political economy, I should note that historically Muslim scholars spent a good amount of effort compiling references to financial matters found in the Quran, the statements of the Prophet, the actions of companions, and the practices of various caliphs. Among the most prominent references is the book under the title *Al-Amwal* (translated as finances) compiled by Abu Obaid Al-Qasim Bin Salam who lived in the period 767-838 AC (AH 150-224). In the book *Al-Amwal*, Abu Obaid collected all references related to money, financial transactions, property ownership, money distribution, and related subjects. *Al-Amwal* is a very resourceful reference for any student or scholar seeking to understand the economics of Islam. Another major reference is the book under the title *Al-Kharaj* (translated as land taxation) authored by Imam Abu Yousuf Yakub Al-Ansari[81] (730-799 AC, AH 113-182). Abu Yousuf wrote *Al-Kharaj* based on the request of Caliph Harun Al-Rasheed,[82] who was looking for a good reference for managing the financial matters of the state. *Al-Kharaj* talked in details about the revenues of the state, the state budget items, and the means of distributing the wealth among the constituents of the state. Besides the financial matters addressed in the book of *Al-Kharaj*, Abu Yousuf included policies and strategies for managing the finances of the state.

In addition to the books of *Al-Kharaj* and *Al-Amwal*, the Islamic library has countless of references to financial matters embedded in the compilation and writing of various scholars within the schools of the prominent Imamas, such as Abu Hanifah,[83] Ja'far,[84] Malik,[85] Al-Shafi',[86] and Ibn Hanbal.[87] Throughout the history of the Islamic state of khilafah, the financial and economic matters in the state were resolved and addressed by scholars who were fluent in the process of deriving rules on various matters by utilizing well established tools for derivation. The rules derived by the scholars were utilized by the caliphs through a direct request as was the case when Al-Rasheed asked Abu Yousuf to provide a comprehensive set of rules. Alternatively, the ruler would just use the rules which have been derived over time by various scholars and have been established as laws through practice.

The scholars from the various schools of thought continued to address all matters in the state including financial and economic matters and provide the appropriate rules and laws. Almost without exception, each and every *fiqh* (Islamic laws) book would include specific chapters and sections on trade, loans, *riba* (*usury*), sale, land property, land taxation, war budgeting and funding, proceeds of war, zakah collection and distribution, partnerships, common or public properties, and much more.

Since the collapse of the Islamic state of khilafah in 1924, the systems of Islam were abruptly deactivated in the countries previously ruled by the Islamic laws. The economic and financial systems are no exception. The colonial powers of Britain, France, and other European countries introduced to these countries new laws and rules which replaced the Islamic ones. The only Islamic financial practice which survived during and after the colonial period was the practice of *zakah*, because in Islam zakah is considered a ritual and one of the pillars of Islam. Even the practice of the zakah during this period became more of an individualistic practice rather than a state-sponsored activity as used to be since the establishment of the first state in Medina by Prophet Mohammad (PBUH). As a result, the Islamic principles of the economic and financial system lost their practical norm in Muslim majority countries. Over time, the theoretical principles of the Islamic economy blurred and became rather fuzzy not only for the average Muslim, but also for some Muslim scholars and academics. This is a natural result for abandoning the implementation of the economic as well as the political system for almost a hundred years.

The few studies that addressed the economic system in Islam in the last few decades contributed in a significant manner to reconstruct an image of a system which has been clouded for over a century. One study appeared as early as 1953 under the title *The Economic System in Islam*[88] by Taqiuddin al-Nabhani. Another book (The Perfect Political Economy) appeared in the early 1960s and addressed the political economy in Islam.[89] In the early 1970s another book appeared under the title *Iqtisaduna* which stands for "Our Economy."[90] A fourth book *(Al-Amwal in the State of Khilafah)* appeared in the 1980.[153] These books laid down a solid foundation for the Islamic economic system, although they seemed very theoretical given the political conditions in the Muslim world at the time these studies appeared. Interest in the subject of Islamic economy began to increase in the 1980s, especially after the Islamic revolution in Iran. The creation of the Islamic Republic of Iran created a sense in the region for the first time that the economic system of Islam has more practical merit than previously thought. Since then, tens of studies bearing titles such as "Islamic Economy," "Economic Thinking in Islam," "Economic Styles in Islam," "Islamic Economic Methods," "Islamic Finances," "Finances of the Islamic State," and the like showed up in the Islamic literature.[91]

4.2.1 Property Ownership

Perhaps the most outstanding feature of political economies is that which defines property ownership in the society. Private ownership was recognized as the distinctive feature of capitalism. Public ownership of the means of production is the main characteristic of socialism. The Islamic political economy recognizes three forms of ownership, namely, the private ownership, the public ownership, and the state ownership. The scope of each of these forms of ownership is exclusively defined.

Before proceeding to explain these forms of ownership, it should be noted that neither socialism nor capitalism was able to exclusively stand by their definitions of ownership. The socialist rulers in the Soviet Union were forced to relax their strict view of public ownership and open the door for limited private ownership, especially in the farming industry. By the same token, the Chinese socialists have also allowed a limited private ownership in the manufacturing industry. Within the world of capitalism, nationalization of private property for different reasons is more than common. The government takeover of banks, insurance companies, and auto industries in the United States and some European countries has become an acceptable response to financial crisis and economic problems. The scope of property ownership in a world dominated by the ideas of socialism and capitalism can be visualized as shown in the diagram in figure 31. State economies based on private ownership end up adding public ownership to their systems; those with public property ownerships end up adding private ownerships.

Practically this shows that optimal and stable political economies are the ones that deploy more than one form of ownership. The proper mix of ownerships and the scope of what constitute a private and what makes a public ownership cannot be obtained through a trial-and-error, wait-and-see kind of process. This mix should be more formally defined so that the resulting political economy can be a stable one and can lead to the desired objectives of resolving poverty and hunger.

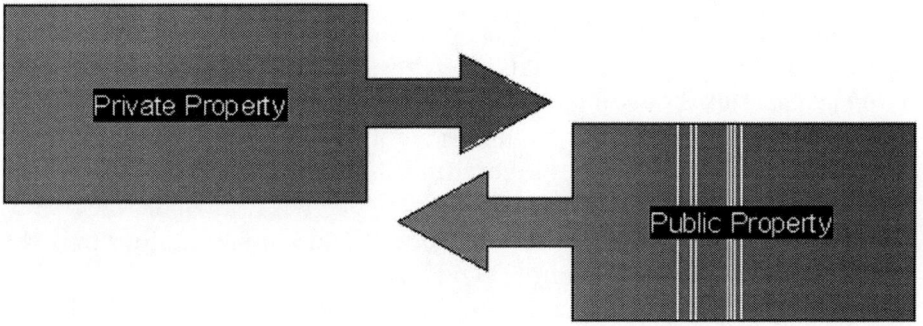

Figure 31: Private and Public Ownership Slide

What defines the proper mix of ownerships is the way the society is formed and viewed by different ideologies. If the society is perceived as being as a group of individuals, then it is natural to emphasize the private ownerships of individuals and to partially or completely exclude other ownerships. If the society is perceived to be as a single material unit with individuals being only as parts of the whole unit, then it is natural to emphasize the collective ownership in the society. However, if the society is perceived as a structure composed of distinct and independent components, then property ownerships will diverse according to the diversity of its components.

The Islamic view of society is such that the society has three distinct components. Each has its specific needs which are different form the needs of the other ones. The first of these components is the individual human being who possesses specific instincts and biological needs which need to be satisfied on a continuous basis. Each individual in the society has his own needs for food, shelter, health, rest, mating, worshiping, and breeding. In order to satisfy these needs, the individual must own the means and tools necessary to satisfy each of these needs. When the means and tools are owned by one person, or by the community at large, there will be no guarantee that the needs of another person who does not own them will be satisfied. For example, if John, Ali, and Adam each has a loaf of bread, but Sam does not have any, then Sam may go hungry while John, Ali, and Adam are full. By the same token, if four loaves of bread are collectively owned by John, Ali, Adam, and Sam, then it is possible that one of them can go hungry as well. To guarantee the satisfaction of the individual basic needs, the individual must be able to own the commodities and tools which are necessary to fulfill these needs.

The only philosophy that verily denied the property ownership of individuals is the Marxist philosophy which viewed the individuals as materialistic parts of a larger materialistic entity called the society. It maintained that individuals posses no instincts of any kind, and therefore property ownership of individuals is an illusion. The reality of human daily living proves this theory incorrect. Islam rejects this theory and insists that the human strife to own the commodities and tools to satisfy his basic needs and instincts are intrinsic and inherent to the creation of the humans.[92]

The second component in the society which has its own distinct needs is the public. The public is not the sum of individuals. Rather it is the group as a whole which requires its own resources such as the land, water resources, atmosphere, minerals, and the like. The needs of the public as one unit differ from the needs of the individuals. The public does not have instincts or biological needs like those of hunger, thirst, shelter, and the like. However, it has its own requirements which must be satisfied in order to sustain the integrity of the public. The public needs include security, maintenance of resources, protection of the land which hosts the public, maintenance of the atmosphere, maintenance of homogenous relations between the members of the society, and the like. The satisfaction of these needs cannot be guaranteed as a result of the satisfaction of the needs of individuals. Just like the individuals who must own property in order to fulfill their needs, the public needs to own in order to meet the requirements of its needs. Public ownerships cannot be substituted by individual ownerships. Islam recognized the public requirements and insists that the public must have its own ownership. It is reported that Prophet Mohammad had said, "The people collectively have the ownership of water resources, forests, and fire.[93]" This narration confirms the public as an independent entity in terms of ownerships.

The third component in a society which should be recognized with its specific needs for ownerships is the state. The state is the political entity which is responsible for caring for the affairs of the individuals and the public alike. The state has its own specific needs which are different from the needs of individuals or the needs of the public. The state needs include its ability to organize, administer, and conduct the affairs of the individuals and the public. As an independent entity, the state must have its own property. This property must be well defined and guaranteed not only by the power of law, but also by the core principles of the ideology. Islam recognized the state as an entity which has its own specific properties.

It is true that all political economies in the world have used a mixture of individual, public, and state ownerships in various forms. But it is also true that the policies have been more random than systematic. Privatization of public property has been used excessively in many countries in the world to convert publicly or state-owned property to private ones. The rules for conversion have been driven mostly by the states' need for immediate cache flow rather than by fundamental principles of the economy. By the same token, the nationalization of private properties which prevailed in the second half of the twentieth century was mostly driven by revolutionary regimes and aimed at reducing the influence of multinational corporations.

In the most recent financial crisis in the United States and Europe, the nationalization of banks and other industries was mostly driven by temporary policies aimed at preventing a major crash of the financial industry. In other words, the contemporary political economies under the dominance of both socialism and capitalism have accepted the three types of ownerships. However, they have not specified the domain of each in a fundamental way. On the other hand, Islam has clearly accepted and defined the three types of ownerships at the core foundation of its political economy. It has also prevented the transfer and conversion of one type of ownership into another one. Under Islam, it is not allowed to privatize the public ownership. It is also prohibited to nationalize the private property. Furthermore, the state is not allowed to tap into the wealth of individuals or the wealth of the public, since it has its own funds and property. In the subsequent sections, we discuss each type of property ownership in Islam.

Private Ownership

In a world dominated by the capitalist ideology, the private ownership of commodities, goods, and means of production is the default norm of ownership. However, within the realm of socialism, private ownership is considered to be against the norm. When I lived in the Soviet Union in the mid-1970s, I had a hard time convincing my colleagues that private ownership was a normal human behavior. It was not easy to belong to a religion, like Islam, which protects private ownership to the extent that it invokes the harshest punishment against the crime against the private property ownership. My experience in the capitalist world was totally the opposite; private property was the norm, and anything else was the exception.

Unlike socialism, Islam recognizes the innermost characteristic of a human which calls for the acquisition of wealth and the means to produce wealth. But it also differs with capitalism in the sense that it restricts the scope and the range in which private ownership is allowed to operate. Islam does not allow an individual to own or produce things which are categorized as prohibited goods in Islam. For example, it is not allowed under Islam to produce or own drugs, alcoholic drinks, or a casino. Islam also restricts individuals from acquiring property which is considered to be a public property such as oil fields, forests, or rivers.

Essentially, Islam does recognize the intrinsic nature of humans and admits that private ownership is a natural manifestation of the human instinct for survival. In the meantime, it recognizes that certain properties should remain in the hands of the public at large in order to guard against the imbalance caused by the variations in capabilities of individuals to acquire wealth. It is not uncommon for some people in a society to acquire more skills than others, or some people to have more motivation for wealth acquisition, or even for some people to have certain disabilities or handicaps which prevent them from acquiring enough wealth to provide for their needs. Various conditions such as wars and internal upheaval, natural disasters such as earthquakes and tsunamis, slavery and discrimination, and political and economic injustice can also contribute to the case where some people lag behind in terms of ownerships.

A quick reading of the progress and growth of societies throughout history shows that some portion of the society always remains completely or partially deprived of property ownerships. In order to account for this imbalance, Islam limited the scope of private ownerships and restricted certain categories of wealth to be exclusively owned by the public, such that the deprived individuals can benefit from the revenue generated by the publicly owned wealth resources.

Explaining the necessity to create a balance between the individual rights and the rights of the public, Prophet Mohammad (PBUH) gave the following example:

> *Your example is like a group who happen to travel on a boat. Some travelers were seated at the upper deck and others were seated at the lower level deck. Passengers at the lower level deck had to pass by the upper deck in order to access the sea water. One passenger, out of inconvenience, thought to dig a hole at the lower deck and access the sea water directly instead of climbing to the upper deck every time he needed to access water. If the rest of the group allows him to go ahead with his plans, saying it is his property and right, then the boat will sink with all*

on board. *If the rest of the group prevents him and stop his plan, then the boat will be saved and so all the passengers.*[94]

This narration points to the significance of maintaining a balance in the society. The rights of the individuals, although protected, should not override the rights and safety of the whole.

Private ownership of wealth is well established in the Quran and repeated in numerous verses. The Quran makes references to the wealth of the individuals when it requests the people to spend part of that wealth for good causes. In Surah Al-Baqara (chapter 2, verses 261-271), the Quran treats the issue of privately owned wealth and the responsibility bestowed upon the owners of the wealth. Following is a brief account and explanation of the concepts derived out of these verses.

> *[2:261] The likeness of those who spend their wealth in the Way of Allah, is as the likeness of a grain (of corn); it grows seven ears, and each ear has a hundred grains. Allah gives manifold increase to whom He wills. And Allah is All-Sufficient for His creatures' needs, All-Knower.*

Note how the verse makes a reference to "their wealth," meaning that the wealth is owned by these people who are requested to spend. In verse 264, the Quran makes a direct reference to the fact that the wealth owned by the people is also earned by them, indicating that wealth earning and ownership is acknowledged by Islam.

> *[2:264] O you who believe! Do not render in vain your charity by reminders of your generosity or by injury, like him who spends his wealth to be seen of men, and he does not believe in Allah, nor in the Last Day. His likeness is the likeness of a smooth rock on which is a little dust; on it falls heavy rain which leaves it bare. They are not able to do anything with what they have earned. And Allâh does not guide the disbelieving people*

Verse 266 points to the fact that ownership of wealth and goods is part of the human intrinsic characteristics, which naturally drives one to wish for the ownership of gardens.

> *[2:266] Would any of you wish to own a garden with date-palms and vines, with rivers flowing underneath, and all kinds of fruits for him therein.*

Again the Quran in verse 267 reiterates the fact that the wealth owned by individuals is earned by them through labor or through the natural production of the land.

> *[2:267] O you who believe! Spend of the good things which you have earned, and of that which We have produced from the earth for you.*

In Surah Al-Nisa'a (chapter 4, verse 2), the Quran makes a reference to the wealth which belongs to under age orphans and dictates that the wealth and property of the orphans should be given back to them once they reach a certain age.[95] In the Islamic society, private ownership is recognized for all people, irrespective of their belief. Muslims as well as non-Muslims own wealth. In Surah Al-Anfal (chapter 8), the Quran makes a reference to the wealth owned by the disbelievers and the fact that this wealth is often used to hinder the spread of Islam.[96] The Quran also talks about the wealth owned by a special group inside the Islamic society known as the hypocrites (disbelievers but publicly declaring Islam). Islam recognized their privately owned wealth, and the fact that it could be used to discredit and attack Islam, but Islam did not call for freezing or confiscating their wealth.[97] Compare this practice with the current practice in the United States, Europe, and the majority of the countries where the accounts of thousands of people are frozen, their property is confiscated, and their wealth is taken over when these people are suspected of being a threat to the national security.

Furthermore, Islam provided for the protection of the private property and prohibited any attempt to violate the properties of any individual in the society. Islam placed a very harsh punishment (up to the cutting the hand) for the theft of any privately owned property. The Quran prohibited any form of violating the property of the individuals, as stated in Surah Al-Baqara (chapter 2, verse 188):

> *[2:188] And eat up not one another property unjustly (in any illegal way e.g. stealing, robbing, deceiving, etc.), nor give bribery to the rulers (judges before presenting your cases) that you may knowingly eat up a part of the property of others sinfully.*

During the last ceremony of hajj (pilgrimage), Prophet Mohammad (PBUH) stated that the wealth as well as the blood of the people are sanctified and should be protected.[98]

While Islam recognized the private ownership of wealth, it also allowed several means of acquiring and increasing wealth. By acquiring wealth, we mean the process by which an initial ownership of wealth is attained. This is to distinguish acquisition from increasing wealth, where increasing wealth assumes that the ownership of some property has been obtained. For example, trading is a means of increasing wealth, because to be able to trade, you should own something in the first place.

Islam defines different ways for individuals to acquire private property and wealth. In general, there are five different means to acquire property:[99] human labor, inheritance, wealth provided to the poor, state grants, and other means.

Human Labor

Human labor is the first and foremost means of wealth acquisition. Using physical or mental labor, a man or woman can create an original wealth which becomes his or her private property, protected by law and enforced by the state. It is reported that Prophet Mohammad (PBUH) had said, *"Whoever cultivated a dead land, it becomes his."*[100] This statement of the Prophet applies to bare land that has never been used in any form before and had not been owned by any people. By cultivating a piece of land and converting it into a useful piece for farming or development, one becomes the sole owner of the land.

Islam also allowed the individual to own what he can extract from beneath the ground such as stones and marbles, from the sea such as precious pearl,[101] or from the air such as oxygen and nitrogen. An exception would be the minerals which exist in large mines since these minerals are known to be the property of the public. By the same token, wealth acquisition can be attained by hunting of birds, animals, fish, and other sea products. The Quran says in Surah Al-Mai'dah (chapter 5, verse 96), *"Lawful to you is (the pursuit of) sea hunting and its use for food."* In another location, the Quran speaks of hunting on the land as a means of possession.[102]

People can use their mental and physical labor to broker legal deals between trading partners; note that the traders have the original wealth, whereas the broker uses his labor to own part of that wealth. Also people can engage in a specific partnership called *"Mudharaba."* In this form of partnership, one party provides the money and the other party provides only labor. The one who participates with his labor creates wealth for himself. This type of partnership can be extended for farming as well.

The most widely used form of wealth acquisition has been employment, where the employer utilizes the physical or mental labor of the employee. The employer in this case is using the benefit of the employees to increase wealth. The employee on the other hand uses his or her labor to create and possess wealth. Islam allowed employment in general except where the work to be performed is prohibited. There are several references in the Quran and Sunnah for labor work and employment. It is reported that Prophet Mohammad (PBUH) had said, *"Allah (SWT) said: On the Day of Judgment, I will be the opponent of three types of people."* One of these types is *"A man hired a worker; the worker delivered all the work required from him; but the employer did not pay him his full wage."*

There are various ways in which Islam differs from capitalism and socialism in relation to labor and employment. Islam restricts employment to areas where the target benefit is legally permitted in Islam. For example, Islam does not allow any person to use his labor to produce wine out of vine products. It is narrated that Prophet Mohammad (PBUH) had stated that the sin involved in winery extends to the people who make and sell wine.[103] In another narration, the Prophet stated that the one who writes the contracts of usury is as fallible as the ones who participate in the usury transaction.[104] Similarly, Islam does not permit all forms of prostitution, because the obtained benefit is prohibited in Islam. Employment in gambling casinos is not allowed either. The wealth acquired by individuals through employment in areas deemed prohibited in Islam is considered illegal wealth. This is a major difference between Islam and materialistic systems which only look at profitability when considering wealth acquisition.

Another area which distinguishes Islam from other economic systems is the means by which wages are evaluated. In the end this matter boils down to the estimation of the value provided by the employee to the employer. The socialists believe that the value of the labor of the employee is equal to the value of the final product produced by the laborer. Since the labor of many employees collectively produce the final product, the socialists determined that all the laborers collectively own the final products because the value of their labor is equal to the value of the end product. This philosophical view led to the conclusion that the laborers (and by the same argument the farmers) must be the final owners of the end products. Since the labor of individual employees cannot be fairly separated from the labor of others, the Marxist theory decided that all laborers are equally partners in the ownership of the final product. In a socialist society, the wages given to employees are not meant to be in exchange of their efforts and labor which have caused the production of products. Salaries and benefits are estimated by the state based on what the state believes to be sufficient for the employees to cover their basic needs.

Capitalism, on the other hand, extends the theory of marginal value to the value of the labor of an employee. We have discussed this theory in details in the first part of this book. Using the marginal value theory, the capitalists estimate the minimum wage for employees and generalize this value for the entire society. The wage is estimated with the assumption that there is sufficient labor and skills available to produce the final goods. So the value is not estimated when there is a shortage of supply or excessive demand. It is estimated at the point where supply and demand are in equilibrium. As discussed before, the price of goods is assumed to control the level of supply and demand. When living expenses soar, the minimum wages become insufficient for the employees and they may not be willing to sell their labor, which results in a shortage of supply. The equilibrium with demand then gets disturbed. As a result, a reevaluation of the minimum wage occurs. Thus, the wage estimation under capitalism is not based on the real benefit provided by the service or the labor of the laborer. Rather, it measures the level of supply and demand which can fluctuate over time. It also measures the minimum living expenses in the society.

In Islam, the value of the labor is considered a benefit in the same manner the value of goods and commodities is also a benefit. The estimation of the real benefit of the labor is the only base for estimating the value of the labor, and consequently the wage is paid in exchange of that benefit. The real value of the labor benefit is determined by the experts in the field. Whenever a dispute arises between the employer and employee on the wage of the employee due to ambiguity or other reasons, then the opinion of the experts in the field is used in the process of arbitration. This rule was derived in analogy with a rule related to marriage dowry, where the dowry value is determined by a group of experts in cases of dispute or ambiguity. Therefore, the value of labor is not determined on the basis of the value of the produced goods or services; it is not based on the living expenses either. It is true that the contract between the employer and the employee is supposed to explicitly define the value of the labor, but this value should be in line with a general consensus about the value of labor in the specific field. If an employer pays less than the normal value of wages, this will be considered a case of deception *ghubn* and the employer will be forced to pay the difference according to law.[105]

Inheritance

The second means of wealth acquisition is inheritance. Inheritance in Islam is a well-defined process, whereby the wealth of a deceased person is distributed among the children, parents, spouses, brothers, and sisters according to a certain formula.[106] Inheritance rules in Islam allow the wealth to be broken and distributed after the death of the wealth owner. It is possible in the process of economic growth for wealth to accumulate in the hands of a few individuals during their life. The rules of inheritance are then used to break this tendency and cause the wealth to be recycled among several individuals. There are three distinct cases of inheritance in Islam:

1. The first case is when the inheritors take the whole inheritance according to the laws of inheritance, whereby all the wealth is distributed amongst them.
2. The second case is when the inheritors are entitled for part of the inheritance only. For example, the deceased leaves behind only the spouse (husband or wife). In these cases only a quarter or half of the wealth is inherited, while the rest of the inheritance goes to the state.
3. The third case is when the deceased leaves no inheritor behind; in this case the whole property goes to the state.[107]

The wealth is thus broken up and the property is transferred to the inheritors, where the exchange of the property resumes in an economic cycle amongst the people. The property is not kept in the hands of a particular person where the wealth accumulates. Inheritance is a legal means of property ownership, so anybody who inherits a thing owns it legally. Thus the inheritance is one of the means of property ownership, which the Islamic *Shari'ah* has permitted

Wealth Provided to Poor

Despite all measures taken to relieve the society from poverty, it is expected that some individuals will end up in a state of poverty for all types of reasons. In order to attend for the needs of these individuals, Islam recommended the state to provide a suitable opportunity for the employment of those who could not find employment on their own. The Prophet (PBUH) said, *"The Imam (head of state) is a Shepard, and he is responsible for his subjects."*[108] Employment enables individuals to use their labor to acquire wealth. In case it is not possible to find a job due to market conditions, or the person becomes unable to work due to age, sickness, or disability, then his support and sustenance becomes the duty and responsibility of his next of kin such as sons, father, and husband assuming that these parties are able to provide the required support. This is outlined in the books of Islamic jurisprudence under the section of *"Nafaqah"* (alimony).

If the immediate relatives are unable to maintain the required alimony, then responsibility is escalated up to the state. The state uses the funds available from the revenues of the public properties as well as from the *Zakah*. The Zakah is a specific amount of wealth taken out of the property of the rich and relayed to the poor. In Surah Al-Ma'arij (chapter 70, verse 24-25), and Al-Tauba (chapter 9, verse 103), Allah says,

> *[70:24] And those in whose wealth there is a known right; for the beggar and the destitute.*
> *[9:103] Take Sadaqah (alms) from their wealth in order to purify them and sanctify them with it*

In other words, the Zakah allocates certain amount of wealth for the poor from the original wealth of the rich. Islam makes this portion of wealth a right for the poor individual rather than a favor made by the wealthy ones. In Surah Al-Tauba (chapter 9, verse 60), the Quran lists eight categories of people who are entitled to acquire wealth from the Zakah fund:

> *[9:60] Zakah (funds) are only for the poor, and Al-Masakeen (very poor) and those employed to collect (the funds), and to attract the hearts of those who have been inclined (towards Islam); and to free the captives, and for those in debt, and for Allah's Cause, and for the wayfarer (a traveler who is cut off from everything); a duty imposed by Allah. And Allah is All-Knower, All-Wise*

The concern about the plight of poor and their right for wealth acquisition is emphasized in many ways in Islam. Imam Ahmad narrated that the Prophet said, *"Allah and his Messenger will disown a community which allows one of its members to sleep hungry."* It is also narrated that the Messenger of Allah said, *"He who resorts to his bed with full stomach while his neighbor is hungry is not a true believer."* It is also interesting to note that when the conditions of hunger and famine persist in a certain society, Islam halts the implementation of the strict rule of hand amputation for theft.[109] Further stressing the concept of resenting poverty, Abu Dhar, one of the companions of the Prophet, is reported to have said, *"I am most shocked by a poor man who cannot find food at home and does not come out carrying his sword in his hand."* Consequently, Islam lines up several steps in a sequential order to make sure that the poor is never left behind to be totally deprived of the means of ownerships. Thus the wealth provided to a poor person is a legal means for acquiring private property.

State Grants

The Islamic state is allowed to provide grants for people in the society for the purpose of stimulating productivity and enabling people to grow their business to a profitable stage. The state uses both state as well as public property to issue stimulus grants. It is narrated that the second caliph Omar Bin Al-Khattab provided stimulus money for the farmers in Iraq to help them cultivate their farms. The help was in a form of state grant, rather than loans.

Prophet Mohammad is reported to have given land for Abu Bakr and Omar after the migration to Medina. He also gave a piece of land to Al-Zubair. After the death of Mohammad (PBUH), the caliphs continued to give part of the public lands to various individuals in an attempt to utilize unused bare land. It should be noted that the state does not use tax money or the funds of the Zakah for the grants. The only fund the state is allowed to use is the one that comes from the state or public property.

Besides these means of property acquisition, there are other means of private ownership such as gifts and wills of deceased. Prophet Mohammad permitted gift giving[110] and he accepted gifts from both Muslims and non-Muslims. Also, Islam allowed a Muslim to designate part of his wealth in form of a will such that the recipients of a will should not be among those who are entitled for inheritance by law; also the amount of will should not exceed one-third of the total wealth.[111]

Another means of legal wealth acquisition is the compensation a person receives due to injury incurred against him by another person. If a person is killed by someone then his inheritors are entitled for compensation. The compensation for killing a person is equal to the value of one hundred camels.[112] The compensation in return for damage incurred for any part of the body is detailed in the books of Islamic jurisprudence.

Marriage contract in Islam includes certain amount of wealth to be paid to the woman. This wealth is the property of the woman and is not in exchange of a certain benefit, because both men and women have a mutual benefit in marriage; however, only the man is obligated to transfer part of his wealth to the woman. This wealth becomes the property of the woman as a result of the contract of marriage and not as a result of divorce as is the case in contemporary laws and systems.

Lost property found by people can be legally transferred to their property after it has been announced as "last and found" for a whole year. If the found property belongs to the category of precious metals, then only

80% of the property will be owned by individuals and the rest will become state property.

Thus individual private property is a well-structured type of property in Islam. Islam has clearly defined all reasons by which property can be initially owned by an individual. Islam further defined the laws to protect private ownership as well as the laws to increase the privately owned wealth. Islam also prohibited the ownership of property gained through theft, fraud, bribery, illegal trade, usury, and other illegal means of property ownership or growth. Furthermore, Islam prohibited the private individual ownership of property which is defined as either state or public property unless that property is legally granted by the state for an Islamically valid reason.

Private property ownership confers with the human natural drive for ownership which is part of the survival instinct. Islam acknowledges this fact and confirms the human need to own and enables this ownership. Islam provides an organization for private ownership by limiting the scope of the property which can be owned privately, defining the means by which private ownerships can be attained. In the meantime, Islam did not limit the amount of wealth which can be owned privately.

Public Property

Islam recognized the existence of public as an entity which has its own needs. These needs are not the sum of the needs of individuals, and therefore the satisfaction of the public needs cannot be achieved by satisfying the needs of each individual. The security of the public, the integrity of its territory, the cleanness and purity of its atmosphere and environment, the solidarity among its units, the preservation of the seas, river, and water reservoirs, and its image in front of other nations are all needs which pertain to the public as a whole and not to specific individuals. In order to preserve the public as one unit in the society, Islam defined certain types of property and declared them as a public property.

The category of public property includes water resources, forest preserves, and energy resources.[113] Old tribal societies used to move and change their location based on the availability of water and green meadows for their cattle. Whenever water springs dry out or fall under the dominance of another tribe, the tribe would be forced to move and search for a location where water is plenty. The same happens when the forests dry out and leave less food for the cattle of the tribe. Realizing that water resources and meadows are essential for the survival of the whole group, Islam announced that these resources should be owned by all and not by any single individual. If these resources fall in the hands of one or few, then the integrity and unity of the public may be compromised. The same applies to energy sources. Earlier Muslims scholars interpreted the word "fire" in the statement of the Prophet to mean the source of fire like woods (in the older societies). Today "fire" refers more generally to energy resources.

Following this analysis, it is recognized in Islam that all water resources such as rivers, lakes, seas, oceans, gulfs, and underground water basins are the property of the public. No single individual or enterprise is allowed to privately own any of these properties. The revenues generated due to the use of these resources will be returned to the public property fund in the state treasury. The state in its capacity as a caretaker of the affairs of the public will be responsible for delivering drinking water for all the people at the cost of pumping and delivering. Similarly, the state will deliver electricity generated from water resources at the cost of generating and delivering electricity. The state will not sell water or electricity for profit; it will not allow individuals or companies to sell water or electricity generated from public resources. However, the state will enable individuals to directly benefit from water resources through pumping water, generating electric power for their own use, or navigating the water pathways given that this will not diminish the ability of others to use and utilize water resources.

Similar to water resources are the wild forests. The woods, grasses, and meadows of the forests will be left for all people to utilize and use as freely as possible. Assaults on the forests and woods by building, pollution, or burning are considered a crime against the public and it is the state's responsibility to protect the forests. Revenues generated from the use and utilization of wild forests are returned to the public property fund in the treasury.

By the same token, all energy resources such as waterfalls, oil and gas fields, and coal mines are considered public property. The state exploits these resources and makes their products available to the public. The people pay to the state the cost of production, maintenance, and delivery. The state does not generate profit out of the sale of the energy products to the public. Note that the public includes both Muslims and non-Muslims. All are treated in the same way. Sale of energy products to foreign countries can be profit based. The state will make profit out of the sale to foreign countries even if the population of the foreign country includes Muslims. Muslims who do not live within the boundaries of the Islamic state do not have the same right for ownerships of public property.

The energy resources are extended to include solar and wind energy. These are considered to be public property because by their nature they cannot be owned by individuals, and because they belong to the category of "fire" defined in the Hadeeth of the Prophet. Individuals can directly benefit from these resources and can use solar panels or build windmills to generate power. However, windmills and solar panels cannot be placed in public forests or lands, and the power generated cannot be transmitted through publicly owned forests and lands. In other words, personal and private use of solar and wind energy are allowed for the personal use only. The public use and utilization of solar and wind energy is the state responsibility. The people will only pay for the cost of production, maintenance, and delivery. Sale of wind and solar energy products for foreign countries can be profit based. The revenue generated out of the sale of oil, gas, wind, and solar energy is returned to the public property fund in the state treasury.

The category of public property is extended, by analogy, to the roads, highways, railroads, airways, and water pathways. The common element between these items and the original items is the fact that private ownership of any of these items may restrict or prevent other people from using them. For example, the private ownership of a road or a water pathway may prevent vehicles belonging to other people from using these paths. Any property whose nature is such that if owned by individual then the others' ability to use the item is diminished is considered a public property, given that it is essential for the public. As such, roads and pathways in general are public property and cannot be owned by individuals. By the same analogy, the radio frequency spectrum which is used in the telecommunication and wireless industry is also a public property.

Another category of public property is the category of minerals of all kinds which exist in large quantities in nature. This category was reported in an incident where a man asked the Prophet to grant him a piece of land known for containing salt.[114] When the Prophet approved the grant, some of the companions told the Prophet that the granted land was in fact a mine of salt, and was not simply a land with a small quantity of salt. The Prophet then revoked the land and canceled the grant, implying that the salt which exists in large quantities should remain under the public ownership, although administered by the state. Islamic scholars extended the category of "salt" to include all minerals which exist in large quantities.[115] This category of public property includes the mines of gold, diamond, iron, silver, phosphate, oil, gas, and others. Note that oil and gas belong to two categories of public property.

These categories of public properties are established based on specific references to Islamic original sources, for example the statements of the Prophet (PBUH). In other words, the classification of public property is an Islamic law. Therefore, it is not permitted to change the status of a public property and make it private under any condition. The revenue generated out of the public property is used for the general benefit of the public. For example, public property benefits can be used to build schools, hospitals, roads, parks, mosques, child care facilities, and any services deemed necessary for the overall public well-being. The revenues of public property can also be used by the state to accommodate the needs of the poor and needy to enable them to find jobs, establish their own businesses, and pull them out of poverty. The revenues are also used for the security of the state and public.

State Property

Islam designated certain types of property to be owned directly by the state. The main difference between state and public property shows in the way the property revenues are used. The public property is administered by the state but not owned by the state. The state may use revenues of the public properties to spend on state's functions only when the state own revenue falls short of meeting its needs. The state property, on the other hand, gives the state full authority to spend as it sees fit to conduct its affairs and the affairs of the citizens.

Throughout the history of the Islamic state, the largest source of income for the state has been the revenue generated from the property ownership of land called *Kharaj* (the lands annexed to the Islamic state through war). Kharaj literally means output. The term *kharaj* replaced the term *fai'i*, which was used for the land annexed without a fight. Abu Obaid narrated in his book *Al-Amwal* on the authority of Az-Zuhri that Prophet Mohammad (PBUH) considered the lands of Bahrain after its conquest a land of Kharaj even after the people in Bahrain had converted to Islam.[116] Kharaj land is defined as a land added to the territory of the Islamic state and whose ownership belongs to the state. The state grants the right to use the land for farming or development in exchange for a predefined fee. The fee is due to be paid by the user of the land whether he was able to benefit from the land or not. The fee is not in exchange for the product of the land; it is in exchange for the right to use it. If the user of the land is a Muslim, he still has to pay the *Zakah* portion of the products. If the user of the Kharaj land is not a Muslim, he only has to pay the Kharaj fee.

During the reign of Caliph Harun Ar-Rasheed,[117] the land of the Islamic state was enormous due to the expansion of the state into Africa, Central and East Asia, and well into Europe. The caliph requested his chief judge Abu Yousuf [118] to write a book detailing the rules related to the wealth associated with the land of Kharaj, and to explain the various ways of spending the Kharaj money. Following the footsteps of Abu Yousuf, several other books on the subject of Kharaj were compiled.[119] The famous book of Hadeeth compiled by Abu Dawoud, known as *Sunan Abu Dawoud*, contains a section titled "The Book of Kharaj." Referring to the huge land of the caliphate state, Harun Ar-Rasheed once addressed a passing cloud over the city of Baghdad saying, "You may drop your rain wherever you wish; your Kharaj will eventually come back to me."

It was the second caliph Omar Bin Al-Khattab who first constituted the laws of Kharaj. Abu Yousuf narrated in his Kharaj book the following incident. In the year AH 16, the Muslim armies of the caliph Omar occupied a huge land in Iraq after the battle of Qadisiyyah. Prominent Muslim companions and army generals Bilal Al-Habasihi, Abderrahman Bin Awf, and Zubair Bin Al-Awwam divided part of the occupied land among the fighting soldiers. They treated the occupied land as spoils of war and thought to divide it among the fighters according to Islamic method for dealing with spoils of war. The caliph Omar had another opinion. He wanted the land to remain a property of the state and convert it into a land of Kharaj. After consulting with his advisers in Medina, Omar proclaimed,

> *I want to keep the land of Iraq and let the people who currently own it continue utilizing it in exchange for a Kharaj fee. The Kharaj money will be for all Muslims including the fighters, their offspring, and the generations to come. I want the Kharaj money to pay for the cost of securing the long borders, and protecting the large cities of Sham, Jazirah, Basra, and Egypt. If we divide the land among the fighters now, the state will not be able to pay the salaries for the soldiers who will have to protect the land and the borders.*

But for this opinion to become a law, Omar had to support his proclamation with an evidence from the Quran or the Sunnah of the Prophet, especially since the Prophet in a previous occasion did distribute the land among the fighters (the land of Khaibar, for example).

After consulting prominent scholars in Medina, Omar used verses 7-10 from Surah Al-Hashr (chapter 59) in the Quran to prove his point.

The verses talk about the rules related to spoils of war including the land. Following is the text of the verses:

> *[59:7] What Allah gave as booty (Fai') to His Messenger from the people of the townships—it is for Allah, His Messenger, the kindred of Messenger Muhammad, the orphans, Al-Masakeen (the poor), and the wayfarer, in order that wealth may not remain a fortune circulated between the rich ones among you. And whatsoever the Messenger gives you, take it; and whatsoever he forbids you, abstain (from it). And fear Allah; verily, Allah is Severe in punishment.*

This verse establishes the principle that the returns of war are for the Messenger to use and distribute among the most needy ones (orphans, poor, wayfarers). The Messenger in this case is referred to in his capacity as a head of the state; the spiritual and religious aspect is covered by the part which refers the booty to Allah.

Furthermore, this verse established a major principle in the political economy in Islam which guards against the accumulation of wealth in the hands of the richest ones in the society. This is reflected in the portion of the verse which reads, *"In order that it may not remain a fortune circulated between the rich ones among you."*

The second verse in this series further describes the groups of people who are entitled to receive the dividends of the booty and proceeds of war. The first group is the poor among the Muslims who migrated from Mecca to Medina leaving all their wealth behind. They receive a portion of the spoils of war to help them get over the poverty status they gained as a result of the sacrifices they made.

> *[59:8] (And there is also a share in this booty) for the poor emigrants, who were expelled from their homes and their property, seeking Bounties from Allah and to please Him, and helping Allah (i.e. helping His religion) and His Messenger. Such are indeed the truthful (to what they say).*

The next verse describes the second group of people who are to receive a portion of the proceeds of war. This group belongs to the Muslims in Medina who subjected their wealth and property to sanctions imposed by Quraish and the Jews in Medina. They also shared their wealth with their fellow brethren who migrated from Mecca. For all of these sacrifices, they deserve to be compensated in order to keep them out of poverty.

> [59:9] And (it is also for) those who, before them, had homes (in Medina) and had adopted the Faith, love those who emigrate to them, and have no jealousy in their hearts for that which they have been given (from the booty), and give the emigrants preference over themselves even though they were in need of that. And whosoever is saved from his own covetousness, such are they who will be the successful.

The next verse is what caught the attention of Caliph Omar. It describes a group of people who are entitled to receive part of the proceeds of war, including the land, but this group is yet to exist. The group belongs to future generations who love and appreciate all what has been accomplished by the first generation of immigrants and hosts. Omar declared that this verse had established the right to own part of the returns of war for the future generations of Muslims. The fact that the verse did not specify a time period in which the group would live implies that all Muslim generations without any limit are entitled to receive dividends from the land gained through the war.

> [59:10] And (it is also for) those who come after them and say: "Our Lord! Forgive us and our brethren who have preceded us in Faith, and put not in our hearts any hatred against those who have believed. Our Lord! You are indeed full of kindness, Most Merciful.

Citing these verses, Omar told the soldiers and generals who were in favor of distributing the land that the only way he can guarantee that the third group mentioned in verse [59:10] receives their rights is to treat the land as a Kharaj land; this way the wealth generated from the Kharaj fees will return to the state treasury. Then the state will spend this money in the best interest of the public. The companions of the Prophet unanimously agreed with Omar's verdict and this has become the law. Abu Yousuf narrated in the Kharaj book that the Kharaj revenues from the southern part of Iraq during the reign of Omar reached one hundred million dirhams (a dirham is equal to 2.98 gram silver).

The majority of the land in the Muslim world is considered a Kharaj land. Examples of lands which are not subject to Kharaj include the islands of Malay, Indonesia, and the Arabian Peninsula. The Kharaj land in the Muslim world is extraordinarily large. The Kharaj revenues from this huge land are a significant source of income for the Islamic state.

Besides Kharaj, Islam designated other types of properties to be owned by the state. One such category is known in Islamic jurisprudence as *Rikaz*.

Rikaz refers to minerals and precious metals found in relatively small quantities beneath the ground. If such metals are found by any person, then he ought to pay one-fifth of the found material to the state. The rest is the property of the one who finds it.

The state is the sole owner of bare mountains and hills, beaches, deserts and wildland which has become bare and deserted over the years. The state also becomes the legal inheritor of anyone who dies without being survived by any legal inheritor. Note that the deceased may write no more than one-third of his wealth as a will to whomever he desires. Also part of the wealth of a deceased survived by only a spouse will go to the state. Any wealth acquired by individuals through fraud, illegal trade or acquisition, bribery, or any invalid means of growing wealth will be confiscated by the state and becomes the property of the state.

It should be noted that taxation is not a means for property acquisition by the state, and in principle, the state is not supposed to place taxes on the citizens. If the state cannot allocate the necessary wealth required to perform its functions, then it can use the wealth of the public property to account for any shortage or deficit. If both the state and public property fall short of meeting the needs, then the state turns to the wealth of the individuals and collect taxes. Taxation in the Islamic state is governed by the following principles. First, the taxation must be made to finance a project which is known to be an obligation upon the Muslim society, for example, to house and feed victims of a natural disaster (earthquake, tsunami and the like). Second, taxes are collected for specific projects and hence must be temporary and cannot be permanent. Third, taxes will be collected from the richest first. In any case, the state before imposing any taxes will provoke the Muslims' eagerness to spend in the cause of Allah, so as to collect the required wealth through mere donations and contributions. The Quran made so many calls for Muslims to spend in the cause of Allah and to give generously. It is reported that Prophet Mohammad (PBUH) was able to finance most of the battles through volunteer contributions and charity.

It is therefore evident that the political economy in Islam recognizes the three types of property (private, public, and state). The triproperty structure provides a balanced mix between productivity, social responsibility, and society integrity. Individual property ownership provokes the innermost drives of humans to produce and own, while public and state property ownership makes up for any imbalance that could arise due to variations in skills, motivations, or abnormal conditions. While the individual property ownerships call for the prosperity and well-being of many in the society, the public and state property guards against the persistence of poverty.

4.2.2 Productivity

There are two sides for the economic productivity: one is technical and the other is ideological. The technical side has to do with the scientific means and ways of increasing production and improving the quality of products. Included in this part are the management sciences, automation, information technology, decision support systems, enterprise resource planning, industrial engineering, and similar sciences. These sciences are universal and do not carry any religious or ideological connotation. Scientific methods can be used within the scope of any ideology, whether Islam or capitalism or socialism, to increase the quantity and quality of products. Therefore, the discussion of technology and the scientific means of increasing productivity do not fall within the scope of the economic system discussion. During the first rise of Islam, the Muslims found no harm in using the scientific techniques advanced by the Greek or Egyptian civilizations before Islam.

The other side of productivity is indeed a systemic one and is closely related to the ideological world view of peoples. The Islamic political economy provided several principles, which in the sum tend to create an environment for increased productivity. By productivity, here, I mean the production of goods and services which are used directly or indirectly to satisfy the needs of people within a given time frame.

It is interesting to note that some of the productivity issues carry both scientific as well as ideological character at the same time. Take for example innovation and invention. The invention of steam engine is a scientific breakthrough. But the political and economic environment which led to the creation of the engine is not pure scientific. Commenting on the relation between innovation and ideological framework, Carly Fiorina[120] described Islam as a civilization which harnesses innovation. It has been noted by scores of historians and writers that the Islamic civilization as a whole was so conducive for innovation, invention, and productivity.

Before getting into the economic part of the productivity, I should mention that the spiritual part of Islam has a great impact on productivity both in quantity and quality. Let's not forget that the Islamic society as a whole is established upon the creed of the belief in Allah as the only god and the necessity to adhere to his commands which are revealed through his messenger Mohammad (PBUH). Therefore, whatever Allah reveals either in the Quran or the Sunnah has a direct and strong impact on the Muslims who take note of this revelation.

In the Quran, Allah defines the main objective behind creating man, in the first place, is to exploit the abundant resources in this earth. In Surah Al-Baqara (chapter 2, verse 30), Allah says in reference to the creation of the first human (Adam):

> *[2:30] And when your Lord said to the angels: "Verily, I am going to place a viceroy on earth (one who exploits resources on earth)"*

This is further emphasized in references made in the Quran to the fact that Allah had created in the earth and in the heavens enormous amount of resources and he wants the people to reach out and exploit these resources for their own benefit. An example is the following verse from Surah Al-Jathia (chapter 45, verse 12):

> *[45:12] Allah it is He Who has subjected to you the sea, that ships may sail through it by His Command, and that you may seek of His Bounty, and that you may be thankful.*

The Muslims understand these types of verses both as a statement of fact and as a command to do. It is no surprise, then, that as soon as the Islamic state stabilized, the Muslims engaged in all types of innovations and production.

Stressing the importance of production, the messenger of Allah (PBUH) commanded his companions to continue doing what they are doing in the field to the last minute of their life. In one narration, he said that one should continue planting a tree even if he sees the signs of life ending in front of his eyes.[121] In another narration, the Prophet stated that any one who plants a tree will receive a reward from Allah every time someone eats the fruits of the tree; even if animals eat of it, the reward will be granted. Muslims in the early days of Islam took the statements of the Prophet seriously and pushed the production to the furthest limits.

On the quality side, the Prophet had called for perfection of the work done by people when he said, "Allah loves the one that perfects his job."[122] The Prophet also had said that no one will enter heavens on the Day of Judgment unless he had perfected the work he was charged to do. Along this line, Islam prohibits the sale of any merchandise with a known defect. If a defect is detected after the sale, then the sale is revoked and the merchandise is returned, and the seller will have to pay the losses incurred due to the sale of a defected product. As such, the quality of production is an obligation in Islam for which Muslims are rewarded when they achieve it and defaulted when they violate it. The Quran further stresses the issue of quality when it says that the work performed by anyone will be monitored by Allah, his messenger, and the group of believers.[123]

The intellectual foundation of Islam, i.e., the belief in Allah and his Messenger, sets the stage for high-quality productivity. Productivity was one of the immediate fruits of the first rise of Islam and its civilization. When Islam declined, so did productivity (both quantitatively and qualitatively).

Besides the intellectual framework provided for productivity, Islam also provides a set of economic principles which facilitate productivity in the society. The components of the political economy which contribute to productivity are discussed in the next sections.

The Prohibition of Usury

Usury, otherwise known as *Riba* in Islamic terms, or interest in capitalistic terms, is categorically prohibited in Islam. When Islam made the first critical assault on usury, it observed that usury allows the cycle of wealth growth to exclude production. In other words, the money grows as a result of monetary exchange only. The Quran explained that usury (Riba) is a process by which the monetary wealth of one human entity grows at the expense of the monetary wealth of another human entity.[124]

Usury in ancient civilizations, e.g., Babylonia and Assyria, produced what was known as debt slavery. Lenders could lend their money to people who would bind their persons as collateral security and sell them into slavery, in the event of nonpayment.[125] The same practice existed in old Greek cities of Athens and Sparta where the peasants were oppressed by the rich and encouraged to get into debt and then were reduced to slavery and exile.[126] This practice continued in different forms within the Roman Empire and tribal societies of Arabia before Islam.

Perhaps the most outstanding and dramatic visualization of the evil impact of usury on societies is the famous play by William Shakespeare *The Merchant of Venice*.[127] Shakespeare dramatized the personality of Shylock, the Jewish banker, who lends money with larger interest rates versus Antonio, the merchant, who lends money without interest. The usurious Shylock was willing to take the life of Antonio for unpaid or delayed debt.

Most recently, Richard Wolf in a speech at the University of Massachusetts exposed the impact of usury on the working class in the United States and on productivity.[128] The average wages of the workers continued to flatten since the 1970s, while the consuming habits continued to rise, which pushed the majority of the Americans into a borrowing spree. Borrowing money with high interest rates (credit card interests average over 20%) against the already-low wages and the real estate possessions exhausted the workers and turned them into what amounts to a "labor slave." Labor slavery allows the master to own the labor without having to care about the laborer.[129]

The impact of usury on productivity was most visible when large corporations, such as General Motors, decided to lend the huge amount of accumulated profit to its workers. Corporations were able to make profit twice. On one hand, they are no longer under the pressure of raising the wages, since the workers are getting more money, albeit in terms of loans. On the other hand, the loans generate profits in the form of interest (usury). Over time, it turned out that generating profit through interest is much easier and more guaranteed than making money through selling cars. Consequently, the auto industry was compromised for the benefit of the usury based banking industry. When General Motors filed for bankruptcy and asked for government bailout money, its bank (GMAC) was indeed making profit.

Money generated through usury is one major cause for the creation of virtual wealth, where money grows at much higher rate than production. The claim that interest baring loans constituent a strong mechanism for financing projects is a mere myth. Say for example, a bank provides one million dollars loan to finance a machine shop with 10% annual interest rate. Assuming everything goes well with the project, the amount of real money which goes to the project is $900,000 instead of the million which was borrowed. The other $100,000 is retained by the bank. So the usurious part of the loan does not go into the production cycle at all. The principle of the loan alone is what participates in the production of goods. Islam did encourage loan giving without interest; Islam called such loan "a good loan." Allah praised the believers who provide good loans and promised to multiply the rewards for them. Allah considered a good loan giving to anyone in the society as if it was a loan given to Allah Himself.[130]

The bank, which lends money with interest, makes everything possible to guarantee the return of its money plus interest in full; even when the projects fail, the bank still takes back its money in full. In other words, the bank is the least party interested in the production of goods because its money and profit is guaranteed either thorough collateral, or through government-backed insurance. In the case of Shakespeare's character Shylock, the guarantee was the flesh of the merchant. In the older civilizations, the guarantee was the freedom of the person or his family members.

In contemporary economic systems under the dominance of capitalism, it has become a common practice for the same amount of money to be loaned multiple times such that bank A lends the money to bank B, and bank B lends the money to bank C, and so on. Every bank in the process gets a share of the usury in the cycle of loans. The main victim in this cycle, besides the people who have to pay the interest, is the production itself.

Profit generation through money lending adversely impacts productivity. Over time, societies which excel in the banking and usurious practices tend to move away from the more complex production economy, which requires factories, machining, management of employees, and so on. The United States provides one of the best examples, where big corporations like GM have shifted their weight to money lending with interest more so than making cars for people to use. Outsourcing of a large portion of the industry in the United States to China and India is another example, where large corporations turned into investors rather than producers.

Islam considered *Riba* (usury) a disastrous practice in the society. And thus it made any practice of usury in any form or format illegal and prohibited. In one verse in the Quran, Allah vows to destroy and eradicate whatever is built upon usury.[131] What really this means is that the virtual economy which is built upon usury cannot survive and is bound to collapse and vanish. After the collapse of Lehman Brothers Bank in 2009, the assets and wealth and power of the bank vanished in no time.

When *Riba* is prohibited, then the only way money finds its way to the market is either through good loans, or partnerships. Good loans are typically provided by people in support of friends or relatives for whom the money lender cares. So the loan giver has a direct or indirect interest in the success of the people whom he provides the loan to. The fact that no interest is retained by the giver allows the use of the full amount of money in the project for which the loan was given.

The other, and more common, practice is to provide the money in the form of investment and partnership in the project. The investor in this case receives profit from the project. The investor shares the profit as well as the losses of the project. The only way the investor can benefit is through the success of the project. In this case, the money can grow only if there is a product which results out of the investment. Thus, productivity is guaranteed to increase through a non usurious participation in the production cycle.

It is interesting to note that Islam did not prohibit *Riba* until the Islamic state was created after the migration of Prophet Mohammad and his companions to Medina. Although, the Quran condemned the practice of *Riba* while in Mecca. But it was not until the migration took place that the verse in Surah Al-Baqara was revealed saying, *"Allah permitted trade and prohibited Riba.*"[132] After the conquest of Mecca, the Prophet made a public declaration by which he demanded the end of all usury practices in Mecca. This was done on the day of pilgrimage.

The point here is that the Islamic rules on *Riba* will be able to generate the expected results of enhanced productivity only when the entire political economy of the society adheres to the principle of "no *Riba* or zero interest." The coexistence of *Riba*-free financial institutions side by side with interest-based banks will only produce mixed results and have marginal impact on the overall health. When individuals abstain from receiving loans with interest, they at least protect their property and avoid the ugly consequences of interest-bearing loans.

With the prohibition of *Riba,* Islam eliminated one of the main hurdles to productivity. To guarantee the deployment of wealth in the production cycle, Islam further prohibited the hoarding of wealth.

The Prohibition of Hoarding

Hoarding is defined as the process of collecting and putting away wealth such that it may no longer be used in the production of goods and services. Islam categorically prohibited the hoarding of wealth when it prohibited the hoarding of gold and silver, being the main currency of the Islamic state.[133] The prohibition of hoarding of gold and silver is a major principle in the political economy of Islam aimed at sustaining productivity. Paying the *Zakah* charity does not change the status of hoarding to a permissible act. Zakah is one principle aimed at eliminating poverty, while the prohibition of hoarding is aimed at sustaining productivity. These two principles cannot be at odd with each other. Rather, they complement one another and allow for a more stable economy.

The gold and silver during the early days of Islam were the currency used for financial transactions. Gold and silver continued to be the currency of the Islamic state until the state collapsed in 1924. So when Islam prohibited the hoarding of gold and silver, it really prohibited the hoarding of money, or wealth. The concept of hoarding does not apply for regular jewelry used by women. Putting money aside for a particular project, such as building a house, performing hajj, or preparation for wedding is not considered hoarding as well. Hoarding, in essence, is a means of keeping money outside the production cycle for indefinite time.

When a person accumulates a large amount of wealth and keeps that money in a safe deposit box or in any account where the money is not used in any project, whether for buying merchandise, a real estate, a business, or any other project of financial merit, then that stockpiled money is a big loss for the economy. Production can only be sustained if the wealth generated as a result of production is reused in the cycle of production. The produced wealth can be used either for consuming goods, commodities and services, or for producing more goods, commodities, and services. In either case, the production cycle grows in strength and rate. The moment part of the produced wealth leaks out to be hoarded, the production cycle will suffer weakness and may come to a complete halt if wealth leak does not stop; see figure 32.

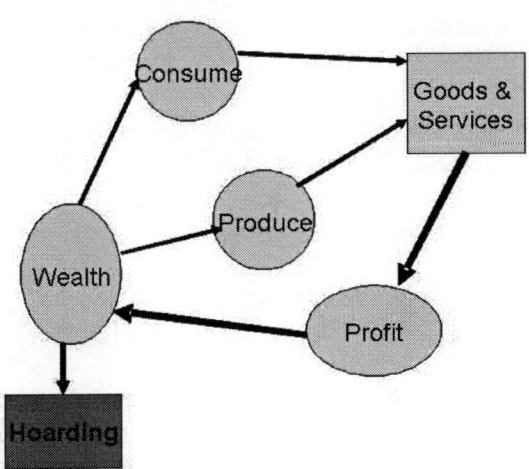

Figure 32: Production Cycle with Hoarding

In the normal production cycle, the wealth is used to consume products and services, which in turn generate profit for the producer who produces the goods and services. As a result, the economy of production grows in terms of produced goods and services and in terms of wealth, which is necessary for the production and consumption. When hoarding occurs, part of the wealth leaks out of the cycle, which reduces the amount of wealth available for consumption and production. Essentially, Islam prohibited this phenomenon, where part of the wealth is removed from the production cycle through the process of money hoarding.

One of the causes of the most recent financial crisis in the world of capitalism was in fact the hoarding of wealth. Investing firms and banks in the United States and Europe decided to withhold a large portion of their money investment and drastically reduced the amount of loans issued to the public. A major motive for the stimulus packages and bailout money given by the government to banks was to encourage or force the banks to resume the process of giving loans to the public. In other words, the banks withheld a large portion of the money and kept it away from the production cycle. Of course, there are reasons for this behavior; but whatever the reasons are, when part of the wealth of a nation is stacked away from the production cycle, the production slows down, the economy downturns, and the financial system suffers a great deal.

The Islamic political economy prevents all forms of hoarding, no matter what the reason was. Hoarding continues to be prohibited, even when a Muslim spends part of his wealth in support of the cause of Islam, and pays the Zakah dues in full. Al-Qurtubi, the famous Quran commentator, says that the "hoarding verse" at once prohibits hoarding and obligates the spending in the cause of Allah; in other words, the verse contains two separate rules.[134] One rule makes the hoarding of money a prohibited act; and the second rule makes the spending in support of the cause of Islam an obligation. Within the Islamic society, hoarding will be prevented by two forces. The piety of a Muslim and the full obedience to Allah in pursuit of his pleasure and reward and in evasion of his wrath and punishment is a strong motive for many Muslims to abstain from hoarding and to keep their wealth in the market. Besides the internal Islamic drive, the Islamic state will enforce the "no hoarding" rule by the power of law, since it is the responsibility of the Islamic state to guarantee the full implementation of the Islamic code. In the same manner, as the state will prevent monetary transactions involving usury, it will prevent acts of money hoarding.

Partnership between Labor and Wealth (Mudharabah)

As discussed above, hoarding is a process which keeps money and wealth outside the production cycle; instead of investing the money, the hoarder will stack it up and deprives the economy form investment opportunity. The prohibition of hoarding automatically calls for investment of the accumulated wealth, especially when the amount of wealth is excessively large. Since wealth is not allowed to grow through usury, then the only means of growing the accumulated wealth is to keep it in the production cycle. One of the mechanisms introduced by Islam is a form of partnership called "Mudharabah."

Mudharabah is a form of company in Islam where one partner provides wealth and the second partner provides labor. The wealth partner(s) can be one or more individuals. The labor partner can also be one or more individuals. The wealth provider is typically someone who has more wealth than he can spend and does not have sufficient time or skills to invest his money. The labor partner is typically someone who has the time and skills but does not have enough wealth to invest and produce. The Mudharabah partnership brings both parties to the market such that the wealth is invested rather than hoarded, and the labor, skills, and knowledge are utilized. Unlike the employment of labor and skills, the Mudharabah partnership exploits the maximum energy of the labor partner, since he becomes one of the owners of the company.

Mudharabah partnership eliminates one of the common reasons for hoarding. The wealthy person, who may refrain from investing his money in the market due to lack of time, skills, or knowledge of investment, will be forced to seek a partner who lacks the wealth. In essence, Mudharabah boosts production from both sides: the money and the labor.

In the Mudharabah partnership, both partners (the laborer and the investor) are equally responsible for the success or the failure of the company. If the company fails, then the one who supplied the money loses his wealth investment and the laborer loses his labor investment. Under the rules of partnership in Islam, the labor partner does not receive any salary, no matter what role he plays in the company. He is only entitled to receive dividends based on the amount of share he holds in the company. Note that the shares in the company do not have to be equally divided between the labor part and the money part; usually, an agreement between both sides will determine the shares of each. No matter what the share distribution is, the responsibility for the company is equally shared by both parties. The rules of Mudharabah in Islam are such that each partner in the Mudharabah is vigorously interested in the success of the company. This should, in principle, increase the confidence of the money partner and reduce his concern for his investment. Since the labor partner does not receive any compensation for his effort, he should be more interested in the profitability of the company, because this is the only way he can get rewarded for his effort.

While there are other ways in Islam to channel both wealth and labor investments, the Mudharabah partnership provides an economic opportunity for a class of wealthy people and a class of skillful laborers to merge and contribute to the production cycle. In its simplest form, the Mudharabah allows the investor to invest his wealth and avoid hoarding, and allows the laborer to become an owner of wealth and the means of production. In a more complex form, Mudharabah provides a mechanism for project funding, especially when the projects require a large amount of money. In this case, a group of wealthy investors partner with a group of variety of labor skills. It is envisioned that Mudharabah partnership will substitute the role currently played by banks and financial institutions.

A major difference, of course, is that banks provide loans which are recoverable in full plus usurious interest.

In essence, the Islamic political economy sustains the highest level of productivity by utilizing the three principles: prohibition of usury, prohibition of hoarding, and Mudharabah. Money cannot make money without being invested in the cycle of goods and services production; otherwise, the gained money will be considered Riba or usury, which is categorically prohibited in Islam. The profit gained through the cycle of production must come back to the same cycle, either by consuming some of the produced goods and services or by producing more of the goods and services. Otherwise, hoarding will occur and that is not allowed. When the money owner lacks the skills and knowledge for proper investment, he can resort to Mudharabah, instead of investing in usury, which is prohibited, or hoarding, which is also prohibited. Thus, the wealth in the society will remain in the production cycle, and the skills of individuals will be part of this cycle. Consequently, Islam guarantees the utilization of both components of productivity: money and labor. On top of that, Islam provides the moral and spiritual framework for production and perfection of products as explained earlier: produce until the last moment of life, and perfect whatever you do.

II.4.3 The Monetary System in Islam

In principle, an economic system is concerned with the process of production and consumption of goods and services, while the political economy provides it with the proper political framework. The monetary system is not necessarily a part of the economic system. Money is a tool used to measure the value of goods and services during the production and consumption processes. This measure is required during the exchange of products and benefits between the producers and consumers. Ancient groups of peoples (tribes and primitives societies) were able to produce all the goods they needed to live and survive, and hence did not require a standard measure for the values of their goods and services. Money, therefore, was not part of the system of production and consumption.

The progress and advancement of societies created the need for people to exchange goods and services within the same society as well as across societies. Initially, the trade of goods and services was conducted using barter methods through the exchange of goods for goods, goods for services, or services for services. One such example reported in the Quran is when Prophet Moses (PBUH) paid eight years of services in exchange for marrying the daughter of his employer, Prophet Shuaib (PBUH).[135] The exchange of goods and services for a specific unit of exchange, called money, was introduced in the period 600-650 BC.[136] Money came to be a standard measure for the benefit found in goods and services. However, money did not replace barter exchange methods but provided a new method. Therefore, money is defined as the medium by which goods and services are measured. The capitalists called the value of goods and services "price" when this value is measured by money. So the price under capitalism is another name for the exchange value of goods and services. Under Islam, the price given in money is not an intrinsic value of things; rather it is an estimate of that value.

The price of a commodity and the wage of a worker, for instance, each represent the society's estimate of the value of that commodity and the effort of that worker. This estimation of the value of goods and services is expressed by well-defined units. These units become the measure by which the benefit obtained from a commodity and the benefit obtained from a service is measured. These units would act as a medium of exchange, and these units are money.

Islam approved barterlike method as well as money for conducting trade transactions. People are allowed to choose either method for the exchange of goods and services based on mutual agreement and the best interest of the trading parties. Either way, using barter or money, the price of the goods or services has to be explicitly defined in the process of exchange. For example, a person can purchase a horse in exchange for working a week in the horse stable of the seller, given that the number of hours of work per day is well defined, or he can pay an ounce of gold for the horse.

Islam did not leave the monetary system undefined; rather it specified the gold and silver as the base units for the monetary system. Both gold and silver were extensively used by societies and civilizations before Islam due to the intrinsic value of these precious metals. The Roman Empire used gold as the main currency and struck several gold-based units at a well-defined shape and weight; one of these units was the "denarius" or the dinar, which was the main coin issued by republican and imperial Rome. The gold dinar was used throughout the Roman Empire and its satellite states.

The Persian empire used silver as its main currency and issued three types of silver coins, called dirham, with different shapes and weights. The Arab tribe of Quraish, where Mohammad the Prophet was born, did not have a currency of its own; rather Quraish used the Roman gold dinar and Persian silver dirham, which they received in exchange of their merchandise. The Arabs used the weight of the gold and silver coins as units of exchange instead of the number of coins.

After the rise of Islam, Mohammad (PBUH) approved the use of gold dinar and silver dirham as was used by the Arabs in Mecca. He also approved the weight of the gold dinar which was the standard weight used by the Quraish merchants in Mecca. It is narrated that Mohammad (PBUH) said, "The weight (of the gold Dinar) is the same as the weight used in Mecca."[137] The Islamic consideration of gold and silver as a base for currency is further evident in the following cases:

1. When Islam prohibited the hoarding of wealth, it only prohibited the hoarding of gold and silver despite the fact that wealth includes any property that can be owned. Wealth includes money (gold and silver), land, cattle, grains, and much more. However, hoarding applies only to monetary wealth; it does not apply to other forms of wealth. It is possible for people to stash away certain goods and commodities such as food items, but this act falls under the term *monopoly* rather than hoarding, which aims at raising the prices of goods. The prohibition of monopoly is referenced in other places in the Quran and Sunnah. It is the hoarding of money alone which interrupts the production cycle of goods. Therefore, prohibiting the hoarding of gold and silver is an indirect reference to the fact that gold and silver constitute the monetary currency in the Islamic state. Hence the verse which prohibits the hoarding of gold and silver in fact refers to the hoarding of money and established gold and silver as the money base.

   > [9:34] *And those who hoard gold and silver and do not spend them in the way of Allah, let them know that a severe punishment is awaiting them.*

2. Islam has linked gold and silver to a set of rules which involve monetary transactions. For example, Islam named a specific amount of gold as a fine to be paid in lieu of a killing by mistake (known as *Diyyah* or blood money). Messenger of Allah was reported to have said, *"The blood money for one soul would be 100 camels . . . and for those who deal in gold is 1000 Dinars."*[138] Other fines were estimated in terms of gold and/or silver as well.

   The minimum amount of stolen wealth which invokes the punitive rule of hand amputation is also estimated in gold. Al-Bukhari reported on the authority of Aisha that the Messenger of Allah said, *"The hand is cut for the theft of one-quarter (gold) dinar and up."*[139]

The attachment of certain financial rules with the *dinar* and the *dirham* makes the *dinar* with its weight in gold, and the *dirham* with its weight in silver, the monetary unit by which the values of goods and services are measured. This monetary unit constitutes the base for the money currency in the Islamic state.

3. The messenger of Allah has determined that gold and silver be used as money, and exclusively made them the monetary measure to evaluate goods and services, and ensured that all transactions be conducted with them as their basis. He also established the units of this money, which were well-known and widespread during the lifetime of the messenger of Allah and they were widely used by all people. It has also been established that the messenger of Allah approved of them. All trade and marriage transactions were conducted in gold and silver, in their quality as money, and this has been documented in numerous Hadeeths of the Prophet. The Messenger of Allah has determined the weight of gold and silver with a specific weight, which was the weight of the people of Mecca. Abu Dawud and An-Nisai reported on the authority of Ibn Umar that the Messenger of Allah said, *"The weight should be that of the people of Mecca."*
4. When the Zakah dues on money was decreed, Islam determined the minimum amount of money which qualifies for Zakah in terms of gold and silver. This is another reference to money as being the gold and silver.
5. The rules of currency exchange specified the rules of exchange between gold and silver currencies only; this serves clear evidence that money should be based on gold and silver only. Tirmidhi reported that the Messenger of Allah said, *"Trade gold for silver as you wish, but hand to hand (without delay)."* Bukhari also reported that the Messenger of Allah said, *"Gold for silver would be Riba, unless it was hand to hand (without delay)."*

A solid base for monetary foundation is essential for the stability of both the financial and economic systems, and thus Islam has laid down the rules for the monetary foundation and did not leave them undefined or subject to the fluctuation of the economic conditions. The *Shari'ah laws* have always referred to gold and silver whenever the subject matter involved monetary transaction. Consequently, the currency within the Islamic political economy would be gold and silver, or based on gold and silver. The rise of the next Islamic state is expected to witness a decisive return to a more solid and stable gold and silver standard as a base for the financial system.

The gold and silver standard does not exclude other forms of exchange. Products could be exchanged for products and services in a barterlike method. The value of products and services will continue to be estimated based on the benefits inherent in these goods. The gold and silver standard only applies to money and monetary exchange.

The first rise of Islam utilized the use of gold and silver as a base for monetary exchange. During the early days of Islam, the Islamic state under the leadership of Prophet Mohammad (PBUH) used the gold and silver coins produced by the Romans, Persians, and Yemeni dynasties. The Muslims, like the Arabs before Islam, used these coins in terms of their weights rather than numbers. The fact that the Prophet approved their use as such makes the use of gold and silver coins an Islamic rule, although they were in use before Islam. The use of Roman, Persian, and Yemeni coins continued for the first seventy-five years of the rise of the Islamic state, until Caliph Abdul Malik Bin Marwan[140] struck new Islamic gold and silver coins. He minted the dinar in gold and the dirham in silver and he used Islamic Arabic script to distinguish the Islamic coins from others. The weight of the dinar was 4.25 grams of gold and the weight of the dirham was 2.98 silver grams. These weights were consistent with the weights of the coins struck by the Romans and Persians and used by the Arabs in Mecca before Islam. The gold and silver standard continued throughout the existence of the Islamic state until it was abolished in 1924 in Istanbul.

Besides the use of gold and silver, the Islamic state also used copper coins for buying and selling negligible low-cost items. However, the copper coins were always convertible to gold dinars or silver dirhams. The point is that Islam allows the use of currency printed in any form (gold, silver, copper, paper, digital tokens) as long as that currency is convertible to gold, i.e., backed by gold. Because the gold and silver standard is a Shari'ah Islamic law, it would be prohibited for the Islamic state to issue paper money which is not completely backed by gold or silver, and it would be prohibited for the state to devalue the paper money against the pre-established gold and silver equivalence. The integrity of the Islamic currency, and hence the confidence in such currency, should serve as a stabilizing force in the Islamic political economy. This should also sustain and increase the trustworthiness of the Islamic financial system, especially since the world had suffered a great deal from currency fluctuations under the dominance of capitalist economy.

Under capitalism, the gold standard had suffered several setbacks even when the world community had agreed on the gold standard at the end of the first and second world wars. Islam considers the use of gold and silver a base for currency, an Islamic rule which cannot be violated by the executives of the state and is not subject for the conditions of the market or the international affairs.

Benefits of the Gold Standard

Besides the fact that the gold standard is an Islamically lawful rule, it has several benefits, which if considered, would make the gold standard a viable global standard for the world community at large. Throughout the history of money and up until the First World War, the whole world operated the gold and silver standards. No other standards were known to the world until then. The heavy cost of the war and the imperial colonial world affairs which persisted after the war led to the collapse of the gold standard and the introduction of paper money with no gold or silver backup. Realizing the importance of the gold standard for the financial and economic stability, several European countries and the United States tried in 1933 to restore the gold standard but failed under the heavy pressure of depression. At the end of the Second World War, the United States and Europe and several other nations concurred that a gold standard is essential to the stability of the global economy and hence to world peace and subsequently signed the Bretton Woods Agreement.[141]

In 1971, the United States unilaterally abrogated the gold standard and forced almost every other nation to stack US dollars instead of gold reserves. Since the seventies, there have been numerous calls for a revamped international system to tackle the problem of unfettered capital flows. However, it wasn't until late 2008 that this idea began to receive substantial support from leading politicians. On September 26, 2008, French president Nicolas Sarkozy said, "We must rethink the financial system from scratch, as at Bretton Woods."[142] On October 13, 2008, British prime minister Gordon Brown said world leaders must meet to agree to a new economic system: "We must have a new Bretton Woods, building a new international financial architecture for the years ahead."[143] Undoubtedly, the gold standard has numerous benefits for the global community. These benefits include the following:

1. The gold basis necessitates the free circulation, import and export of gold, which leads to monetary, financial, and economic stability.

2. The gold standard ensures the stability of exchange rates between the currencies of various countries (less than 5% variation per Bretton Woods). This stability in turn leads to a boom in international trade, for traders would no longer fear the expansion of foreign trade, with potential loss of money reserve values.
3. The gold standard prevents the explosion of virtual monetary wealth because central banks and governments would refrain from printing excessive amount of banknotes money. The authorities would fear that if they exceeded limits in issuing banknotes, the demand for gold would increase and they would not be able to meet this demand. Therefore, they would always tend to maintain a reasonable ratio between what they issue in terms of banknotes and gold reserves.
4. Under gold standard, the movements of money, goods, and labor across countries would become easier due to the fixed exchange rates between currencies of various countries. The constraints imposed by hard currency regulations would disappear, giving rise to a more stable global trade.
5. The gold standard would help preserve the gold preserve in each country by eliminating the incentives for gold smuggling from one country to another. Gold moves between countries only as a result of trade.
6. International trade will not suffer due to currency exchange rate fluctuations. This provides a more balanced and fair trade environment for all nations.

These are some of the benefits of the gold standard. Thus the Islamic insistence to return to the gold standard is in line with the natural financial norms and should be met with global appreciation. This was the normal standard up until the First World War, when the whole world was operating the financial system under the gold standard. At the start of the First World War, the most prevailing monetary system in the world was based on the gold standard, and money in circulation at the time was in fact gold coins and paper money readily exchangeable for their equivalent value in gold. The silver standard also operated alongside the gold standard. The implementation of this standard facilitated productive and stable global economic relations.

When the gold standard was applied throughout the whole world, it did not experience any serious problems. On the contrary, problems began to rise when the gold standard was violated and eventually removed and then replaced by nonexchangeable paper money. Worst of all, the world superpowers began to use their currency as a weapon in their warfare against other nations. The United States, emerging after the Second World War as the largest global economy, forced the US dollar to play the role previously played by gold as a basis for the monetary system.

The return to a gold standard, despite all the expected benefits, may face serious challenges from the states which demolished the gold and silver standard in the first place. The United States had built virtually large financial giants with hundreds of trillions of dollars whose value exceed multiple times the entire world reserve of gold. The existence of such huge virtual wealth poses the most serious challenge to the return of gold standard. The total gold reserve in the world above the ground is estimated at 150,000 tons. At the current price of gold, $1,150 at the time of writing this part of the book, the total dollar value of the gold is $5.4 trillion. This is less than 40% of the total US foreign debt (estimated at $14 trillion). The United States has less than 8,200 tons of gold which is worth less than $300 billion. So the US gold reserve is barely enough to cover 2% of its total debt. Thus, the United States has created a strong and high barrier in the path of a return to gold standard.

Another challenge is the potential flow of gold into the direction of states which have turned into a reservoir of goods, expertise, services, and manufacturing tools. China and India are good examples of such countries. Today, China and India provide the world with most of the consuming goods and services through a network of factories, outsourcing companies, and experts. A return to gold standard without careful consideration would lead to the accumulation of gold in the treasury of few states such as China, India, Germany, and Japan. Of course countries with large supplies of raw materials and energy resources like oil and gas can also see a flux of gold into their markets.

The fear of gold polarization (accumulation of gold in the hands of a few states) may potentially lead to the implementation of more protectionist policies by many states in order to protect their reserve of gold. Protection can take the form of high rate tariffs, high custom taxes, and export and import restrictions among other policies. In order to calm down this fear and avoid polarization, barterlike methods of goods and services exchange should be encouraged at the earlier stage of the return to the gold standard. For example, states with abundance of raw materials such as minerals, oil, and gas can exchange these products for manufactured goods and food from states which produce these goods. Also, the states which use the gold standard will be encouraged to reduce their dependence on imports by increasing their own local production and satisfying their basic needs locally. Eventually, the adoption of a gold standard while striving to preserve the national gold reserve will lead to a more balanced international trade and the trade deficits between nations will decrease. The challenges to the implementation of gold standard are more likely to occur only if few states adopt the gold standard, while many others continue to rely on monetary systems not supported by either gold or silver.

The Islamic state is not expected to face serious challenges when implementing the gold standard since the state will reside over the largest reserves of oil and gas in the world. The state can easily exchange oil and gas for manufactured products and services. The political economy of the Islamic state also calls for self-sufficiency in the production of the basic needs, particularly food, medicine, and education. Furthermore, the industrial policy of the state calls for the creation of heavy industrial base which provides the necessary machining and tools for production. These policies will help the state become rather self-sufficient and less dependent on imports which in turn helps to preserve its gold reserves. The Islamic lands host some of the largest gold mines in the world, which is expected to provide a continuous source of gold, thus making the return to gold standard much more feasible.

Despite the urgent need of a monetary system based on gold and silver, and the repeated calls for the return to gold standard by scores of politicians and economists, this return is not expected to occur within the current conditions and under the rules of capitalist world order. The return to the gold standard requires courage and determination by states and their leadership. That is because the return to a gold standard could be perceived by many as defiance to the current financial world order, and thus would pose a challenge to the interests of the countries which benefit the most of the current order. Indeed, it takes a great deal of valor, courage and determination to issue currency and back it by gold and silver. In fact, a decisive return to the gold standard despite all difficulties and challenges requires an ideological commitment, which makes the implementation of the gold standard a necessity rather than an option and an obligation rather than a courtesy.

Because the gold and silver based currency constitutes a law under the Islamic jurisprudence, it can be argued that under the current world conditions, the rise of the Islamic state is the only viable hope for the rise of a new monetary system based on gold and silver. We have witnessed major countries like France, Britain, India, and China calling for a monetary system based on gold, but none had the sufficient courage and the ideological commitment to carry through their call.

The ideological commitment is readily embedded within the rules of Islam. As argued earlier, the use of gold and silver as a base for the monetary system is an Islamic rule which cannot be overruled by the executives of the Islamic state. This is part of the Shari'ah laws. Moreover, the challenges of the implementation of the gold standard within the Islamic state are, by and large, less than those for any other state, due to the inherent wealth of the state. There could be some challenges during the first phase of the rise of the Islamic state. However, once the state reaches its expected steady state by unifying many of the Islamic lands and becoming more self-sufficient, the challenges will begin to disappear. On the long run, the gold standard will become a source of power and stability for the Islamic financial system, which will encourage many other states to follow the course of the Islamic state and convert to a gold standard.

The Methods of Issuing Currency

In the Islamic economic framework, the price is defined as the society's estimate of the value of goods, and the wage is defined as the society's estimate of the value of services. Money, on the other hand, is the medium by which this estimate is expressed. It is the medium which enables people to measure various goods and services and refers them to one common base, thus facilitating the process of making a comparison between various goods and between various services by referring them to one general unit which serves as the general standard. Prices are paid for goods and wages are paid for workers on the basis of this unit, which is money.

The value of money is estimated by its purchasing power, i.e., by how many goods and services a person could buy with one unit of the money. Therefore, the medium by which the society estimates the value of goods and services must have a purchasing power in order to qualify as money, i.e., a power with which any person could acquire goods and services.

This medium must originally have its own intrinsic power, or be dependent on an intrinsic power, i.e., it should itself have a value recognized by the public, in order to be considered as money. This is exactly what grants gold and silver the power to serve as a base for money; gold and silver have intrinsic value which has been recognized by societies throughout the history of man. It has been used as a precious metal, as jewelry for men and women, as collateral items and loan guarantees, and as units of exchange. However, the process of issuing money (units with purchasing power) is not the same for all countries in the world. Some countries may adopt money which possesses intrinsic power (gold and silver) or which depends on an intrinsic power. Other countries may adopt conventional money (nonconvertible), i.e., they agree upon a medium to be considered as money and they give it a buying power by means of legislation or government decree; in this case, the money does not possess a real value on its own.

Countries which operate the gold and silver standard use metallic money, paper money, or both. Metallic money is gold or silver coins minted at a certain weight, shape, and style. For example, in the Islamic state, the dinar is a 4.25 gram gold piece struck in a circular shape with Islamic Arabic script. The dirham is a 2.98 gram silver piece struck in a circular shape with Islamic Arabic script. Fractions of the dinar and dirham (for example one-half dinar, one-fourth dinar) can also be struck and minted in certain shapes and styles. In essence, the dinar (gold) and the dirham (silver) are the two basic units from which all other money coins are derived.

Countries which operate the gold and silver standard, like the Islamic state, can also issue paper money in lieu of the gold and silver. The dinar can be issued in the form of a paper printed in a certain style. Each paper dinar will be matched at the state's treasury by 4.25 grams of gold. Each paper dirham will also be matched by 2.98 grams of silver. Besides paper money, the state can issue metallic coins made of copper or other cheap metals; by the same token these coins will be matched by an equivalent gold or silver. With the advancement of technology, the state may issue electronic currency, where the currency will be provided in digital form. But in all cases, the money in circulation, whether paper, digital, or coins, will not exceed the gold and silver reserves owned and possessed by the state. This type of paper or digital money is called intrinsic money. The state may prefer this method to issue currency for cost saving and security reasons.

The second method relies on partial coverage of gold and silver for the paper money in circulation. The paper money in this case is only partially covered by gold or silver. The issuing house, be it a bank or a government treasury, would however maintain a lesser amount of gold and silver than the claimed value of the paper money, or its nominal value. For instance, a bank or the state's treasury would issue paper money worth 500 million *dinar*s and maintain in its treasury only 200 million *dinar*s worth of gold and silver. In this case, 40% of the money in circulation is covered by gold. This type of paper money is known as fiduciary paper money. A country which issues money under these conditions would still be considered as operating the gold standard. The idea behind this method is that not all money in circulation needs to be converted to gold or silver at once, so the state estimates a probabilistic ratio for potential conversion and, based on that, issues more money than it actually can convert into gold. The state expects that in the worst-case scenario, only a portion (say 40%) of the money in circulation will have to be converted to gold. The state should be able to meet that demand without too much difficulty. If a situation arises such that more than 40% of the money needs to be converted to gold, and the state cannot meet that demand, the currency then faces the consequences of devaluation. This is one of the risks of using fiduciary money.

The countries which operate a nonexchangeable paper money standard issue bills which are not convertible to gold or silver or any precious metal. The institution which issues these bills is not required by law to exchange these banknotes for gold at a specific price. Gold in such countries is treated just like any other commodity; the price of gold fluctuates from time to time according to supply and demand. Since 1971, when the United States severed the link between gold and the US dollar, the price of gold had risen from $35 per ounce to more than $1,200 per ounce, that is, almost thirty-five times. It is interesting to note that during the two hundred years prior to 1971 (1771-1971), the gold price ranged between $20 and $35 per ounce.

The banknotes, issued in paper-based money are not backed by a metallic reserve, and thus cannot be exchanged to metallic money at a preset rate. They only hold a legal value and do not possess an intrinsic power, nor do they depend on an intrinsic power. They merely represent a unit that has been agreed upon as a means of buying goods and services, and it is the law that gives it the power to become a means of circulation, with which a person may acquire goods and services. Its power is derived from the power of the state which issues the currency. If the government issues a decree canceling one of the circulated money bills, then that bill would lose its buying power immediately. People holding a quantity of the canceled bill would lose that money unless the government allows the exchange of the canceled bill by another legalized one.

In essence, any country could agree upon a particular unit which expresses the society's estimate of the values of goods and services. A decree issued by the government enables the unit to become a purchasing power for goods and services. Therefore, any country could issue a currency that has a fixed and a distinguished quality, which expresses the society's estimation of the value of goods and services, i.e., money with which any person could acquire goods and services in the issuing country, according to the value given to that money. It is the issuing country which forces other countries to recognize its currency so that these countries could acquire the goods and services produced by the issuing country.

In principle, a country does not need to depend on the International Monetary Fund, the World Bank, a federal reserve bank, or any other institution for issuing currency and giving the currency a specific buying power. The strength of the unit and its ability to obtain goods and services would be sufficient to turn it into a currency either by itself, such as gold and silver, or by its dependence on gold and silver, e.g., intrinsic paper money which represents its nominal value in gold and silver, or through having a certain amount of gold and silver held in reserve, as is the case with fiduciary paper money. The same can also happen for the nonexchangeable paper money with a certain economic and political power which enforces its acceptability and allows people to use it for acquiring goods and services.

Throughout history, three types of money existed in the world: metallic money made of gold and silver, intrinsic paper money (covered by gold and silver), and nonexchangeable banknotes. Since the end of the Second World War and until 1971, countries in the world used to operate two main types of money, the metallic and the paper money with full or partial gold cover. Since 1971, the whole world began operating exclusively the nonexchangeable paper money standard, with enforced acceptability, when the US President Nixon aborted the Bretton Woods declaration, thus severing the link between the dollar and gold.

Exchange Rate of Currencies

Currency exchange is the process of converting one currency for another. This would be either exchanging one currency for another of the same type, such as the exchange of gold for gold, and silver for silver, or the exchange of one currency type for another one of a different type, such as the exchange of gold for silver or vice versa.

The exchange of currencies which belong to the same type is allowed in Islam under two conditions. First, the exchange has to be for the exact same amount, and second, the exchange has to take place at the same time. The Prophet (PBUH) is reported to have said, "The exchange of gold for gold must be done with equal weight and exact amount; otherwise the difference is *Riba* (usury)."[144] The same rule applies to the exchange of silver coins for silver coins. For example, assume that some person has a one-hundred-gram piece of gold and wants to exchange it for five smaller pieces of gold. This transaction is permitted only if the five smaller pieces of gold have a total weight of one hundred grams. Also, the exchange has to take place at the same time, i.e., the person with the one-hundred-gram piece should hand in his piece at the same time when he receives the five smaller pieces. In other words, it is not allowed to give the large piece and receive the five pieces in installments at different times. Islam considers this transaction illegal and treats it as a form of Riba. This rule is extended to all types of currencies. So, if someone wants to buy dollars with dollars or euros with euros, then the amount of exchange must be the same and the money should be received in full at the time of executing the transaction.

When the exchange occurs between two distinct types of currencies, e.g., gold for silver, or dollar for euro, then the weight or quantity can vary because these are two different types of currencies with different values; but the exchange of money must be completed at the same time when the transaction is executed. If the receipt of any of the exchanged currencies is deferred to a different time, then that would be considered Riba according to Islamic law. The Prophet (PBUH) is reported to have said, *"Sell gold for silver the way you wish, hand in hand"*[145] meaning that the rates can vary but the sale should be instantaneous. This rule extends for all types of currencies; for example, the exchange of dollars for yen, or dinars or euros can take place per the rate of each currency, given that the transaction of sale is completed at the time of exchange.

Islam requires that the exchange of the currencies be completed at one time; as such, it prevented any loss due to potential fluctuation of the rates of one currency in relation to the other. When the transaction is completed at the time of exchange, the negotiated prices for both currencies are guaranteed for both the seller and the buyer. However, if one of the currencies is not received at the time of transaction, then its rate may change in the future which means that one of the traders will lose while the other one will gain more or less than what was negotiated at the time of executing the transaction. This is especially true when the currencies are measured by weight rather than numbers; metallic money may lose weight over time due to circulation or due to change of altitudes of the sale locations. The restrictions imposed by the Islamic law on the currency exchange transactions intend to protect both the seller and buyer of currencies and to avoid any conflicts which could arise from the sale of currencies. Furthermore, it leads to more stable currency exchange rates which forces the economists to focus on productive economy for achieving financial growth rather than on currency exchange rate fluctuations.

Currency exchange inside the same country is not expected to cause any economic problem, since the rates of exchange are clearly set and fixed by the same government. The exchange occurs between currencies issued under the same standard, which is normal and conflict free. What could be a potential problem is the exchange between different currencies in two or more countries. That is because countries operate different standards; some countries may operate the gold standard, while others may operate the nonexchangeable paper money standard. When both countries operate the gold standard, the exchange rate between these countries or the ratio of exchange between their currencies would remain almost stable. If the currencies in both countries are based on metallic gold or silver coins, then the exchange of currencies is rather simple. It will be conducted on the basis of the weight of currencies in both countries. The ratio between the weights will determine the exchange rate. The exchange rate could only fluctuate within minimal margins which depend on the transfer charges of gold between countries. Since these charges are minimal, the exchange rate between countries operating the gold standard is virtually stable.

Similarly, the exchange rate between paper money backed by gold or silver remains rather stable, since the paper money is very much similar to the metallic money. The only difference is that the paper money circulates in lieu of metallic money and acts as a representative of gold or silver. Therefore, the intrinsic paper money would be dealt with in exactly the same way as far as the exchange rate is concerned. In fact the rule of intrinsic paper would in all aspects be the same as metallic money.

If a country operated fiduciary paper money, i.e., banknotes, the gold in this case would only be covering some of the fiduciary money's value and not all of its value, even though the country would be operating the gold standard. Therefore, the value of the fiduciary paper money would differ according to the amount of gold covering it, and this would determine the exchange rate between them. This exchange rate is also a rather stable one and easy to monitor, because it depends on the percentage rate of gold backing the paper money.

When countries operate the nonexchangeable paper money standard, the exchange rate between the currencies of these countries may pose a serious challenge. Fixing the exchange rate of paper currency in relation to gold is rather impossible, because the paper money has no intrinsic real value to be fixed against a certain weight of gold or silver. The value of paper money is measured by its buying power in the country which issues the paper money notes. As an example, assume that country A uses paper money of type A and country B uses paper money of type B. Assume that ten units of currency A are needed to buy one loaf of bread in country A, and one unit of currency B is required to buy one loaf of bread of the same quality in country B. Then the exchange rate between the two currencies would be 1 B unit = 10 A units. If the prices of goods and services in country A increase, while they remain stable in country B, then the exchange rate between the currencies will change in favor of currency B; for example 1 B unit becomes equal to 20 A units if the prices double in country A. In other words, the exchange rate between currencies fluctuates based on the fluctuation of goods and services prices in the countries issuing the currencies. This, of course, is subject to the governments and central banks not interfering to protect the exchange rate of their currencies despite the diminishing buying power.

Government interference in the affairs of the currency exchange rates has become a well-known phenomenon, especially during wartime and financial crisis. The absence of the gold standard leaves the price of a currency and its exchange rate subject to political and economic conditions. The imbalance between world currencies and the abilities of governments to raise or reduce the ratio of their currencies against the currencies of other nations have become a source of concern for many nations in the world. In the most recent financial crisis, China, for example, had serious concerns about its large reserve of US dollars. The reduction of the value of the exchange rate of the US dollar by say 10% would cause China to lose $140 billion of its $1.4 trillion reserve.

The main concern in regard to currency exchange rate is associated with paper money. The Islamic state, which operates the gold and silver standard, will be in a position to avoid much of that trouble and concern. The Islamic state is compelled to abide by the gold and silver standard because it is a *Shari'ah* rule upon which many other *Shari'ah* rules depend (Zakah, punitive rules, hoarding, and others). When dealing with other states which operate gold and silver currencies, the Islamic state will proceed according to the rules of exchange in a rather smooth manner. Also, Islam allows the purchase of a paper-based currency under the assumption that this currency is of type different from gold and silver. The state applies the rules of exchange between currencies of different types. In evaluating the exchange rate between the Islamic dinar or dirham and the foreign currency, the Islamic state needs to estimate the power of the foreign currency to buy gold and silver or to buy the goods and commodities deemed necessary by the state. At any rate, the Islamic state policy is to avoid as much as possible exchanging its gold—and silver-based currency for a nonmetallic currency.

In the current foreign trade and commerce practices, countries accumulate the currencies of foreign countries in order to be able to buy the products produced by those countries. The truth of the matter is that when a state has a gold based currency, it will have no problem buying the products of any country using its own currency, thus avoiding the need to exchange its gold-based money for a pure paper money.

The policies for self-sufficiency and increased productivity should help the Islamic state avoid the conflicts of monetary exchange between the Islamic gold dinar and the non-Islamic paper money. In essence, the implementation of the Shari'ah laws regarding the gold and silver monetary base and regarding the currency exchange provides a solid protection to the Islamic state's currency and to the political economy at large.

5

Satisfaction of Basic Needs

Recall that the main objective of the Islamic political economy is to satisfy the basic needs of each individual and to enable each individual to satisfy his luxury needs. From the Islamic perspective, the basic needs of any human are the same irrespective of the place or the time era the people live in. These needs are directly related to the survival and the well-being of people. Islam recognizes these needs and makes them a right for each and every individual. Essentially, the basic needs of a human are the food and water, clothing, secure housing, and health; some may argue that health is a by-product of the other basic needs (food, clothing, and housing). Beyond these needs, human strive for more comfortable and luxurious life, which is perfectly all right in Islam.

In a reference to the basic needs of individuals, it is reported that Prophet Mohammad (PBUH) said, *"Whoever ends his day, with security at home, splendid health, and enough food, is a person who obtained all that he needs in life."*[146] This narration by the Prophet indicates that food, secure shelter, and health constitute the essentials of life which each and every individual must attain. A reference to clothing as a basic need is found in Surah Albaqara (chapter 2, verse 233): *"The father of the child shall bear the cost of the mother's food and clothing on a reasonable basis."* Although the reference is to a family type responsibility, but the context is related to the needs of an individual. Thus Islam makes it a must that each and every individual in the society receives sufficient food, sufficient clothing, secure housing, and health protection. Beyond these basic needs, each individual should have access to the tools and resources which enable him to seek more of the luxurious needs.

The Islamic approach to the complete satisfaction of the basic human needs differs fundamentally from the approach taken by the socialists or capitalists. The socialists focused on the equality of property ownership, rather than the requirement to fulfill the basic needs of the people. The socialists would still consider the objectives of the political economy achieved even when the people in the society fall short of satisfying their basic needs while they enjoy equal ownership of the means of production. In theory, one can expect that this equality of ownership naturally leads to the satisfaction of the basic needs; however, practice proves otherwise. Under the leadership of socialists in the Soviet Union, the public ownership of the means of production did not guarantee the satisfaction of the needs of individuals. The Soviet Union suffered a great deal of poverty and millions of people lacked some of the basics and essentials of life such as food, health care, and shelter. We have to always remember that these needs are needs of specific individuals and it is the right of each to attain these needs. And these needs must be addressed directly; they should not be treated as the by-product of another objective. In the case of socialism, it was assumed that the equality of ownership of the means of production automatically caters for the needs of individuals. The practice of socialism in the Soviet Union and China proved this assumption wrong.

Capitalism made a similar mistake in the sense that it left the satisfaction of the needs of people to depend on another goal. The main goal pursued by the capitalist political economy is the economic growth which calls for increasing the scarce products and services. The growth of the economy measured in terms of the increase in the gross domestic product (GDP) or gross national product (GNP) is the main objective of the capitalist political economy. The economy under capitalism goes in recession or depression when economic growth slows down below a certain value. It goes into recovery when the growth resumes for a given period of time. Whether in recession, depression, or recovery, millions of people may continue to lack the basic needs of food, health protection, shelter, and clothing. The number of people who fall below a poverty line (earning less than $1.25 a day in many countries) continues to grow even when the overall health of the economy is in good shape. In other words, the assumption that the more goods, services, and wealth the society produces, the more likely for people to receive enough food, health care, housing, and clothing is incorrect. This has been proven with abundance of data; the first part of this book provided all types of data and statistics which support this conclusion. Again, capitalism, similar to socialism, has failed to consider the essentials of life for each individual as an objective that stands on its own, which ought to be pursued by the political economy. Instead, capitalism considered the satisfaction of the needs of individuals as a by-product of another goal, which is the economic growth and the increase of production.

Islam, as discussed earlier, treated each individual in the society as a subject which needs to be addressed on its own. Islam recognized that the satisfaction of the needs of the society at large does not necessarily guarantee the satisfaction of the individual units of that society. In a reference to this fact, the Prophet (PBUH) declared that a community that has plenty of food and resources remains in a sinful error if at least one of its members does get enough food (by the same token he does not get shelter, health care, and clothing). In essence, Islam does not tolerate the existences of homelessness, hunger, or sickness in the society.

In the process of satisfying the basic needs of individuals, Islam deploys several mechanisms. The first mechanism assigns for each individual in the society a responsible party to guarantee that the individual meets his or her basic needs. The second mechanism establishes an obligatory fund, known as Zakah, which augments the first mechanism and seeks to fulfill the needs of individuals. This mechanism is further enhanced by other forms of charity (*sadaqat*). The third mechanism is provided by the public and state ownerships. The second part of the objectives of the Islamic political economy, which is the satisfaction of more than the basic needs, is achieved through the private ownership as discussed earlier in this book. These mechanisms are further discussed and elaborated in the following sections.

Children, Parents, and Relatives Support

Islam assigns for each individual in the society a hierarchical order to take care of his or her basic needs. The first level of support falls upon the individual himself. Islam made it an obligation upon able men to work and provide for themselves and their dependents. Allah (SWT) in Surah Al-Mulk (chapter 67, verse 30) urges people to take advantage of the plenty of resources in the earth; He says, *"He it is Who has made the earth subservient to you (i.e. easy for you to walk, to live and to do agriculture on it); so walk in the path thereof and eat of His provision. And to Him will be the Resurrection."* Prophet Mohammad (PBUH) is reported to have said, *"Rather than asking people for support, which may or may not be granted, a man should go out and seek work such as bringing wood on his back from the forests and selling wood."*[147] It is established that all able men are required to seek work and provide for their own basic needs and for those who depend on them.

This rule applies exclusively to males in the society. Women in Islam are not required to work in order to provide for their basic needs. Islam mandated alimony support for all women, whether they are able to work or not; women support comes under the category of support for daughters, wives, or mothers. In the same manner, Islam mandated alimony support (called N*afaqah* in Islamic terms) for all men who are unable to work due to disability or being unable to find work.

The hierarchy of alimony (*Nafaqah*) responsibility is established in a reverse order of inheritance. That is, the legal inheritor of a person is also legally responsible for taking care of the basic needs of that person. The inheritor responsibility principle is stated in the Quran in Surah Al-Baqara (chapter 2, verse 233): *"No person shall have a burden laid on him greater than he can bear. No mother shall be treated unfairly on account of her child, nor father on account of his child. And on the inheritor is incumbent the like of that (which was incumbent on the father)."* In essence, the male inheritor who is eligible to inherit a person after he/she dies is also responsible for taking care of that person, if he becomes poor before his/her death.

Of course this is true only if the person is unable to attend for his or her own needs. If a deceased person has no legal inheritors, the state becomes his legal inheritor, and by the same logic, the state is the legal caretaker of such a person. It is narrated that the Prophet (PBUH) had said, *"I inherit whoever has no legal inheritors."* It is established in the Shari'ah that when the Prophet refers to himself in a legal manner, it is taken that he is actually referring to the state.

To understand the principle of reverse inheritance caretaking, let's look at some examples. A married woman, for example, is to be supported by her husband, as indicated in the Quran and the Sunnah. In Surah Al-Talaq (chapter 65, verse 6) it says, *"Provide them (wives) with the same housing as you provide for yourselves."* It continues to say in verse 7, *"Let the rich man spend (on his wife) according to his means; and the man whose resources are restricted, let him spend according to what Allâh has given him."* Prophet Mohammad also said, *"Their right (wives) upon you is to provide them with good housing and clothing,"* emphasizing the basic needs of woman as an individual in the society. The basic needs of each woman, whether rich or poor, are guaranteed by either by the husband (if married), the father, the sons, or the brothers. Note that the husband, the sons, the father, and the brothers are legal inheritors of a woman. If none of these parties are able to provide for the basic needs, the support is escalated to the state. The state uses one of several funds, as explained later on, to provide for the basic needs of a woman whose immediate relatives are either absent or unable to provide the necessary support.

The basic needs of a male individual are guaranteed as follows. A healthy and able adult male is required to work and support his own self and those who depend on him. When a man asked the Prophet for support, it is narrated that the Prophet had provided the man with food for the day and an ax and asked the man to cut woods and make money and provide for himself and his family.[148] The father is in charge of his own children for support when the children are young and remain unable to work and satisfy their own needs. When the parents grow old, their support falls upon their able sons. The right of support for parents upon their sons is established in the Quran and Sunnah. It says in Surah Al-Isra (chapter 17, verse 23), *"And your Lord has decreed that you worship none but Him. And that you be dutiful to your parents (including support). If one of them or both of them attain old age in your life, say not to them a word of disrespect, nor shout at them but address them in terms of honor."* The Prophet (PBUH) is narrated to have said in response to a question posed by one of his companions as to who deserves the highest level of support, *"Your mother, then your mother, then your mother, then your father, then your closest relatives."* The close relatives are taken to be the brothers and sisters and their children. One of the companions of the Prophet (PBUH) narrates that the Prophet had said, *"Allah commands you to take care of your mothers then your fathers and then your relatives, the closest first."*[149] In response to another question on the issue of support, the Prophet explained that support should be provided to the mother, father, sister, and brother.[150]

Essentially, Islam assigned for each poor individual a party, which, if not poor itself, should be responsible for fulfilling the basic needs of that individual. Islam went to the extent of giving preference for paying alimony support over debt payment. In other words, if a person is in debt and at the same time has a wife, a child or parents to take care of, he is first required to satisfy the needs of his immediate relatives and then he can take care of the debts. This is not to diminish the significance of paying debt; it simply shows the importance of satisfying the needs of each individual in Islam. The support provided to children, parents, brothers, and sisters is enforced under the Islamic law by the Islamic court and state. In other words, this issue is not left to the discretion of individuals. In the meantime, Islam recognized the possibility that some individuals may remain out of the scope of the support of immediate relatives due to the poor status of their responsible party or the fact that some individuals do not have any immediate relatives. For these reasons, Islam provided other mechanisms to compensate for such situations such as the Zakah and the state-sponsored funds.

Zakah: A Fund for Satisfying the Needs of Individuals

The Zakah (Obligatory Charity) is one of the main pillars of Islam. It is narrated that Prophet Mohammad (PBUH) had said, *"Islam is constructed upon five"*;[151] one of the five pillars is the Zakah. The Zakah is a particular and well-defined portion of wealth deducted out of the wealth of rich individuals and devoted to the poor ones. It is narrated that Prophet Mohammad (PBUH) had told his companion Muath Bin Jabal when he sent him in a mission to Yemen to inform the new Muslims that one of their duties is to deduct a Zakah from the wealth of the rich ones and give it to the poor ones.[152] To guarantee the proper functionality of the Zakah, Islam made this form of charity as one of the main forms of worship carried out by a Muslim; it is frequently cited along with the prayer in the Quran. Furthermore, Islam mandated the state to be in charge of collecting the Zakah funds and distributing the funds according to preestablished rules of distribution. The Quran designated eight categories of people who are entitled to receive the Zakah charity.

In Surah Al-Tawbah (chapter 9, verse 60), the Quran says, *"As-Sadaqât (here it means Zakah) are only for the Fuqarâ' (poor), and Al-Masâkin (the very poor) and those employed to collect (the funds), and to attract the hearts of those who have been inclined (towards Islâm); and to free the captives, and for those in debt, and for Allâh's Cause (i.e. for Mujâhidûn—those fighting in a holy battle), and for the wayfarer (a traveler who is cut off from everything); a duty imposed by Allâh. And Allâh is All-Knower, All-Wise."* Five of the eight categories are devoted to the satisfaction of the basic needs of people who may have a problem taking care of their own needs.

The poor (Fuqara) category covers a segment of the population who do have income but due to extreme conditions, their income is not sufficient to cover the basic expenses of lodging, shelter, health, clothing, and food. This category of people is eligible for Zakah funds. The second category is the very poor (Miskeen), covers a group of people who are deprived of any source of income and lack the basic needs of life. Typically, this group covers orphanage, disabled people, older people with no living or able sons, war victims, victims of natural disasters such as hurricanes, earthquakes, tsunami, and the like. These people are eligible to receive Zakah funds. The category of captives includes any captive individual whose freedom requires the payment of ransom or compensation. In the past, this category included the slaves whose masters demanded money in exchange of their freedom. Allowing the Zakah funds to be used for this category, Islam recognized that freedom is a basic need for humans which must be guaranteed and satisfied. Today, the captive category includes prisoners of war and victims of piracy.

The category of people who are "in debt" covers those who experience certain hardships which force them to carry debts beyond their capacity to satisfy the demands of their creditors. For example, if a person is involved in an accident which results in the death or injury of another person, then a ransom has to be paid to the survivors and legal inheritors of the deceased. If the ransom is beyond the capacity of the person causing the accident, then the Zakah funds may be used to compensate for the deficiency. Financial crisis, natural disasters, economic downturns, accidents, health conditions, education expenses, and other reasons may bring a person huge debts beyond his normal capacity to pay for the debts. Islam recognized this category of "indebted" people and allowed them to receive Zakah funds to pull them out of debt.

Islam also recognized a category of people called the wayfarer (*Ibn Al-Sabeel*). This category covers in particular students who travel away from their homeland in search for knowledge and education. It also covers any person who is traveling and has a temporary need for food, shelter, and basic expenses to continue his trip.

The distribution of the Zakah funds elegantly defined the types of people who need the immediate help and support like the poor and the very poor (Miskeen). It also defined the condition, which may force people to move in a situation where they need help and support (captivity, in debt, travel). As explained earlier, the first level of support to any of these categories must come from the immediate relatives (sons, fathers, brothers). If the first level of support is unable to provide the full amount, the Zakah funds will be utilized to make up for the remaining balance.

The Zakah in Islam is accurately defined for each category of wealth. The Zakah rate for all monetary wealth (gold, silver, paper money) is 2.5% given that the total monetary wealth is equal or larger than 85 grams of gold or 595 grams of silver. The Zakah is computed at the end of each year. All types of trade and commerce revenue are subject to Zakah at 2.5% of the estimated revenue at the end of the year. The products of farming lands have different rates depending on whether the land is irrigated by rainwater, natural rivers, or privately drawn water canals. Cattle and livestock have their own Zakah rate as well. More details of the Zakah rules and details can be found in the book *Al-Amwal*.[153]

With the absence of the Islamic state and a comprehensive Islamic economic system, it is difficult to estimate the amount of available Zakah funds. However, it is estimated that the monetary wealth of investors from the rich-oil gulf states exceeds $1.25 trillion.[154] The annual Zakah funds computed against this wealth is $31.25 billion. This Zakah fund, although much less than the real wealth in the Muslim world, is sufficient to cover the vast majority of the basic needs of most of the poor people in the entire Muslim world. History reports that the Islamic state during the first hundred years of its rise was able to collect more Zakah funds than the needs of its ever-growing population.[155]

Public and State Property: No Human Needs Remain Unsatisfied

No human needs should remain unsatisfied. This is a basic principle which Islam honours. This is clearly stated in the Quran in Surah Al-Israa (chapter 17, verse 70). *"And indeed We have honored the Children of Adam, and We have carried them on land and sea, and have provided them with At-Tayyibât (lawful good things), and have preferred them above many of those whom We have created with a marked preferment."* In order to guarantee the satisfaction of the basic needs, Islam added one more level of support in case the first two levels fail to cover the needs of some people. Natural disasters, wars, and hard economic conditions can easily leave many individuals without the proper support of their immediate relatives and can easily dry out the funds of Zakah due to revenue depletion of the rich and wealthy. The third level of support provided by the Islamic economic system is the public and state property, which was discussed in section 4.2.

The revenue of the public property is administered by the state. Public property is equally owned by all citizens, rich and poor alike. Therefore, the proceeds of this type of property are used to finance projects of common interest for all the population. Examples of such project include health, education, roads, bridges, railroads, communication infrastructure, utilities and the like. Hence, the public property revenues contribute towards the satisfaction of health and education basic needs for all citizens of the society, rich and poor alike.

The public property revenue is also used to support the basic needs of poor individuals in the society. This is derived from the fact that the Muslim society at large is responsible for each and every poor individual. Prophet Mohammad (PBUH) declared that a community which leaves one of its members hungry is in direct violation of rules of Islam and warrants a severe punishment from Allah. The scope of the community can be extended to include the entire society. Thus it is an obligation upon the whole society to make sure that the basic needs of each individual are satisfied. It is also narrated that Prophet Mohammad (PBUH) had said, *"If a deceased person leave wealth, then that wealth goes to his survivors. If he leaves survivors without leaving them wealth, then I will be responsible for them."*[156] This establishes the rule that the state will be in charge of those who do not have any family support. The state will first use the funds of Zakah in its capacity as administrator of the Zakah. If the Zakah fund is not sufficient to take care of the needs of all those who need the support, the state will use the funds of the public and state property.

Whether the public property revenues are first spent on the needs of the society or on the needs of poor individuals is a debatable issue among scholars. The guiding principle, however, is the urgency of the need. The state as an administrator of the public property revenue is responsible for spending the revenues and prioritizing the projects. In all cases, the basic needs of hunger, shelter, and clothing come first. If the Zakah funds and the wealth of wealthy individuals are not sufficient to provide for these needs, the revenues of the public property are used immediately to compensate for the deficit. It is only when the security of the entire society is at risk when the caliph of the state may give precedence to national security over individual basic needs. It is narrated that Caliph Omar Bin Al-Khattab (the second caliph in Islam) used the revenue of the state-owned and publicly owned land to provide food for all during famine which hit part of the Islamic state in the seventeenth AH year.

Currently, the public property wealth is enormous given that this wealth includes revenues from oil, gas, minerals, and real estate properties. During the financial crisis, which hit the world in 2008, the oil and gas industries were among the few industries which remained profitable. Given the vast amount of oil and gas reserves in the lands of Islam, it is expected that these funds alone can cover all the basic needs of each individual in the state. Nevertheless, the hierarchy of alimony support should be preserved. The first level of support, which relies on the relationship between immediate family members, is sought to strengthen the family ties in addition to providing the necessary financial support. The Zakah funds also are used to strengthen the faith and belief base of those who contribute the Zakah, because the Zakah is an essential pillar of Islam. So the fact that the public and state property funds may be abundant, the support should proceed in the order given above: family support, Zakah funds, and then the public and state properties revenues.

It should be noted that the support hierarchy is a right for each poor individual in the society and not an option. It is also an obligation upon the state under the Islamic law to guarantee this hierarchy of support; it is not an option for the state. The satisfaction of the basic needs of individuals should not be part of the politics of the state, or a matter of political struggle between ideologies as was the case between capitalism and socialism.

Despite all the rhetoric about human rights, which dominated the political scene throughout the twentieth century, the basic rights of humans for food, shelter, and clothing remained in despair for a large percentage of the world population. Both socialism and capitalism have seriously failed to satisfy the basic needs of hundreds of millions of people around the globe. Both ideologies have used the basic human rights as a means to challenge the politics of the opponent ideologies. The rights of humans for food, shelter, and clothing are integral part of the Islamic system. Islam intertwined the support issue with the family intimate relationships, as well as with the fundamental of worshiping through the Zakah. It also established the category of publicly owned property in order to compensate for any deficiencies that may arise in the family relationship or the Zakah worship.

Private Property: Beyond the Basic Needs

On top of the basic needs, humans naturally strive for the achievement of more and beyond the basic needs. Islam recognized the fact that people may develop this love and eagerness for more wealth and luxurious life. In Surah Al-Imran (chapter 3, verse 14), the Quran says, *"Beautified for men is the love of things they covet; women, children, much of gold and silver (wealth), branded beautiful horses, cattle and well-tilled land. This is the pleasure of the present world's life; but Allah has the excellent return (Paradise with flowing rivers) with Him."* It is narrated that Prophet Mohammad (PBUH) had said, *"Allah likes to see the favors he bestowed upon his servants."*

Islam did not restrict the individuals from seeking the expansion of their wealth in order to attain a better life. For this purpose, Islam legalized and permitted the private property ownerships. It also permitted different means of growing private wealth, while restricting some other means such as usury investment, the sale of drugs and alcohol, prostitution, and sex trade.

Islam did not establish any upper limit on the amount of wealth, which can be earned by any individual. In some narrations, the Prophet said if some person had the equivalent of a mountain of gold, in reference to extra large amount of wealth. The only limits imposed by Islam are related to the means of acquiring or growing wealth. The Quran explicitly permitted trade as a means of growing wealth. Other rules in Islam defined the rules of trade and the boundaries of what constitutes a legal or illegal trade. But within the boundaries of legal trade, an individual can grow his wealth as much as he could. It is reported that Othman Bin Affan, the companion of the Prophet and the third khalifah, managed a caravan trade which amounted to thousands of camels' worth of goods.

Although Islam allowed individuals to grow their wealth and enjoy the outcome of that wealth, it continued to emphasize that the joys attained in this life are negligible in comparison to the endless joys of the life after death. This comparison between the luxuries of this life and the ones to be attained in paradise is repeated time and again in the Quran. The idea is to protect the personality of individuals from the negative and destructive traits such as greed, haughtiness, selfishness, and repression. The reference to the haughty rich Qarun in the Quran is a good example, where the request is made to Qarun saying, *"Use the wealth given to you by Allah to seek the pleasure of the hereafter, while not forgetting to enjoy your current life."*[157] Prophet Mohammad (PBUH) is reported to have said, *"Allah likes the humble rich man."*

Throughout the history of the Islamic state and civilization, the signs of wealth and luxury are visible through the marvels of architecture, cities, libraries, schools, medicine, road infrastructure, navy fleets, and much more. The cities of Baghdad, Damascus, Samarqand, Alhambra, Andalusia, and Istanbul provide a living evidence of the luxuries attained by Muslims under the Islamic civilization. In the meantime, the absence of poverty and hunger was remarkably recorded by historians of both Islamic and non-Islamic orientation. Throughout the vast Islamic lands, Muslims established rest areas where travelers can lodge and eat for free during their journeys.

The resurgence of Islam and the second rise of Islam as an ideology, civilization, and way of life are expected to revive the story of a human whose basic needs are fully guaranteed and whose endeavor for luxury is fully recognized and made possible.

PART 3

Is Islam a Threat or Benefit?

And We have sent you (O Mohammad) not but as a mercy for the mankind.

—Quran 21:107

The base of a new Islamic caliphate will extend throughout the Middle East, and which would threaten legitimate governments in Europe, Africa, and Asia and US interests.

—Rumsfeld, former secretary of defense

I believe that if a man like Mohammad were to assume the dictatorship of the modern world, he would succeed in solving its problems in a way that would bring it the much-needed peace and happiness.

—Bernard Shaw

1

Unfounded Fear

The collapse of the Wall Street's giant world trade center and the collapse of Wall Street's giant financial institutions spectacularly raise two images of Islam: An image that spreads fear and carries threat; and an image that shines with life and prosperity. The terrorist attacks which demolished the world trade center on 9/11/2001 have made it very difficult to portray the true Islamic view of the world. Despite the repeated calls by politicians, philosophers, and thinkers to distinguish between Islam as a religion and those who carry the attacks, the distortion of the image of Islam was quite significant. Seven years after heightening the war on terrorism, wall street financial market collapsed, but this time the terrorists were economists and were from within the system, and were not Muslims. As a result, the public is stuck with two views and two images; one portrays Islam as a threat and the other one as a benefit. This part of the book addresses this dilemma. It is not the intention of this part to discuss the issue of terrorism at length; this will be dealt with in another publication. It will only be discussed within the limits and the scope of this book.

When the issue of terrorism is widely debated, many people continue to draw a hard line between Islam as a global religion and the acts of terrorism. With this type of distinction and clarity, there should not be a serious fear from the rising trend of Islam. This view, however, was not the case with the former Defense secretary, Donald Rumsfeld. In one of his comments, he portrayed the rise of the Islamic political system as a threat to the west in general, as reported in an article published by The New York

Times on December 12, 2005, under the title "21st-century Warnings of a Threat Rooted in 7th Century."[158] In this article, Bumiller shows how score of high level politicians view Islam as a threat to western civilization and democracy. Capitalizing on the issue of radicalism, fundamentalism, and terrorism, Wayne Kopping produced in 2006 the film "Obsession—The Threat of Radical Islam."[159] The purpose of the movie was to warn against the threats presumably posed by radical Islam.

The war against terrorism and the myriad of media outlets, blogs, web pages, radio talk shows, and publication have helped create what amounts to an "Islamophobia" at the public as well as the official levels in Europe and the USA. In France, a resolution was passed against wearing Islamic head dress by Muslim women in public schools. Several European countries contemplated a law against Muslim women wearing the veil. The United States adopted several security related laws including profiling, spying, wire tapping, patriot law, and other laws, all of which have been indirectly related to Muslims.

The point here is that a significant element of fear has clouded the atmosphere of Islam and its potential rise. Dealing with this phenomenon is not a simple task, especially when the identities of people who carry some of the worst attacks are revealed and found to be Muslims. Terrorism as such is a horrible crime; it cannot be condoned or accepted or justified in any way. This is said; it must also be clear that Islam as a religion and a comprehensive ideology is not the cause or reason behind terrorism. On the contrary, Islam, in its capacity as a comprehensive system, can play a decisive role in eliminating terrorism and the environment which breeds terrorism.

The argument throughout this book has been that Islam as an ideology functions as a whole system. For Islam to produce the expected outcome, it needs to be implemented at more than one level. Even the economic and financial systems, which have received a great approval from several parties around the world, are not expected to provide the stability and prosperity unless coupled with the social, political, and ethical components of the ideology. The fact that Islam as a comprehensive system is not practiced or implemented in the Islamic world, makes it difficult to attach global societal behavior to Islam, whether in the fields of war or peace. It is not a coincident that Islam for the first thirteen years of its initial rise left out a great part of its legislation, rules, and regulations. In fact, all of the rules which are directly related to the organization of society and societal behavior were revealed during the last ten years of the life of the Prophet when a state for Islam was created.

Except for the rituals and personal aspects of Islam, the practical aspects of the Islamic state were superseded throughout the twentieth century and the first decade of the twenty-first century. As a result, the civilization of Islam, which flourished for the previous thirteen hundreds years, was replaced by a mixture of civilizations. Since the caliphate was abolished in 1924 in Istanbul, various types of nationalism coupled with variations of capitalism and socialism dominated the world of Islam. The dominance of these civilizations was reflected in many aspects of life including the government structure, the economic system, the educational institutions, the lifestyle, and international relations. It was also remarkably visible during the era of anticolonial national liberation movements, which swept the majority of third world countries. For the majority of the twentieth century, the dominant ideologies and civilizations were stamped by national socialist movements, which characterized Egypt Nasirism, Palestinian national movements, Indo-Pakistani movements, Indonesian movements, Turkish nationalist movements, and the like.

Traits of Islam began to appear in the national movements towards the end of the twentieth century when the shah of Iran was toppled by a revolution led by Ayatollah Khomeini in 1979. During the same period, the Soviet invasion of Afghanistan prompted a counterrevolution characterized by Afghan nationalism, local Islam, and Western liberal idealism. Later in the century, the collapse of socialism and the Soviet Union shifted the national socialist movements in the Muslim world to national democratic movements.

The point here is that the Islamic civilization was not the main driver of events and societal behavior in the Muslim world for the past one hundred years. The main events were driven by nationalism, socialism, and later in the century by democracy and liberalism. A mixture of these civilizations created almost every environment in the entire Muslim world. This includes the environment of poverty in countries like Egypt and Indonesia or prosperity in countries like Qatar and Bahrain. It also includes lack of economic developments in many parts and political instability and oppression in other parts. The responsibility of Islam for the conditions which prevailed throughout this period of time is almost null and negligible. In fact, part of the conditions which persisted in many places in the Muslim world included the persecution of Islamic activists and forced ejection of Islam from the practical life of people. Turkey, for example, continues to ban some Islamic public practices like the Muslim women dress code.

During this period, which is characterized by an exclusion of Islam as a civilization and ideology, an environment of militancy and violence was created in some parts of the Muslim world. Part of this militancy was an outgrowth and continuation of previously created liberation movements under conditions of occupation, colonialism, or social repression. Al-Qaeda, for example, grew out of the womb of the Afghan anti-Soviet jihad movement, which was in part supported and funded by US covert operations. Hamas, in Palestine, was born in the midst of uprising against Israeli occupation of Palestinian lands, which had instigated the creation of several brands of Palestinian national liberation movements. Despite the apparent Islamic character of these militant movements, Islam did not contribute to the environment in which any of these movements was created. Islam was used in the majority of these movements as a recruiting vehicle and a source of inspiration for the members.

Before Islam was drawn into the front, nationalism and sense of patriotism inspired the same crowd which supplied the fighters of the earlier periods. In other words, the environments of violence, war, repression, terrorism, occupation, poverty, economic deprivation, and political instability were predominant throughout the majority of the third world including the Muslim world, without Islam being part of the mosaic of the land. In response to these conditions and environments, the nations of these lands used many ideologies and political agendas; when an ideology fails or runs out of energy, another one comes into play. The Palestinian movements provide the best example of this phenomenon, where the nationalistic and patriotic drivers were slowly replaced by Islamic ones. In Afghanistan, Islam helped fuel the tribal motives of the Afghan people. The point here is that Islam as an ideology is not the one to blame or praise, to commend or to condemn for whatever activities and movements which culminated in the last one hundred years.

When Islam ruled and the Islamic civilization was the main and dominant one in the lands of Islam, historians could easily attribute many events, conditions, and environments to Islam. This was true even when the Islamic state was at its weakest point during the crusade wars, because Islam continued to provide the law of the land. There is no dispute that during the period of Islamic dominance and until its decline at the end of the nineteenth century, Islam was responsible for the ups and downs, the despair or hope, the stability or chaos, the economic progress or downturn, the violence or peace, the scientific advancement or the lack of it. The inventions made in Baghdad or Samarqand, the architecture in Andalusia or Istanbul, the libraries in Alexandria or Baghdad are undoubtedly the results of Islamic civilization. Today, there are thousands of Muslim innovators, scientists, writers, and scholars. But the truth of the matter, which is recognized by any observer in the field, is that these brilliant people are not the product of the Islamic civilization, despite the fact that many of them are devout Muslims. There is no question that Islam helps molding the personality of scientists and innovators and contributes to their productivity; but the environment, which created their ability to invent and excel, is a product of the contemporary civilizations, which in turn are mix of nationalism, liberalism, socialism, capitalism, and democracy.

In essence, a Muslim who wins a Noble Prize in literature or science achieves this performance under the conditions and systems created by ideologies other than Islam. And it is not fair to attribute such achievements to Islam when Islam is not the driver of the laws of land or the maker of the civilization of the land. In societies ruled by non-Islamic laws, Muslim achievers are simply not the product of Islam. By the same token, a Muslim who blows up a market full of people or carries a bomb on an airplane is not a product of Islam either. Both are the products of the laws, regulations, systems, and civilizations which dominate the societies in which both brands—scientists or terrorists—grow.

Until and unless Islam becomes the source of laws and systems in the land, and becomes the main guide for the civilization and the societal behavior, it will be ideologically incorrect to attribute any of the contemporary events to Islam. As any ideology, the theoretical foundation of Islam alone cannot produce its expected outcome unless it begins the practical period by implementing the systems that emanate from this foundation. This principle applies to the economics of Islam as well as to its politics. During the first thirteen years of the first rise of Islam, there was an extensive discussion on many aspects of the societal behavior and issues such as poverty, justice, morals, wealth distribution, war, peace, family ties, and much more. And Islam did not take the responsibility over the actions of people living and practicing any of these issues, although some of the Muslims were part of these actions. For example, some Muslims living in Mecca during that era continued to be part of the usury practices, which were condemned by Islam.

Even after the creation of the Islamic state in Medina, the Islamic society and state did not assume responsibility for Muslims who continued to live outside the scope of the Islamic society and the state. This is important to know, because Islam, when it assumes the responsibility over an issue, it must have the complete authority to impact the outcome of that issue as well as all the parameters that contribute to it. When Prophet Mohammad (PBUH) conducted a peace treaty with the Quraish tribe of Mecca, he agreed to expel any Muslim who migrates to the Islamic state against the will of Quraish. It is narrated in the biography of Mohammad, as compiled by Ibn Hisham,[160] that a Muslim fled Mecca and ran into Medina seeking the protection of the Islamic state; but the Prophet forced that man to return to Mecca based on the request of Quraish. When that man fled again and began to carry militant assaults against Quraish, the Prophet (PBUH) distanced himself from his actions and refused to provide him with any type of support.

In the meantime, the Prophet as a leader of a state conducted the relations between his state and other states with complete responsibility. The rules of engagement between his state and the rest of the world were well defined, whether in peace or war. Islam provided a full and complete script for the rules of engagement. But these rules are carried out at a state level, and not at the levels of individuals or groups. The responsibility for the acts are centralized and well defined. The Islamic state or system does not assume the responsibility or bear the consequences over the acts of individuals or groups outside the scope of the state. The point I want to make here is that for Islam to be fully responsible for Islamic acts or events, it must be in control of the society and the rules of the lands. Once Islam is in control, and the laws of the land are driven and controlled by Islam, and a central leadership in the form of a caliph is in charge, then and only then we can attribute general behavior and actions to Islam. While Islam is not in power, and a central leadership is absent, the sporadic, fitful, and spasmodic acts of many Muslims in the world will continue to be outside the scope of the Islamic system and ideology; each individual will be responsible for his own acts.

Aside from the first thirteen years of the life of Mohammad (PBUH), this is the first time, throughout the history of Islam, where Muslims find themselves living in societies and states which are not governed by Islam and its systems. The difference, though, is that during the first thirteen years' period, the systems of Islam were not completely revealed and the Islamic state was never created before. This time around, the systems of Islam have already been compiled and can be found in original texts of the Quran, the Sunnah, and many books of jurisprudence; moreover, a history of more than thirteen centuries of real practice is readily available for all. Fundamentally, though, the two eras are similar, because the existence of the Islamic state and central leadership is essential for the implementation of Islam. The fact that the rules and laws of Islam are compiled and can be found in many sources does not mean that these laws perform on their own or by the power of conviction in the hearts of those who believe in these laws. Laws and rules need a central state and governance to activate them. By the same token, the systems of economy, governance, social life, and jurisprudence do not run on their own in a society; in order for these systems to be active and produce their results, they require a political system to install these systems, monitor their performance, and protect them from corruption.

The point here is that the fear that some people may have regarding the implementation of Islam is not realistic. This fear is created out of the false perception that Islam stands behind the actions that people have been accustomed to attribute to Islam. This fear is real, but it is not founded on real grounds. It is based on the premise that the Islamic ideology is an active participant in the affairs prevailing in the world including those of extreme nature. The truth of the matter is that Islam has not been part of the mix of ideologies, which have shaped the world affairs and politics for the last one hundred years. On the contrary, Islam has been rising, and in many cases with great difficulty, to challenge the current ideological mix. Consequently, Islam should be viewed and scrutinized from the perspective of an ideology seeking a foothold in the world affairs. The basis of this scrutiny should be the theoretical foundation of Islam and the history of Islam in action.

The validity of any ideology should be first tested at the level of its theory. If the ideology had been practiced for a sufficient period of time, then it should also be tested at the implementation level. The theory of Islam is complete and had been compiled and can be found in numerous sources; therefore, it can be verified and tested. Islam also had been implemented and has a history of implementation over thirteen hundred years (more than any other single ideology). Therefore, the practical implementation of Islam can also be tested and verified.

2

Theoretical Foundation

The theoretical foundation of Islam is summarized in one statement reported by Prophet Mohammad (PBUH). He said, "Islam is constructed upon five tenants":

- → Believe that Allah is the only God and that Mohammad is his Messenger.
- → Establish prayer.
- → Pay the Zakah dues.
- → Fast the month of Ramadan.
- → Perform pilgrimage to the Sacred House in Mecca.

The first of these tenants provides the intellectual foundation of the ideology of Islam. It is the base upon which everything else in Islam is constructed. Furthermore, it provides what is called an intellectual leadership, because once this foundation is established, the human behavior is naturally molded by whatever laws that emanates from this foundation.

Islam requires the belief in the existence of god to be based upon a mental reasoning process. In this regard, Islam devalues any type of belief if it is a mere imitation and continuation of the beliefs of older generation. In numerous occasions, the Quran belittles the beliefs of people which simply rely on the beliefs of fathers and previous generations. In Surah Al-Maidah (chapter 5, verse 104), it says, *"And when it is said to them: Come* to what Allah has revealed and unto the Messenger. They say: Enough for us is that which we found our fathers following, even though their fathers had no knowledge whatsoever and no guidance."* This notion is repeated in other places in the Quran; see for example the verses in references.[161, 162, and 163]

Instead of following a belief that has been simply inherited from older generation without careful scrutiny, the Quran invites the people to ponder and use their minds to establish a firm belief in the existence of one Almighty Creator. In Surah Al-Ghashiah (chapter 88, verse 17-20), the Quran says, *"Do they not look at the camels, how they are created? And at the heaven, how it is raised? And at the mountains, how they are rooted (and fixed firm)? And at the earth, how it is outspread?"* Along these lines, the Quran makes numerous references to universal phenomena and physical realities to instigate the human thought and draw the attention to the essence of creation. See for example the direct invitation to mental reasoning in Surah Al-Baqara (chapter 2, verse 164): *"Verily! In the creation of the heavens and the earth, and in the alternation of night and day, and the ships which sail through the sea with that which is of use to mankind, and the water (rain) which Allah sends down from the sky and makes the earth alive therewith after its death, and the moving (living) creatures of all kinds that He has scattered therein, and in the veering of winds and clouds which are held between the sky and the earth, are indeed proofs, evidences and signs for people who reason."* Another reference to the products of land draws the attention of the mind to ponder on the reason behind the variation in kind and quality of fruits and vegetables which grow in the same garden.[164] There are more than three hundred references in the Quran to various signs, physical phenomena, and natural events which compel the mind to think and ponder about the creation, in order to establish a firm belief in the existence of the one Creator for man, life, and the universe.[165]

The numerous references in the Quran always draw the attention of the mind to the fact that all existing materials share the qualities of being limited in time and space, and in being self-insufficient. None of the existing bodies, whether in the outer universe or in the realms of life, can sustain its own existence. All existing material beings depend on external factors to exist and to be sustained. The idea is that Islam wants the people to appreciate the concept of creation and to have a deep and thorough conviction in the core idea of belief.

Because the belief in the foundation of Islam is based on reason, Islam does not force people into belief. It leaves the matter of belief for the human mental discretion.[166] The conviction in the foundation of belief is required because upon this foundation, Islam builds an entire system for life. Building and sustaining such system requires a tremendous amount of energy, which can only be drawn if both the mind and the heart of the people are totally engaged in this system.

An important aspect of the belief in god is the belief in the attributes of god. The main attribute, which qualifies Islam as an ideology, is the notion of sovereignty of god. In essence, this attribute places god as the only source of laws and rules, which shape the behavior of individuals and societies. This notion is clearly stated in the Quran. In one verse, it says, *"It is He (Allah) Who is the only God to be worshiped in the heaven and the only God to be worshiped on the earth. And He is the All-Wise, the All-Knower."*[167] In another verse, it says, *"The command (or the governance) is for none but Allah. He has commanded that you worship none but Him; that is the (true) straight religion, but most men know not."*[168]

The delivery of the systems of Islam from the Creator to the people comes in the form of revelation to the messenger Mohammad (PBUH). Repeatedly, the Quran emphasizes that the revealed message is the only code which should be followed by all, including the Prophet himself. See for example Surah Al-Araf (chapter 7, verse 203), where the Quran says, *"I (Mohammad) but follow what is revealed to me from my Lord. This (the Quran) is nothing but evidences from your Lord, and a guidance and a mercy for a people who believe."* The Quran, in turn, received special attention such that it had a unique lexical, syntactic, and semantic structure. This uniqueness enabled the preservation of the Quran over time albeit unaltered and unchanged. Besides, the uniqueness of the Quran is perceived as an evidence and proof that the Quran is indeed revealed by god. It is stated in the Quran that no one will ever be able to replicate the Quran or any part of it; this challenge is valid until today. In Surah Al-Isra'a (chapter 17, verse 88), the Quran says, *"If the mankind and the jinn were together to produce the like of this Quran, they could not produce the like thereof, even if they helped one another."* Since the revelation of the Quran in the seventh century, no replica of the Quran had ever been made, and the original text of the Quran had been preserved. Until today, there is only one copy of the Quran in the Arabic language. The translations of the Quran into other languages are numerous, but there is only one version in Arabic.

Besides the Quran, the revelation includes the Sunnah of Prophet Mohammad which consists of his biography and narrated texts. The Sunnah was compiled by a group of scholars who devised new methods for authentication and validation of the Sunnah of Prophet Mohammad.[169]

Since the early days of revelation, it was recognized that the revealed text (in the form of Quran or Sunnah) provides a base for deriving rules and laws. The text of the Quran was analyzed and interpreted in a manner to allow more accurate derivation of rules and laws. Several books of the interpretation of the Quran, known as the Tafseer, were authored since the early days of Islam.[170] Based on the original texts of the Quran and the Sunnah as well as the books of interpretation, Muslim scholars developed the knowledge base of jurisprudence, known in Islam as the science of *Fiqh*. Essentially, this base includes the set of rules, regulations, laws, ethics, daily practices, and general ideas derived from the Quran and the Sunnah. Over an extended period of time, several methods of derivation were developed. Based on these methods of derivation, several schools of *Fiqh* emerged.[171] Since the seventh century and throughout the rise of Islam and until the end of the nineteenth century, thousands of books in the areas of Tafseer, Sunnah interpretation, jurisprudence (Fiqh), and creed were authored. Many of these books survived despite the great loss incurred during the Mogul and crusade wars.[172, 173]

The theoretical foundation of the Islamic ideology is intelligibly and without any ambiguity detailed in the vast collection of literature produced over thirteen centuries. The soundness of the theory is vigorously established through a well-defined reasoning process which applies to the foundation of faith: God, Messenger, and the Quran. The correctness of the systems of laws and regulations is established on the basis of a correct derivation methodology. The power of this idea lies in the notion that only the base upon which the derivation is processed needs to have an original proof. The system of laws is deemed correct if the base from which it emanates is correct, and the method of deriving the system is correct. In other words, it is not required to prove that praying five times a day is a correct practice. Rather, it is required to prove that praying five times a day was revealed in a valid Quran or Sunnah text, and the method of interpreting that text follows a sound and correct method. By the same token, it is not required to prove the correctness of the law banning usury in financial transactions. Rather, it is required to prove that the antiusury law is found in the texts of Quran and Sunnah, and the method of generating the law from these texts is a valid and correct method.

The fact that Islam demanded a mental reasoning for the belief in its core ideas and principles demonstrates the confidence of Islam in the soundness of the intellectual base of its ideology. The rationalistic nature of the Islamic foundation was recognized and acknowledged by French historian and scholar Edward Montet.[174] Montet makes the following conclusion: "Islam is a religion that is essentially rationalistic in the widest sense of this term considered etymologically and historically." He further explains, "The Qur'an has invariably kept its place as the fundamental starting point, and the dogma of unity of God has always been proclaimed therein with a grandeur a majesty, an invariable purity and with a note of sure conviction, which it is hard to find surpassed outside the pale of Islam." Montet describes the rationality of the creed as "a creed so precise, so stripped of all theological complexities and consequently so accessible to the ordinary understanding might be expected to possess and does indeed possess a marvelous power of winning its way into the consciences of men." The extended proofs of the core ideas of Islam are beyond the scope of this book. This will be dealt with in another publication by the author. In the meantime, the reader can refer to numerous publications which address this issue in greater details.[175]

3

History of Implementation

It is true that a practical model of the Islamic ideology does not fully exist in the contemporary world. However, Islam is not a new religion or ideology. On the contrary, Islam has the longest record of implementation for any single ideology. Socialism has less than eighty years of experience in its record. Capitalism, in any of its forms or shapes, barely has two hundred years of practical implementation in its record. Islam, on the other hand, had more than thirteen hundred years of implementation. During this period, it experienced strength and weakness, victory and defeat, progress and decline. In other words, the duration of the Islamic ideology in practical life has sufficient data to validate the ability of Islam to cope with various aspects of life, to deal with crisis, to resolve human-related problems, to organize the life of humans, to administer warfare relations, and to manage peaceful interrelations.

Throughout the implementation period of Islam, several nations came under the rule of Islam with diverse languages, ethnicity, religions, colors, and races. So the record of implementation of Islam is far more rich than required to test any ideology. This section will provide a brief account of the history of the Islamic ideology in action. For more detailed information on the history of the Islamic state and civilization, the reader can consult a wide spectrum of publication on the Islamic history.[176]

To illustrate the success of the Islamic ideology in achieving its objectives in creating a stable and just system, I will rely on historical witnesses of scholars and historians. I will resort to the witnesses of non-Muslim historians and scholars to add more reliability to the discussion and conclusions.

Quite few historians devoted part of their account to the personality of Mohammad the Prophet as a creator of a civilization based on the ideology and religion of Islam. The personality of the leader and his ability to mold a society based on his ideas and beliefs demonstrates the practicality of the ideology. Edward Gibbon in *The Decline and Fall of the Roman Empire*[177] writes about Prophet Mohammad and says, "The good sense of Mohammad despised the pomp of royalty. The Apostle of God submitted to the menial offices of the family; he kindled the fire; swept the floor; milked the ewes; and mended with his own hands his shoes and garments. Disdaining the penance and merit of a hermit, he observed without effort of vanity the abstemious diet of an Arab." Edward Gibbon and Simon Oakley, in another account, extend the observation from the unique stewardship traits of Mohammad to his followers and their ability to sustain a civilization for more than twelve hundred years.[178] The moral force of Mohammad the Prophet is cited as a major contributor to the success of the civilization he created. Gibbon and Oakley write with great esteem and admiration, "It is not the propagation but the permanency of his religion that deserves our wonder, the same pure and perfect impression which he engraved at Mecca and Medina is preserved after the revolutions of twelve centuries by the Indian, the African and the Turkish proselytes of the Quran." The consistency of the theoretical foundation of the ideology with the practical implementation is noticed by Gibbon and Oakley in their writings. "The Muslims have uniformly withstood the temptation of reducing the object of their faith and devotion to a level with the senses and imagination of man." With great elegance, the historians maintained that the simplicity of the creed of Islam (I believe in One God and Mohammad the Apostle of God) had a great impact on the successful implementation of the simple and invariable ideology of Islam. "The intellectual image of the Deity has never been degraded by any visible idol; the honors of the Prophet have never transgressed the measure of human virtue, and his living precepts have restrained the gratitude of his disciples within the bounds of reason and religion."[179]

In 1878, Reverend Bosworth Smith,[180] after a thorough investigation of the history of Islam and the man behind the successful implementation of Islam, described Mohammad as "head of the State as well as the Church (or religion)" in a reference to the integration of the state functions within Islam. According to Rev. Smith, Mohammad was Caesar and pope in one; but he was pope without the pope's pretensions, and Caesar without the legions of Caesar, without a standing army, without a bodyguard, without a police force, without fixed revenue. Rev. Smith concludes his finding with the following testimony: "If ever a man ruled by a right divine, it was Mohammad, for he had all the powers without their supports. He cared not for the dressings of power. The simplicity of his private life was in keeping with his public life." In other words, the comprehensive ideology of Islam was backed by a strong and intelligent leadership, which created a story of success. In the Reverend's words, "after his mission had been proclaimed, we have a book (Quran) absolutely unique in its origin, in its preservation, on the Substantial authority of which no one has ever been able to cast a serious doubt."

Another investigation of the history of the implementation of Islam was conducted by Arthur Stanley Tritton.[181] He examined the claim made by some historians that Islam was spread by the sword, and that Muslims forced other nations into Islam after the conquest of their lands. In 1951, A. S. Tritton wrote, "The picture of the Muslim soldier advancing with a sword in one hand and the Qur'an in the other is quite false."[182] The same conclusion was made by De Lacy O'Leary[183] in his publication *Islam at the Crossroads*[184] where he wrote, "History makes it clear, however, that the legend of fanatical Muslims sweeping through the world and forcing Islam at the point of sword upon conquered races is one of the most fantastically absurd myths that historians have ever repeated." This conclusion was also made by James Michener,[185] where he says, "No other religion in history spread so rapidly as Islam. The West has widely believed that this surge of religion was made possible by the sword. But no modern scholar accepts this idea, and the Quran is explicit in the support of the freedom of conscience." Lawrence E. Browne[186] also dismisses the myth surrounding the spread of Islam by force and makes the following remarks: "Well-established facts dispose of the idea so widely fostered in Christian writings that the Muslims, wherever they went, forced people to accept Islam at the point of the sword."

The claim that Islam used the sword to spread the religion has no evidence whatsoever as asserted by several historians. Historian K. S. Ramakrishna Rao, in *Mohammed: The Prophet of Islam* (1989), says that this claim is a distortion of history and it is not even worth the investigation. He confirms the conclusions of other historians about the incorrectness of the claim that Islam had spread by the power of the sword.

Perhaps, one of the most thorough accounts of the history of Islam in terms of the ideological foundation, the Prophet of Islam (Mohammad PBUH), and the Islamic civilization was provided by Alphonse de Lamartine.[187] In his famous article "Historie de la Turquie,"[188] Lamartine made the following conclusion about Prophet Mohammad (PBUH): "Never has a man set for himself, voluntarily or involuntarily, a more sublime aim, since this aim was superhuman; to subvert superstitions which had been imposed between man and his Creator, to render God unto man and man unto God." Lamartine admired the ability of Mohammad to "restore the rational and sacred idea of divinity amidst the chaos of the material and disfigured gods of idolatry." On coupling both theory and practice, Lamartine wrote, "Never has a man undertaken a work so far beyond human power with so feeble means, for he (Mohammad) had in the conception as well as in the execution of such a great design, no other instrument than himself and no other aid except a handful of men living in a corner of the desert." Translating a theoretical foundation and ideology into a revolution and constructing a long-lasting civilization was noted by the French historian with great appreciation: "Never has a man accomplished such a huge and lasting revolution in the world, because in less than two centuries after its appearance, Islam, in faith and in arms, reigned over the whole of Arabia, and conquered, in God's name, Persia, Khorasan, Transoxania, Western India, Syria, Egypt, Abyssinia, all the known continent of Northern Africa, numerous islands of the Mediterranean Sea, Spain, and part of Gaul."

Concluding his remarks, and drawing analogy with contemporary systems and ideologies, Lamartine decidedly bestows the title of greatness upon Mohammad, not only for the solid and sound theory he proclaimed, but also for the system he built upon that foundation. His remarks are summarized as follows: "If greatness of purpose, smallness of means, and astonishing results are the three criteria of a human genius, who could dare compare any great man in history with Mohammad? The most famous men created arms, laws, and empires only. They founded, if anything at all, no more than material powers which often crumbled away before their eyes. This man moved not only armies, legislations, empires, peoples, dynasties, but millions of men in one-third of the then inhabited world; and more than that, he moved the altars, the gods, the religions, the ideas, the beliefs and the souls." The power of Islam and its ability to mold nations and create unity among people by the virtue of its own ideas is further explained by Lamartine, where he says, "On the basis of a Book, every letter which has become law, he created a spiritual nationality which blends together peoples of every tongue and race. He has left the indelible characteristic of this Muslim nationality the hatred of false gods and the passion for the One and Immaterial God. This avenging patriotism against the profanation of Heaven formed the virtue of the followers of Mohammad; the conquest of one-third the earth to the dogma was his miracle; or rather it was not the miracle of man but that of reason."

Lamartine commented on the power of the Islamic creed of the unity of God, and purported that it was in itself such a miracle that upon its utterance from his lips, it destroyed all the ancient temples of idols. This dogma was twofold the unity of God and the immateriality of God: the former telling what God is, the latter telling what God is not; the one overthrowing false gods with the sword, the other starting an idea with words.

Mahatma Gandhi,[189] the great Indian reformer, gave his interpretation of the Islamic civilization and ideological foundation under the leadership of Prophet Mohammad (PBUH), asserting that the spread of Islam was due to the power of ideas rather than the power of sword. Gandhi sums up his findings in these words: "I wanted to know the best of the life of one (Mohammad) who holds today an undisputed sway over the hearts of millions of mankind. I became more than ever convinced that it was not the sword that won a place for Islam in those days in the scheme of life. It was the rigid simplicity, the utter self-effacement of the Prophet the scrupulous regard for pledges, his intense devotion to his friends and followers, his intrepidity, his fearlessness, his absolute trust in God and in his own mission. These and not the sword carried everything before them and surmounted every obstacle. When I closed the second volume (of the Prophet's biography), I was sorry there was not more for me to read of that great life."

The Irish Noble Prize winner Sir George Bernard Shaw[190] makes the following remarks on the ability of Islam to deliver its declared objectives of justice and fairness: "If any religion had the chance of ruling over England, nay Europe within the next hundred years, it could be Islam." Bernard Shaw further explains, "I have always held the religion of Mohammad in high estimation because of its wonderful vitality. It is the only religion which appears to me to possess that assimilating capacity to the changing phase of existence which can make itself appeal to every age. I have studied him—the wonderful man and in my opinion far from being an anti-Christ, he must be called the Savior of Humanity." His study of Islam in action and the Islamic ideology in practice led Shaw to express his feelings about the ability of Islam to deliver a system capable of addressing the needs of humans at any time and at any place; he says, "I believe that if a man like him were to assume the dictatorship of the modern world he would succeed in solving its problems in a way that would bring it the much needed peace and happiness: I have prophesied about the faith of Mohammad that it would be acceptable to the Europe of tomorrow as it is beginning to be acceptable to the Europe of today."

Michael Hart[191] placed Prophet Mohammad on the top of the first one hundred most influential people in the history of mankind. Hart justified his decision to pick Mohammad to top the list of the greatest people by giving the following account: "He was the only man in history who was supremely successful on both the secular and religious level. It is probable that the relative influence of Mohammad on Islam has been larger than the combined influence of Jesus Christ and St. Paul on Christianity. It is this unparalleled combination of secular and religious influence which I feel entitles Mohammad to be considered the most influential single figure in human history." Similar to Michael Hart, Dr. William Draper[192] asserts that Prophet Mohammad has exercised the greatest influence upon the human race. In the preface to his translation of the Holy Quran, John Rodwell[193] made similar observations on Prophet Mohammad's career as a wonderful instance of the force and life that resides in him who possesses an intense faith in God and in the unseen world. Rodwell asserts that "he (Mohammad) will always be regarded as one of those who have had that influence over the faith, morals and whole earthly life of their fellow men, which none but a really great man ever did, or can exercise; and whose efforts to propagate a great verity will prosper."

Commenting on the common view held by Western people about the life of Mohammad and his ability to lead a nation into prosperity, stability, and global outreach, W. Montgomery Watt[194] admires Mohammad's integrity which is manifested through his readiness to undergo persecution for his beliefs and through the high moral character of the men who believed in him and looked up to him as a leader, and the greatness of his ultimate achievement. Further to these remarks, Montgomery believes that embedded in the Quran and other expressions of the Islamic vision are vast stores of divine truth from which he and other occidentals have still much to learn. In his views, Islam is a strong contender for the supplying the basic framework of the one religion of the future.

One of the greatest contributions and achievements of Islam was its ability to transform nomad Arab tribes into a civilized society with global reach. Before Islam, the Arabs were mostly scattered tribes across the desert that did not leave any significant trace of civilization. The Islamic transformation of the Arabs into a new global entity with a well-defined mission and a civilized method was recognized by British historian Arthur Glyn Leonard in *Islam, Her Moral and Spiritual Values*. He observes, "It was the genius of Muhammad, the spirit that he breathed into the Arabs through the soul of Islam that exalted them. That raised them out of the lethargy and low level of tribal stagnation up to the high watermark of national unity and empire. It was in the sublimity of Muhammad's deism, the simplicity, the sobriety and purity it inculcated the fidelity of its founder to his own tenets, that acted on their moral and intellectual fiber with all the magnetism of true inspiration."

The ideological transformation of Arabs into a nation with an outstanding character, which surpassed many of the existing ones at the time, was also recognized by professor emeritus of Semitic literature at Princeton University Philip K. Hitti[195] in is book *History of the Arabs: From the Earliest Times to Present*. According to Hitti, "Within a brief span of mortal life, Mohammad called forth of unpromising material, a nation, never welded before; in a country that was hitherto but a geographical expression he established a religion which in vast areas suppressed Christianity and Judaism, and laid the basis of an empire that was soon to embrace within its far flung boundaries the fairest provinces the then civilized world."

One of the main reasons for the successful implementation of the Islamic ideology is the strict separation of the personal selfish motives from the overall objectives of the mission of Islam. This was observed by American historian Washington Irving[196] in his article "Mahomet and His Successors." Irving sums up the integrity and ideological character of Prophet Mohammad in these words: "In his private dealings he was just. He treated friends and strangers, the rich and poor, the powerful and weak, with equity, and was beloved by the common people for the affability with which he received them, and listened to their complaints." This unique character granted Islam a powerful momentum which lasted for centuries ahead. Irving continues saying, "His military triumphs awakened neither pride nor vain glory, as they would have done had they been affected for selfish purposes. In the time of his greatest power he maintained the same simplicity of manners and appearance as in the days of his adversity. So far from affecting a regal state, he was displeased if, on entering a room, any unusual testimonials of respect were shown to him. If he aimed at a universal dominion, it was the dominion of faith; as to the temporal rule which grew up in his hands, as he used it without ostentation, so he took no step to perpetuate it in his family."

One of the greatest achievements of Islam throughout its implementation history was its ability to melt multiple nations and races into one Islamic nation (*Ummah*) with bonds of brotherhood and faith. Canon Taylor,[197] in a paper read before the Church Congress at Wolverhampton in 1887, makes the following observation: "Islam gives hope to the slave, brotherhood to mankind, and recognition of the fundamental facts of human nature." This fact was also recognized by historian R. L. Mellema, who notes that the doctrine of brotherhood of Islam extends to all human beings, no matter what color, race, or creed. He further contends that Islam is the only religion which has been able to realize this doctrine in practice. Indeed, Muslims, wherever on the world they are, will recognize each other as brothers, even when Islam as an ideology is not at the ruling level.

The British historian *H. A. R. Gibb*[198] observes that Islam possesses a magnificent tradition of interracial understanding and cooperation, in a manner that no other society has such a record of success uniting in an equality of status, of opportunity, and of endeavors so many and so various races of mankind. Note that this power stems from the foundation of Islam, which, if utilized, still has the capacity to reconcile apparently irreconcilable elements of race and tradition faced by the world community today. The extinction of race consciousness as between Muslims is one of the outstanding achievements of Islam. In the contemporary world, which is ravaged by racial divides, there is a crying need for the propagation of this Islamic virtue. This virtue of Islam gained the appreciation of prominent historians, including Arnold Toynbee,[199] who analyzed with great scrutiny world civilizations.

Contrary to the myth propagated in the mass media that terrorism is rooted within Islam, the history of the Islamic civilization during the periods of Islamic rule points to the other direction. The British historian Wells (1866-1946)[200] appreciated the fact that the Islamic teachings integrate great traditions for equitable and gentle dealings and behavior. According to Wells, the Islamic doctrine inspires people with nobility and tolerance. Wells further admires the highest order values advanced by Islam and at the same time practicable. He also notes that Islam brought into existence a society in which hard-heartedness and collective oppression and injustice were the least as compared with all other societies. The British historian concludes with this testimony, "Islam is replete with gentleness, courtesy, and fraternity."

The Indian politician and activist Sarojini Naidu[201] also appreciated the justice inherent within the message of Islam. She contemplated that the sense of justice is one of the most wonderful ideals of Islam. She wrote, "As I read in the Qur'an I find those dynamic principles of life, not mystic but practical ethics for the daily conduct of life suited to the whole world."[202]

The other area of contention is the way Muslims and Islam deal with non-Muslims. The fear that Islam and Muslims may subjugate non-Muslims to hardships and deny them their basic rights as citizens is not founded. On the contrary, the Islamic civilization throughout its prevailing period is a great testimony to the fairness of Islam towards non-Muslims. Addison James Thayer studied the relations between Muslims and non-Muslims and concludes that even after the crusade wars, Muslim rulers seldom made their Christian subjects suffer for the Crusades.[203] He writes, "When the Muslims resumed full control of Palestine, the Christians were given a good status and experienced enlightened justice." Addison James also notes that under the Crusaders, Christians were forbidden access to the shrines, and not until the Muslim victories could they enjoy their rights as Christians.

The level of advancement achieved by the Islamic ideology throughout its implementation is widely recognized by scholars and historians. UCLA professor of sociology and physiology Jared Diamond[204] remarkably summarized how Islam excelled at the time when Europe lagged behind. He writes, "Medieval Islam was technologically advanced and open to innovation. It achieved far higher literacy rates than in contemporary Europe; it assimilated the legacy of classical Greek civilization to such a degree that many classical books are now known to us only through Arabic copies. It invented windmills, trigonometry, lateen sails and made major advances in metallurgy, mechanical and chemical engineering and irrigation methods. In the middle-ages the flow of technology was overwhelmingly from Islam to Europe rather from Europe to Islam. Only after the 1500's did the net direction of flow begin to reverse."

The testimonials facts on the Islamic civilization in terms of tolerance, brotherhood, justice, fairness, prosperity, advancement, and human rights are abundant. The idea here is not to provide a lesson of history. Rather, it is to quell the fear that has swamped the hearts of many due to links between Islam and terrorism, or Islam and unfair treatment of people, or Islam and backwardness. The observations made by historians, politicians, scholars, and writers all indicate that Islam and its civilization is far from any of these negative connotations.

4

Final Word

The second rise of Islam is imminent. As Patrick Buchanan writes, it is an idea whose time has come. But this should not be taken as an alarm for which the sirens of fear should be blown. Islam is not a religion made out of vengeance or hatred. It is not an ideology made to benefit the few and subjugate the multitude. The overwhelming facts both in theory and practice provide compelling evidence that Islam, once implemented in a system, and practiced in real life, and allowed to build its civilization, will bring the humanity the much-needed peace, security, prosperity, and justice.

Today, more than any other time in history, the world at large is living in a state of despair, a state of falling moral and ethics, a state of the rich ruling over the poor, a state of collapsing empires, a state in which man-made gods are no longer able to sustain sovereignty or keep the worshipers. This is the time for the rise of the one-god system, the god who is full of mercy, who has no biases towards the rich, or the white, or the black, or the west, or the north, or any kind of bias. This is the time for the rise of a new system which creates a balance of wealth distribution, and a balance of the laws with one and only one standard.

This is a call for the people to think and consider alternatives. Islam is not a religion or ideology which imposes itself upon people. It does, however, compel its ideas upon the minds, and it is up to the rationalistic mind to accept or reject.

Completed on Wednesday the 10th of February 2010
Mohammad Malkawi

REFERENCES (PART 2 AND 3)

1. Letter to the Reverend Ensor Walters (1933), as quoted in *Bernard Shaw: Collected Letters, 1926-1950* (1988) by Dan H. Laurence, p. 305.
2. 1. Noah Feldman, *"The Fall and Rise of the Islamic State,"* Princeton University Press, 2008, ISBN:978-0-691-12045-4.
3. 1. Patrick Buchanan, "An Idea Whose Time Has Come," www.Townhall.com June 2006.
4. The List: The World's Fastest-Growing Religions, *"Foreign Policy,"* May 2007, http://www.foreignpolicy.com/story/cms.php?story_id=3835 (Islam is the fastest-growing religion in the world at an annual rate of 1.84%).
5. http://en.wikipedia.org/wiki/Ideology.
6. Kennedy, Emmet (1979) *"Ideology" from Destutt De Tracy to Marx*, Journal of the History of Ideas, Vol. 40, No. 3 (Jul.-Sep., 1979), pp. 353-368 http://www.jstor.org/pss/2709242.
7. David F. Forte, *"Understanding Islam and the Radicals,"* Heritage Foundation Lecture #718, October 12, 2001.
8. Eliade, Mircea. *Encyclopedia of Religion*. New York: Macmillan, 1987.
9. Quran, Surah # 106, verses 1-4 ([1] (It is a great Grace and Protection from Allâh, for the taming of the Quraish, We cause the Quraish caravans to set forth safe in winter [to the south], and in summer [to the north without any fear], So let them worship [Allâh] the Lord of this House [the Ka'bah in MeccaMecca]. [He] Who has fed them against hunger, and has made them safe from fear).
10. Ibn Katheer, "Interpretation of the Quran," Chapter 6 Verse 144. Ibn Katheer reported that Amr Bin Luhay was given the title of "The Lord" in Mecca for his wealth and leadership. He introduced idols to the society of Mecca.
11. http://ar.wikipedia.org/.

12. Al-Qurtubi, "Interpretation of the Quran," Chapter 8 Verse 35. Al-Qurtubi reports on the authority of Ibn Abbas that Quraish and the Arabs used to circulate the Ka'aba whistling and nude.
13. Quran, Surah # 96, verse 1.
14. Quran, Surah # 96, verse 19.
15. Quran, Surah # 28, verses 76-83 (details of the story of Qarun).
16. Quran, Surah # 82, verses 1-5.
17. Quran, Surah # 89, verses 17-20.
18. Quran, Surah # 30, verse 39.
19. Quran, Surah # 68, verse 9-13 and Surah # 111, verse 1-3.
20. Biography of Prophet Mohammad by Ibn Hisham.
21. Quran, Surah #4, verses 1-5.
22. Quran, Surah # 8, verses 1-12; Surah #9 1-5; Surah 47 and 48.
23. Quran, Surah #2, verse 282.
24. Book of Hadith, Sahih Muslim, Narration # 2363.
25. Taqiuddin al-Nabhani, "The Islamic State," 1953.
26. Quran, Surah #3, verse 103 "Recall the favor of Allah upon you: you were once rivals; Allah has united your hearts and created among you brotherhood."
27. Quran, Surah 59, verse 9 "They give them (the emigrants) preference over themselves even though they were in need of that food . . ."
28. Quran, Surah # 34, verse 54 "And We have not sent you (O Muhammad) except as a giver of glad tidings and a warner to all mankind, but most of men know not."
29. Quran, Surah # 49, verse 13 "O mankind! We have created you from a male and a female, and made you into nations and tribes, that you may know one another. Verily, the most honorable of you with Allâh is that who has more piety."
30. Lynn H. Nelson "Lectures for A Medieval Survey," *The ORB: On-Line Reference Book for Medieval Studies*, http://www.the-orb.net/textbooks/nelson/islam.html.
31. Ibn Katheer, *"Al-Bidaya Wal Nihayah,"* History book by Ibn Katheer: The Start and the End.
32. Peter Stearns, et. al. The First Global Civilization: The Rise and Spread of Islma" in "World Civilizations: The Global Experience."
33. Carly Fiorina, speech at a conference in Minnesota under the tile "Technology, Business and our Way of Life: What is Next," September 26, 2001.
34. Ira Marvin Lapidus "A History of Islamic Society" p. 309, Cambridge University Press, ISBN-13: 9780521779333.
35. Lamartine, comments on Prophet Mohammad in his "Histoire de la Turquie," Paris, 1854.
36. Quran, Surah # 3, verse 31 "Say (O Mohammad) if you really love Allâh then follow me. Allâh will love you and forgive you your sins."

37. Quran, Surah # 59, verse 7 "And whatsoever the Messenger (Muhammad [peace be upon him]) gives you, take it; and whatsoever he forbids you, abstain (from it)."
38. Quran, Surah # 6, verse 50; Surah # 7, verse 102; Surah #10, verse 15 and 109; Surah # 11, verse 12.
39. Quran, Surah # 2, verse 245 "Who is he that will lend to Allâh a goodly loan so that He may multiply it to him many times? And it is Allâh that decreases or increases (your provisions), and unto Him you shall return."
40. Taqiuddin al-Nabhani, "Concepts of Hizb Ut-Tahrir," 2005, pp. 3-5.
41. Abdelqadeem Zallum, "How the Khilafah Was Destroyed," 3rd edition 1990.
42. Adeed Dawisha "Requiem for Arab Nationalism," Middle East Forum, Vol.10, No.1 Winter, 2003 available from the web adress http://www.meforum.org/article/518.
43. Bassam Tibi, Arab Nationalism between Islam and Nation State (London: MacMillan,1997).
44. Global Corruption Report 2007, http://www.transparency.org/publications/publications/gcr_2007. Retrieved 2007-10-27.
45. Sir John Davenport, "Arabs Element of Dominance During the Medieval Ages."
46. Human Watch Report "Syria's Tadmor Prison Dissent Still Hostage to a Legacy of Terror," 1996, Vol. 8, NO. 2 (E).
47. http://ar.wikipedia.org.
48. Rashid Rida, "The History of Imam Mohammad Abdo—*Tarikh Alustad Al-Imam Al-Shaikh Mohammad Abdo*," 2nd edition, 2006.
49. Syed Qutb, *Fi Zilal Al-Quran*, (Living under the shadow of the Quran).
50. Syed Qutb, *"Milestones."*
51. Abul A'ala Al-Mawdoodi, *"The Principles of Islam"* and *"Tafheem Al-Islam."*
52. Syed Qutb from (Muslim Brotherhood) executed in Egypt 1966; Abdel Aziz Badr (Hizb Ut-Tahrir) executed in Iraq 1969.
53. Angel M. Rabasa, et al. "The Muslim World after 9/11," Rand Corporation Report, ISBN 0-8330-3534-7, 2004.
54. Hadeeth, "Sunnan Al-Baihaqi," Hadeeth No 17097.
55. Surah # 58, verse 4 "And he who finds not the money for freeing a slave must fast two successive months before they both touch each other. And for him who is unable to do so, should feed sixty poor people. That is in order that you may have perfect Faith in Allâh and His Messenger. These are the limits set by Allâh. And for disbelievers, there is a painful torment."
56. Surah # 59, verse 7.
57. Surah # 30, verse 40.
58. Surah # 35, verse 3.

59. Surah # 30, verse 37-39 "Do they not see that Allah increases the provision for whom He wills and straitens it for whom He wills. Verily, in that are indeed signs for a people who believe. So give to the kindred his due, and to Al-Miskîn (the poor) and to the wayfarer. That is best for those who seek Allah's Countenance; and it is they who will be successful. And that usury which you take in order that it may increase at the expense of other people's money, has no increase with Allah; but that which you give in Zakah (charity) seeking Allah's Countenance, then those they shall have manifold increase"
60. Corinne Asells, "Food Prices Continue to Increase," Suite101.com, http://world-hunger.suite101.com/article.cfm/world_hunger_crisis.
61. Surah # 59, verse 9, "And those who ... had adopted the Faith, love those who emigrate to them, and have no jealousy in their breasts for that which they have been given, and give them (emigrants) preference over themselves even though they were in need of that. And whosoever is saved from his own covetousness, such are they who will be the successful.
62. Surah # 3, verses 14-15, "Beautified for men is the love of things they covet; women, children, much of gold and silver (wealth), branded beautiful horses, cattle and well-tilled land. This is the pleasure of the present world's life; but Allah has the excellent return (Paradise with flowing rivers) with Him. Say: 'Shall I inform you of things far better than those? For Al-Muttaqûn (the pious) there are Gardens (Paradise) with their Lord, underneath which rivers flow. Therein (is their) eternal (home) and purified mates or wives. And Allah will be pleased with them. And Allah is All-Seer of the (His) slaves.'"
63. Hadeeth, narrated by Ahmad in the Musnad under Hadeeth number 4880; and by Al-Hakim.
64. Hadeeth, narrated by Al-Tabarani on the authority of Ibn Abbas, and by Al-Hakim on the authority of Aisha.
65. Surah # 9, verse 60, "As-Sadaqât (here it means Zakah) are only for the Fuqarâ' (poor), and Al-Masâkin (the very poor) and those employed to collect (the funds), and to attract the hearts of those who have been inclined (towards Islâm); and to free the captives, and for those in debt, and for Allâh's Cause (i.e., for Mujâhidûn—those fighting in a holy battle), and for the wayfarer (a traveler who is cut off from everything); a duty imposed by Allâh. And Allâh is All-Knower, All-Wise.
66. Surah # 2, verse 184 "And as for those who can not fast (due to age or permanent illness), they can feed a Miskeen (poor person) for every day of Ramadan."
67. Hadeeth, "Sahih Al-Bukhari," # 6164 and "Sahih Muslim," # 2599.
68. Surah # 5, verse 89 "Allah will not hold you liable for casual oaths, but He will hold you liable for your deliberate oaths; for the expiation of a deliberate oath, you are required to feed ten Miskeen (hungry poor persons), on a scale

69. Surah # 17, verse 26 and Surah # 30, verse 38.
70. Surah # 69, verses 33-34 "Verily, He used not to believe in Allah, the Most Great. And urged not on the feeding of Al-Miskeen (the poor)."
71. Surah # 89, verses 17-18 "Nay! But you treat not the orphans with kindness and generosity. And urge not one another on the feeding of Miskeen (the poor)."
72. Surah 90, verses 12-16 "The real challenge is to give food in a day of hunger (famine); To an orphan near of kin. Or to a Miskeen (poor) cleaving to dust (out of misery)."
73. Surah # 76, verse 8.
74. Abel Rahman Al-Maliki, "The Perfect Political Economy," 1963.
75. Surah # 20, verse 14 "Verily! I am Allâh! none has the right to be worshiped but I, so worship Me, and perform prayer for My Remembrance."
76. Surah # 2, verse 183 "O you who believe! Observing As-Saum (the fasting) is prescribed for you as it was prescribed for those before you, that you may become Al-Muttaqûn (the pious)."
77. Surah # 3, verses 134 "Those who spend in prosperity and in adversity, who repress anger, and who pardon men; verily, Allah loves the good-doers."
78. Surah # 17, verse 70 "And indeed We have honored the Children of Adam, and We have carried them on land and sea, and have provided them with good things, and have preferred them above many of those whom We have created with a marked preferment."
79. Surah # 17, verse 23 "And your Lord has decreed that you worship none but Him. And that you be dutiful to your parents. If one of them or both of them attain old age in your life, say not to them a word of disrespect, nor shout at them but address them in terms of honor."
80. Surah # 28, verses 76-83.
81. Abu Yousuf, Yakub Ibn Habib Ibn Ibraheem Al-Ansari. He lived between AH 113 and 182. Abu Yousuf was the student of Iman Abu Hanifah, the prominent scholar of the Hanafi school of thought. Abu Yousuf served as the chief judge for Harun Al-Rasheed. He wrote *Al-Kharaj* in response to a request from Caliph Harun Al-Rasheed who wanted a detailed reference of the economic principles and system in Islam.
82. Harun Al-Rasheed is the fifth caliph in the Abbasi Islamic Dynasty. He ruled in the period 786-809 AC (AH 170-193).
83. Abu Hanifah Al-Numan (699-767 AC, AH 80-150), the founder of the Hanafi school of thought.
84. Imam Ja'afar Al-Sadiq (703-765 AC, AH 83-148), the founder of the Ja'afari (Shi'i) school of thought.

85. Malim Bin Anas (715-798 AC, AH 93-179), the founder of the Maliki school of thought.
86. Mohammad Bin Idrees Al-Shafi'i (766-819 AC, AH 150-204), the founder of the Shafi'i schoold of thought and the author of the Islamic laws reference "Al-Um" (the Mother of Laws). Al-Shafi'i founded the principles of *Fiqh* (jurisprudence).
87. Ahmad Bin Hanbal (780-855 AC, AH 164-241), the founder of the Hanbali school of thought.
88. Taqiuddin al-Nabhani, "The Economic System in Islam," 1953.
89. Al-Maliki, same as reference 74.
90. Mohammad Baqir Al-Sadr, "Iqtisaduna," Dar Al-Kutb Al-Lubnani, 1978.
91. Adnan Khalid Turkmani, "Islamic Economic Trend," 1990.
92. Surah # 3, verse 14.
93. Hadeeth narrated by Ahmad and Abu Dawoud.
94. Kanz Al-Ummal, Hadeeth # 5533.
95. Surah # 4, verse 2 "And give unto orphans their property and do not exchange (your) bad things for (their) good ones; and devour not their substance (by adding it) to your substance. Surely, this is a great sin."
96. Surah # 8, verse 36 "36 Verily, those who disbelieve spend their wealth to hinder (men) from the Path of Allah, and so will they continue to spend it; but in the end it will become an anguish for them. Then they will be overcome. And those who disbelieve will be gathered unto Hell."
97. Surah # 9, verse 81 "Those hypocrites who stayed away (from Tabuk expedition) rejoiced in their staying behind the Messenger of Allah; they hated to strive and fight with their properties and their lives in the Cause of Allah, and they said: 'March not forth in the heat.' Say: 'The Fire of Hell is more intense in heat,' if only they could understand!"
98. Hadeeth narrated by Al-Bukhari, vol. 5, # 125.
99. See reference 88; pp.75-85.
100. Al-Shafi'i, "Kitab Al-Umm," Bab: Ihia' Al-Mawat, and Musnad Ahmad Ibn Hanbal.
101. Surah # 16, verse 14 "And He it is Who has subjected the sea (to you), that you eat thereof fresh tender meat (i.e., fish), and that you bring forth out of it ornaments to wear."
102. Surah # 5, verse 4 "They ask you what is lawful for them Say: 'Lawful unto you are all kind of foods which Allah has made lawful. And those beasts and birds of prey which you have trained as hounds, training and teaching them (to catch) in the manner as directed to you by Allah; so eat of what they catch for you, but pronounce the Name of Allah over it, and fear Allah. Verily, Allah is Swift in reckoning.'"

103   Hadeeth narrated by Anas Bin Malik "The Messenger of Allah cursed ten types of people regarding alcohol: its presser, the one who asks for it to be pressed, its drinker, its carrier, the one to whom it is carried, the one who serves it, its seller, the one for whom it is sold, its purchaser and the one for whom it is purchased."

104   Hadeeth narrated by Ibn Maja, "That the Prophet cursed the one who takes usury, his agent, its two witnesses and the one who writes the contract."

105   Shafi'i school, Tuhfat Al-Muhtaj Fi Sharh Al-Minhaj, Section on Farming, Volume 6.

106   Surah # 4, verses 11-12 "Allah commands you as regards your inheritance: to the male, a portion equal to that of two females; if there are only daughters, two or more, their share is two-thirds of the inheritance; if only one, her share is half. For parents, a sixth share of inheritance to each if the deceased left children; if no children, and the parents are the only heirs, the mother has a third; if the deceased left brothers or (sisters), the mother has a sixth. (The distribution in all cases is) after the payment of legacies he may have bequeathed or debts. You know not which of them, whether your parents or your children, are nearest to you in benefit; (these fixed shares) are ordained by Allah. And Allah is Ever All-Knower, All-Wise."

107   Hadeeth narrated by Abu Dawoud in the book of inheritance, "I inherit anyone who leaves no inheritors behind."

108   Hadeeth narrated by Bukhari.

109   Hadeeth narrated by Abu Umama, *"There is no amputation in time of famine."*

110   Ibn' Asakir narrated that the Prophet also said, "Exchange gifts amongst yourselves so that you love each other."

111   Hadeeth narrated by Bukhari, "Sa'ad ibn Waqqas said: 'I was ill once to the point I was approaching death. The Prophet came to visit me. So I said: "O Messenger of Allah, I have great wealth, and nobody inherits from me except my daughter. Can I bequeath (in a will) two thirds of my property?" He said: "No." I said: "Half of it?" He said: "No." I said: "One third of it?" He said: "The third is big (enough). It is better to leave your children rich than to leave them poor and begging from the people.""'

112   Hadeeth narrated by An-Nisai, "the Prophet wrote a letter to the people of Yemen and he sent it with Amr ibn Hazm; it included "The blood money for the (killed) person is 100 camels."

113   Hadeeth narrated by Ahmad and Abu Dawoud, "People are partnership in their ownership of forests, water and fire."

114   Hadeeth narrated by Tirmidhi, "Abyadh ibn Hammal came to the Prophet and asked him to grant him a salt laden land, and he granted it to him. And when he left, one person in attendance with the Prophet said: Do you know

what you granted him? You granted him the uncountable water. He then took it away from him."

115 See for example the book of *Al-Amwal* by Abu Obaid, *Al-Kharaj* by Abu Yousuf, *Iqtisaduna* by Al-Sadr, *The Economic System in Islam* by An-Nabhani.
116 Abu Obaid, the book of *Amwal*; section on *Kharaj*.
117 See reference 82.
118 See reference 81.
119 Abu Zakaria Al-Qurashi, book Al-Kharaj, AH 203. Qudamah Bin Ja'afar, book Al-Kharaj and Documentation, AH 328.
120 http://www.hp.com/hpinfo/execteam/speeches/fiorina/minnesota01.htm.
121 Hadeeth narrated by Bukhari, # 479.
122 Haddeth narrated by Al-Tabarani in the book Awsat, # 891.
123 Surah # 9, verse 105 "And say (O Muhammad) 'Do deeds! Allah will see your deeds, and (so will) His Messenger and the believers.'"
124 Surah # 30, verse 39 "And that usurious money which you give to others, in order that it may increase from other people's wealth, has no increase with Allah; but that which you give in Zakat seeking Allah's Countenance, then those they shall have manifold increase."
125 David Astle, "The Babylonian Wow," http://download.cxs2.info/the_babylonian_woe.pdf.
126 Houghton Mifflin (Publishers): *Encyclopedia of World History*, P. 48 ; Boston ; 1940.
127 The Arden Shakespeare, "The Merchant of Venice," edited by H.L Withers, D. C. Heath Company, London.
128 Richard Wolf, "Capitalism Hits the Fan," http://video.google.com/videoplay?docid=7382297202053077236#.
129 June Grem, *"The Money Manipulators,"* Enterprise Publications, 1971.
130 Surah # 57, verse 11
131 Surah # 2, verse 276
132 Surah # 2, verse 275
133 Surah # 9, verse 34
134 Al-Qurtubi, "The Compilation of the Rules of the Quran," Surah # 9, verse # 34
135 Surah # 27, verse 27 "He said: I intend to wed one of these two daughters of mine to you, on condition that you serve me for eight years."
136 Goldsborough, Reid, "World's First Coin," Rg.ancients.info. 2003-10-02. http://rg.ancients.info/lion/article.html. Retrieved 2009-04-20.
137 Hadeeth narrated by Abu Dawoud on the authority of Tawoos and Ibn Omar.
138 Hadeeth narrated by An-Nisai on the authority of Amru Ibn Hazm,
139 Hadeeth narrated by Muslim and Bukhari
140 Abdul Malik Bin Marwan (646-705 AC, AH 25-86) was the ninth caliph in Islam.

141. http://www.imf.org/external/np/exr/center/mm/eng/cc_sub_4.htm.
142. George Parker, Tony Barber and Daniel Dombey (October 9, 2008). "Senior figures call for new Bretton Woods ahead of Bank/Fund meetings."
143. Agence France-Presse (AFP) (October 13, 2008). "World needs new Bretton Woods, says Brown."
144. Hadeeth narrated by Muslim on the authority of Abi Said Al-Khudari, Hadeeth # 1548.
145. Hadeeth narrated by Tirmidhi.
146. Hadeeth narrated by Tirmidhi, # 2346 and by Ibn Majah # 4141on the authority of Salmat Bin Obaid Allah Al-Ansari.
147. Hadeeth narrated by Bukhari
148. Haddeth narrated in the Sunnan book on the authority of Ibn Masoud.
149. Hadeeth narrated in "Al-Fawaed by Abu Al-Faraj Al-Asbhani," # 20 on the authority of Al-Miqdam Bin Madi Karb.
150. Hadeeth narrated in "Sunan Abu Dawoud and Anil Al-Awtar," # 2982, on the authority of Kulaib Bin Manfa'ah.
151. Hadeeth narrated by all narrators on the authority of Ibn Omar "Islam is constructed upon five: witness that Allah is the only God and that Mohammad is his Messenger; establish the prayer; provide Zakah; fast the month of Ramadan; and perform pilgrimage (Hajj)."
152. Hadeeth narrated by Bukhari on the authority of Ibn Abbas "The Prophet designated Muath Bin Jbal to Yemen and asked him to inform the new Muslims that Allah obligated upon them a charity to be taken out of the wealth of the rich ones and given to the poor."
153. Al-Amwal in the Khilafah State by Abel Qadim Zallum, 3rd edition, 2004.
154. Al-Alamiah International Islamic Charity Organization Journal, November 2007, # 211.
155. The era of Omar Bin Abdel-Aziz, the 8th Caliph of Bani Umayya (717-720 AC), http://ar.wikipedia.org/wiki/; http://ejabat.google.com/ejabat/thread?tid =140bef0f6d8e07f5&pli=1.
156. Hadeeth narrated by Bukhari, # 5056
157. Quran, Surah # 28, verses 76-83.
158. Elizabeth Mumiller, "21st-Century Warnings of a Threat Rooted in the 7th Century," *New York Times*, Dec. 12, 2005.
159. http://www.obsessionthemovie.com/.
160. Sirat Ibn Hisham—Biography of the Prophet by Ibn Hisham, http://abdurrahman.org/seerah/sirat_ibn_hisham.pdf.
161. Surah #7, verse 28 "And when they commit an evil deed (e.g., going round the Ka'bah in naked state), they say: 'We found our fathers doing it, and Allah has commanded us on it.'"

162. Surah # 10, verse # 78 "They said: 'Have you come to us to turn us away from that (Faith) we found our fathers following, and that you two (Moses and Aaron) may have greatness in the land? We are not going to believe you two!'"
163. Surah 31, verse # 21 "And when it is said to them: 'Follow that which Allâh has sent down,' they say: 'Nay, we shall follow that which we found our fathers (following).' (Would they do so) even if Shaitân (Satan) invites them to the torment of the Fire."
164. Surah 6, verse # 99 "It is He Who sends down water (rain) from the sky, and with it We bring forth vegetation of all kinds, and out of it We bring forth green stalks, from which We bring forth thick clustered grain. And out of the date-palm and its spathe come forth clusters of dates hanging low and near, and gardens of grapes, olives and pomegranates, each similar (in kind) yet different (in variety and taste). Look at their fruits when they begin to bear, and the ripeness thereof. Verily! In these things there are signs for people who believe."
165. Surah 30, verse 21-32.
166. Surah 2, verse #256 "There is no compulsion in religion. Verily, the Right Path has become distinct from the wrong path."
167. Surah 43, verse # 84.
168. Surah 12, verse # 40.
169. The main scholars who compiled the Sunnah of Prophet Mohammad include Imam Bukhari, Imam Muslim, Abu Dawoud, An-Nassai, Ibn Majah, Imam Malik, Al-Tirmidhi, Ibn Ishaq.
170. Books of Quran Tafseer include the books authored by Ibn Katheer, Al-Qurtubi, Al-Tabari, Al-Razi, Al-Nasfi, and many others.
171. Schools of Fiqh include the schools of Imam Abu Hanifah, Imam Ja'afar, Imam Shafi'i, Imam Malik, Imam Ahmad.
172. The Moguls attacked Baghdad and burned its great library in the year 1258 (AH 656).
173. Crusade wars in the period 1096-1291.
174. Edward Montet, "La Propagande Chretienne et ses Adversaries Musulmans," Paris 1890. (Also in T. W. Arnold in "The Preaching of Islam," London 1913.)
175. See for example "Islamic Personality part 1" by Taqiuddin al-Nabhani.
176. See for example the classical books on the history of Islam such as "Al-Bidaya Wal Nihaya—Beginnin and End in History" by Ibn Katheer and "Tareekh Al-Tabari" by Al-Tabari.
177. Edward Gibbon, "The History of the Decline and Fall of the Roman Empire," written 1776-1789, republished by Bibliolife, 2008.

178 Edward Gibbon and Simon Ocklay, History of the Saracen Empire, London 1870, p. 54.
179 Edward Gibbon, same as reference 20.
180 R. Bosworth Smith (1784-1884), "Muhammad and Muhammadenasim," written in 1878, republished by Atlantic in 1996.
181 Arthur Stanley Tritton (1881-1973) was a British historian and scholar of Islam. He was appointed professor of Arabic at the School of Oriental and African Studies, University of London, in 1938, and also spent some time teaching at Aligarh University. He published several studies related to Islamic history including "The Rise of the Imams of Sanaa (1925)," "The Caliphs and their non-Muslim Subjects: A Critical Study of the Covenant of Umar (1930)," and "Islam: Belief and Practices (1951)."
182 A. S. Tritton "Islam: Belief and Practices," 1951.
183 De Lacy Evan s O'Leary (1872-1957), a British historian and scholar of Islam and the Arabic language.
184 De Lacy Evans O'Leary, "Islam at the Cross Roads : A Brief Survey of the Present Position and Problems of the World of Islam." London: Kegan Paul, Trench, Trubner. New York: E. P. Dutton, 1923 A Short History of the Fatimid Khalifate. London 1923.
185 James Michener in "Islam: The Misunderstood Religion," *Reader's Digest*, May 1955, pp. 68-70.
186 Lawrence E. Browne in "The Prospects of Islam," 1944.
187 Alphonse Marie Louis de Prat de Lamartine (October 1790-1869) was a French writer, poet, and politician.
188 http://fr.wikipedia.org/wiki/Histoire_de_la_Turquie.
189 Mahatma Gandhi, statement published in "Young India,"1924.
190 Sir George Bernard Shaw in "The Genuine Islam," Vol. 1, No. 8, 1936.
191 Michael Hart, "The 100, A Ranking of the Most Influential Persons in History," New York, 1978.
192 Dr. William Draper (1811-1882), "History of Intellectual Development of Europe," New York: Harper & brothers, 1876.
193 John Rodwell translation of the Holy Quran, 1861.
194 W. Montgomery Watt in "Muhammad at Mecca," Oxford, 1953.
195 Philip Hitti, "Arab History: From The Ealiest Times to the Present," 6th edition, London, Macmillan & Co. LTD, 1956.
196 Washington Irving (1783-1859) was an American author, essayist, biographer, and historian of the early nineteenth century.
197 Canon Taylor, paper read before the Church Congress at Walverhamton, quoted by Arnoud in The Preaching of Islam, pp. 71-72.
198 H. A. R. Gibb, Whither Islam, London, 1932.

[199] Arnold Joseph Toynbee (1889-1975) was a British historian whose twelve-volume analysis of the rise and fall of civilizations, *A Study of History*, 1934-1961, was a synthesis of world history, a metahistory based on universal rhythms of rise, flowering, and decline, which examined history from a global perspective.

[200] Herbert George Wells (1866-1946) was an English author. He was a prolific writer in many genres, including contemporary novels, history, politics, and social commentary.

[201] Sarojini Naidu (1879-1949) was a child prodigy, freedom fighter, and poet. Naidu was the first Indian woman to become the president of the Indian National Congress and the first woman to become the governor of Uttar Pradesh. She was active in the Indian Independence Movement, joining Mahatma Gandhi in the Salt March to Dandi, and then leading the Dharasana Satyagraha after the arrests of Gandhi, Abbas Tyabji, and Kasturba Gandhi.

[202] Sarojini Naidu (1879-1949), "Lectures on the Ideals of Islam."

[203] Addison, James Thayer. "The Christian Approach to the Moslem." AMS Press, New York, USA. 1966 (1942).

[204] Jared Diamond: UCLA sociologist and physiologist who won the Pulitzer Prize for his book "The Evolution of Religions."

INDEX

A

Abraham. *See* Ibraheem
Abu Bakr Al-Siddiq, 147–48, 169, 200
Abu Dawoud (scholar), 153, 205, 221
Abu Dhar Al-Ghafari, 178, 199
Abu Ghraib, 86
Abu Hanifah Al-Numan, 155, 186
Abu Obaid Al-Qasim Bin Salam, 186, 204
  Al-Amwal, 186, 204, 240
Abu Yousuf Yakub Al-Ansari, 186, 205, 207
  Al-Kharaj, 186
Afghanistan, 31, 83–84, 90, 99, 162–66, 168–69, 249–50
Africa, 67, 73, 83–85, 87, 151, 205, 245, 260
African Americans, 45, 79, 86–87
AIDS, 78–81. *See also* HIV
Al-Amwal (Abu Obaid), 186, 204, 240
al-Bukhari. *See* Bukhari (scholar)
alcoholic drinks, 154, 192
Ali Bin Abi Talib, 178
alimony, 198–99, 237–38, 242
Al-Kharaj (Abu Yousuf), 186
Allah
  commanding support of parents and relatives, 238

  disowning community which allows hunger, 70, 178, 199
  prohibition of usurious acts, 105–6, 173
  providing wealth, 172–75, 177, 183–85, 193, 206, 210
al-Maliki. *See* Maliki, Abel Rahman al-
alms, 173, 199. *See also* charity
Al-Qaeda, 164–65, 250
Al-Qurtubi (Quran commentator), 216
al-Rasheed. *See* Harun al-Rasheed
al-Sadr, Mohammad Baqir. *See* Sadr, Mohammad Baqir al-
Al-Shafi'i (scholar), 155, 186
Amazon.com, 102
American Indians, 86–87, 90
American International Group (AIG), 121
Amnesty International, 85–86, 89, 132
amputation, 199, 220
Andalusia, 150, 160, 244, 250
Angola, 84–85
An-Nisai (hadeeth narrator), 153, 221
Arabian Peninsula, 147, 151, 207
Arab League, 82
Arabs
  diet, 260
  ideological transformation, 141–42, 264–65

nations, 82–83, 157, 159–60, 162, 166
units of exchange, 219–20, 222
Argentina, 85, 111
Arthur Andersen, 102
Atatürk, Mustafa Kemal, 18, 155, 157, 162
Austria, 113
automation, 43, 209
automotive industry, 62, 95, 102, 120–21, 125, 188, 212

B

Ba'ath party, 162, 166
Bahrain, 24, 204, 249
Baker, James, 84
Balcerowicz, Leszek, 20
Ban Ki-moon, 72
bankruptcy, 97, 102, 110, 121, 212
banks, 104–9, 212–13, 215–18
basic needs, 41–42, 48–49, 59–60, 180, 185, 189, 196
  satisfaction of, 190, 225–26, 234–36, 241–43
  support of children, parents, and relatives, 236–38
  zakah fund for, 239, 241
Bear Stearns, 38, 97, 102, 108, 121, 125
Bernanke (Federal Reserve chief), 38, 97, 108, 121
blood money, 220
Bretton Woods Agreement, 25, 114–17, 119, 223–24, 230
Brown, Gordon, 223
Brown, Larry, 71
  Hunger in America, 71
Browne, Laurence, 261
Brzezinski, Zbigniew, 21, 131
Buchanan, Patrick, 18, 136, 139, 268
Bukhari (scholar), 153, 220–21
Burkina Faso, 75
Bush, George H., 84, 95
Bush, George W., 21, 87, 89
buying power, 227–29, 232

C

caliphs, 147–49, 160, 178, 181, 186, 200, 242–43, 252
capitalism
  in action, 46, 64–65, 67–68, 70–71, 191
  complex system, 33, 35
  concept of value, 52–53
  definition of, 29, 120
  fault model, 33, 35
  faults in system of, 17, 20, 23, 35–40, 42–43, 50, 60–61, 99, 120
  historical perspective, 29–30, 32
  principles of, 38–39
  renaming of, 123–24, 126
  signs of failure, 19, 29, 57, 75, 91, 98, 120, 124, 173, 179
Carter, Jimmy, 21, 84, 128
  Our Endangered Values, 21
cattle, 135, 174–75, 183, 201, 240, 243
central banks, 115–16, 224, 232
Chad, 75
charity, 46, 71, 140–41, 173, 193, 208
  forms of, 58, 236
  zakah, 145, 152, 179, 214, 239
China, 58, 79, 225–26, 233
Christians, 23, 261, 264–65, 267
Chrysler, 121, 125
commodities
  relationship with needs, 38–39
  relative shortage of, 39–40, 48
  values of, 50–52, 99, 181, 183, 197, 219–20
communism, 15, 18–19, 30, 43, 61–62, 85
compensation, 45, 51, 55, 57, 200, 217, 239
Concepts of Hizb ut-Tahrir (Nabhani), 156
consumer price index (CPI), 69–70, 159
consumption, 36, 51–52, 54–57, 59–60, 72, 176, 185–86, 215, 218

corruption, 21, 62–63, 135, 150, 157, 159–60
corruption perception index, 159–60
CPI. *See* consumer price index
credit system, 56, 96, 109, 211
currencies
  exchange rates of, 113–14, 221, 230–33
  methods of issuing, 108, 229–30

D

Davenport, John, 160
debt, 78, 93, 199
  in ancient Greece, 211
  in Islam, 238–40
  national, 63, 109–11
democracy, 17, 30–31, 89–90, 248–49
Depression, 19, 94, 113–14, 117, 223
Diamond, Jared, 267
diamonds, 84–85
dinar, 219–22, 228, 231
dirham, 207, 219, 221–22, 228, 233
discrimination, 44, 86–89
dollar
  convertibility of, 114–16, 230–31
  as reserve currency, 117, 225
Draper, William, 264

E

Ebeling, Richard, 124
economic crisis, 19, 21–22, 37
economic products. *See* products
economic system, 42, 45, 49, 64–65, 223
  in Islam, 170–71, 173, 176–77, 180, 185, 187, 196, 241
  principles of, 72, 81, 122, 124, 126–27, 218
  versus economic science, 43
Economic System in Islam, The (Nabhani), 38, 187
education, 23, 77, 240–41

as basic need, 38, 63, 81, 179, 226
correlation with poverty, 74–75
Egypt, 47, 89, 158, 160–63, 165, 167, 209, 249
electricity, 112, 202
Empire of Wealth, An (Gordon), 22
employment, 195–96, 198. *See also* labor
End of History and the Last Man, The (Fukuyama), 123
energy production, 54, 202
Engel, Ernst, 176
Engels, Friedrich, 14, 30, 36, 93
Enron, 102, 104, 130
Equal Pay Act, 44
Ethiopia, 18, 79, 89, 111
exchange rates, 113, 224, 231–33

F

Fall and Rise of the Islamic State, The (Feldman), 18, 152, 155
Faqueer, 179, 239
fasting, 179, 181
Federal Reserve, 96, 100, 105, 108–11, 116, 121, 229
Feldman, Noah, 18, 136, 152, 154–55
  The Fall and Rise of the Islamic State, 18, 152, 155
financial crisis, 17, 19–20, 24, 37, 65, 99, 119, 121
  how Islam relates to, 24–25
  moral crisis behind, 21–23, 31, 95, 215
  See also economic crisis
Fiorina, Carly, 58, 152, 209
Fiqh (jurisprudence), 186, 257
Fisher, Irving, 100
fluctuations, 53, 99, 105, 117, 184, 197, 221, 232
Food and Agriculture Organization (FAO), 67, 73
Forte, David F., 140
Fountainhead, The (Rand), 60

Fowler, Henry H., 115
France, 57, 82–83, 112–13, 187, 226, 248
Friedman, Milton, 30–31, 38, 45, 120
Fukuyama, Francis, 17, 30, 123
  The End of History and the Last Man, 123
Fuqarâ'. *See* Faqueer

G

Gandhi, Mahatma, 263
Gates, Bill, 103, 124
GDP. *See* gross domestic product
General Motors (GM), 121, 125, 212–13
genocide, 90
Gibb, H. A. R., 135, 266
Gibbon, Edward, 260
  The History of the Decline and Fall of the Roman Empire, 260
globalization, 64–65, 83, 164
GM. *See* General Motors
GNP. *See* gross national product
gold
  hoarding of, 116, 214, 220
  polarization, 225
  price of, 117, 229
  reserves, 115–16, 223–26
  weight of, 221
gold standard, 25, 68, 70, 228, 231–33
  benefits of, 223–27
  and virtual economy, 112–15, 117–20
  See also silver standard
Gordon, John Steele, 22
  An Empire of Wealth, 22
grants, 200–201, 203
gross domestic product (GDP), 40, 111, 158, 179, 235
gross national product (GNP), 40–41, 66, 68, 235
Guantánamo prison, 86
Guinea, 75

H

Hadeeth, 203, 205
Haiti, 65, 67
Hamas, 167, 250
Hart, Michael, 264
Harun al-Rasheed, 186, 205
health, 48–49, 234
  catastrophes in developing world, 78–79, 81
  insecurity of, 76–78
  insurance, 77–79, 88
Hewlett-Packard (HP), 58, 151
Hezbollah, 167
Hispanics, 45, 76–77, 80
History of the Arabs (Hitti), 265
History of the Decline and Fall of the Roman Empire, The (Gibbon), 260
Hitti, Philip, 265
  History of the Arabs, 265
HIV, 78–80. *See also* AIDS
Hizb ut-Tahrir, 156, 162, 165
hoarding
  gold and silver, 220
  money, 214–16, 220
  prohibition of, 214–18, 220, 233
How the Khilafah Was Destroyed (Zallum), 157
HP. *See* Hewlett-Packard
human rights, 85–86
Human Rights Watch (HRW), 85–86, 89
Hungary, 111, 113
hunger, 178–80, 199
  insecurity of food supply, 70–72
  in the world, 72–74
Hunger in America (Brown), 71

I

Ibn Hanbal, Ahmad, 155, 186
Ibn Hisham (biographer), 251
Ibn Katheer (historian), 152
Ibraheem (prophet), 141–43

Ijtihad, 156–57
IMF. *See* International Monetary Fund
imperialism, 83
India, 58, 79, 156, 162, 225–26
Indonesia, 207
InfoSpace, 102
inheritance, 27, 146, 149, 195, 197–98, 200, 208, 237, 240
innovation, 58, 177, 209–10, 267
interest, 39, 102, 105–7, 109, 111, 142. *See also* usury
International Labor Organization, 89
International Monetary Fund (IMF), 49, 65, 81–83, 111–12, 114–15
Internet, 95, 101
investment, 29, 106–7, 147, 182, 213, 217
Iqtisaduna (Al-Sadr), 38, 130, 187
Iran, 18, 84, 160–61, 163, 167–69, 187
Iraq, 90, 99, 161, 165–66, 200, 205, 207
Irving, Washington, 265
Islam
  decline of, 155–57
  economic system, 105, 168–71, 176, 180, 186–87, 227, 251
  expansion of, 150–54
  foundation of, 141, 158, 170, 251, 253–55, 261, 263, 266
  ideology of, 139–40, 148, 169–70, 254
  monetary system, 218–21, 223, 233
  political economy, 63, 185–88, 209, 214, 216, 218, 221–22, 234, 236
  rise of, 16, 135, 137–38, 150, 158, 160–62, 164–66, 244, 247, 268
  structure of, 138, 146–49
  value definition in, 181, 183, 185
Islam, Her Moral and Spiritual Value (Leonard), 264
Islam and the Moral Economy (Tripp), 24
Islam at the Crossroads (O'Leary), 261
Islamic Development Bank, 24
Ismail (son of Ibraheem), 141

J

Ja'afar Al-Sadiq, 155, 186
Jackson, Andrew, 109
Jamaat-e-Islami, 162–63, 165
Jamaica, 111
Jefferson, Thomas, 31, 108
Jennings, Peter, 77
jewelry, 214, 227
Jewish people, 83, 90, 141, 146–47, 160, 206, 211, 265
jihad, 137–38, 165
Jinnah, Muhammad Ali, 162
Johnson (president of the United States), 115
Jordan (river), 159
J. P. Morgan, 102
Juurikkala, Oskari, 21

K

Ka'aba, 141–42
Katrina (hurricane), 99
Kemal. *See* Atatürk, Mustafa Kemal
Kennedy, John F., 44, 109
Keynes, John Maynard, 30, 60, 100, 114, 125
khalifah. *See* caliphs
Kharaj, 204–5, 207
khilafah, 137, 148, 155–57, 162–63, 168, 186–87
Khomeini, Ayatollah, 163, 165, 249
Kimmit, Robert, 24
Köhler, Horst, 25
Kopping, Wayne, 248
  Obsession, 248
Korea, 85
Kuhner, Jeffrey, 22
Kurds, 161
Kuwait, 82, 84, 158, 161, 165, 167, 169

L

labor, 29, 36–37, 57, 194–98
  human, 36–37, 89, 195–97, 212, 216–17
  partnership with wealth, 216, 218
Lagarde, Christine, 24
Lamartine, Alphonse de, 152, 261–63
Lapidus, Ira Marvin, 152
Latvia, 111
lawsuits, 45
layoffs, 15, 94, 96
Lehman Brothers, 102, 108, 110, 213
Lenin, Vladimir, 14, 30, 36, 64, 93
Leonard, Arthur Glyn, 264
  Islam, Her Moral and Spiritual Value, 181, 183, 264
Life Insecurity, 81
Lincoln, Abraham, 109
Lindqvist, Ossi, 24, 129
loans, 105–7, 109, 112–13, 173–74, 212–16
lottery, 154
lynching, 87

M

Malay, 207
Mali, 75
Maliki, Abel Rahman al-, 180
  The Perfect Political Economy, 180, 187
Malik ibn Anas, 155, 186
Malkawi, Mohammad
  as a boy, 13, 15, 92–93
  education, 16, 92
  employment, 94
  speaker, 16
Malloch, Theodore Roosevelt, 23, 46
marginal benefit, 50–51
marginal value theory, 196–97
Marshall Plan, 115
Marx, Karl, 14, 30, 36–37, 61, 93, 183
Masakeen or Masâkin. *See* Miskeen
Maududi, Syed Abul A'ala, 162
McCain, John, 21, 128
McFadden (Pennsylvania congressman), 109
Mecca
  before conquest by Mohammad, 141–46, 157
  financial behavior, 144–45, 172–73, 180–81, 213–14, 251
  monetary system, 220–22
Medina, 143, 145–47, 150–51, 154, 165, 167, 187, 200, 205–7, 213, 251, 260
  flourishing of Islam in, 150–51, 154, 187, 205–7, 251, 260
  migration of Mohammad to, 145–47, 165, 167, 200, 213
Mellema, R. L., 265
Merchant of Venice, The (Shakespeare), 211, 276
Michener, James, 261
Miskeen, 173, 179–80, 199, 206, 239–40
Mohammad (prophet)
  conquest of Mecca, 142, 144–46
  death of, 138, 147, 200
  ideological character of, 138, 260–65
  migration to Medina, 146–47, 165, 167, 187, 200, 213
  references to economic issues, 170–71
  basic needs, 234, 239, 241
  grants, 200
  labor, 195–96
  monetary system, 220–21
  property ownership, 190, 204, 243–44
  support of children, parents, and relatives, 236
  wealth and poverty, 172, 178
monopolies, 30, 59–60, 62, 220
Montet, Edward, 257–58
moral crisis, 21–23, 44, 46
Moses (prophet), 144, 218
Mozambique, 75
Mubarak, Hosni, 89
Mudharabah partnership, 195, 216–18

Mugabe, Robert, 89
mujahideen or mujâhidûn, 84, 239
Musharraf, Pervez, 89
Muslim Brotherhood, 162–63, 165–67
Mustafa Kemal. *See* Atatürk

N

Nabhani, Taqiuddin al-, 37–38, 156, 162–63, 187
   Concepts of Hizb ut-Tahrir, 156
   The Economic System in Islam, 38, 187
Nader, Ralph, 21
Naidu, Sarojini, 266
Nasser, Gamal Abdel, 18, 162
nationalization, 62–63, 122, 188, 191
Native Americans. *See* American Indians
Niger, 74–75
Nigeria, 79
9/11, 16, 132, 152, 247
Nisa'i. *See* An-Nisai
Nixon, Richard, 25, 119, 230
Nobel Prize, 20, 120, 138

O

Obama, Barack, 21, 123
Obsession (Kopping), 248
O'Leary, De Lacy, 261
   Islam at the Crossroads, 261
orphans, 27, 173, 180–82, 194, 206
Othman ibn Affan, 169, 243
Ottoman Empire, 18, 20, 159
Our Economy (Al-Sadr). *See* Iqtisaduna
Our Endangered Values (Carter), 21
ownership, 14, 30–31, 43, 188–89
   coexistence of public and private, 125
   freedom of, 30–31, 46, 60
   private, 38, 60–63, 188–89, 191–94, 200–201, 236
   public, 43, 62, 120–22, 188, 190–91, 203, 235
   state, 61–63, 120, 122–23, 125, 188, 191, 236

P

Pakistan, 89, 112, 161–62, 165–66
Palestine, 83, 90, 160–61, 166, 249–50, 267
paper money
   fiduciary, 228, 230, 232
   intrinsic, 230, 232
   nonexchangeable, 224, 229–33
patriotism, 44–45, 47, 162, 250
Perfect Political Economy, The (Maliki), 180
Persia, 147, 150–51, 219, 222
Phelan, John, 102
Phelps, Edmund, 20
pilgrimage, 145, 181, 194, 214, 254
poverty
   and education, 74–75
   and gross national product, 66–67, 70
   Islamic view, 178–81
   rates, 68, 74–75, 79, 88, 112–13
prayer, 145, 170, 172, 181, 239
Préval, René, 65
price mechanism, 37–38, 40–41, 54–57, 63, 67, 114, 119, 122
   and market regulation, 57, 59–60
Principles of Political Economy and Taxation, The (Ricardo), 30
private property, 38, 126, 191, 193–95, 199, 243–44. *See also* ownership, private
productivity, 50–51, 101–2, 122, 124, 126, 177, 200, 208–9, 211
   impact of usury on, 211–14
   sustaining, 174, 214, 218
products
   and social responsibility, 45–46, 48
   value of, 38, 50–54
profiling, 90, 153, 248
property ownership. *See* ownership
public property, 126, 187, 191–92, 199–204, 241–42. *See also* ownership, public
purchasing power. *See* buying power

Q

Qarun (wealthy follower of Moses), 144, 185, 244
Qatar, 249
Quraish tribe, 141–42, 206, 219–20, 251–52
Quran
  interpretation of, 256–57
  revelation of, 138–39, 141–45, 170–73, 183, 255–56
  style in, 153–55
Qutb, Sayyid, 162

R

racism, 86–87
Ramakrishna Rao, K. S., 261
  Mohammed, 261
Rand, Ayn, 60, 120
  The Fountainhead, 60
ransom, 239–40
Ray, James Arthur, 124
Reagan, Ronald, 71, 80, 118–19
real estate, 95, 122
recessions, 19, 37, 105, 111, 235
Refaie, Majed al-, 24
Reisman, George, 120
relative scarcity, 38, 40–41, 60, 63, 114, 122
resources
  abundance of, 53, 174–77, 179, 225
  energy, 201–3, 225
revenues, 149, 186, 192, 199, 202–4, 241–42
riba (*see also* usury), 105–6, 173, 185, 187, 211, 213–14, 218, 221, 230–31
Ricardo, David, 30, 38, 129
  The Principles of Political Economy and Taxation, 30, 129
Rizq, 171–74, 185
Rodwell, John, 264
Romans, 150, 222
Rosset, Peter, 49, 70

World Hunger: Twelve Myths, 49, 70
Rumi (philosopher), 152
Rumsfeld, Donald, 245, 247
Russia, 23, 31, 47, 79, 82, 126
Rwanda, 90

S

sadaqât, 236, 239. *See also* zakah
Sadr, Mohammad Baqir al-, 37–38
Sarkozy, Nicolas, 223
Shakespeare, William, 211–12
  The Merchant of Venice, 211
Shari'ah, 18–19, 136–38, 152, 154–56, 158, 198, 221–22, 227, 233, 237
Shaw, George Bernard, 138, 152, 245, 263
Sierra Leone, 85
silver standard, 109, 112, 222, 224–25, 228, 233. *See also* gold standard
Smith, Adam, 30, 38, 54
  The Wealth of Nations, 30
Smith, Bosworth, 260–61
socialism, 14, 30, 35, 43, 138–41, 157–58
social responsibility, 31, 38, 44–45, 208
Sorrell, Martin, 20, 128
state grants, 195, 200–201
state property, 61–63, 125–26, 191, 201, 204, 208, 241–42
Stewart, Martha, 104
stock markets, 19, 94, 99–102, 113, 119
Structural Adjustment Programs (SAPs), 66
Sunnah, 146–48, 155–56, 170, 185, 196, 205, 220, 237–38, 256–57
surplus value, 37

T

Taliban, 165, 168–69
Tanzeem e Islami, 165
taxation, 30, 112, 129, 150, 180, 186–87, 208
Taylor (canon), 135, 265
TB. *See* tuberculosis

terrorism, 16, 77, 81–82, 95, 137, 140–41, 152, 247–48
Thatcher, Margaret, 84
Tirmidhi (scholar), 153, 221
torture, 86, 90, 145, 161
Toynbee, Arnold, 136, 266
Tripp, Charles, 24, 129
  Islam and the Moral Economy, 24
Tritton, A. S., 261, 279
Trump, Donald, 97
tuberculosis, 71, 78–80, 131
Turkey, 155, 160–62, 166, 249

U

Ukraine, 111
Umar Bin Al-Khattab, 178, 205, 207, 221
Ummah, 154, 156–57, 265
UN. *See* United Nations
UNESCO, 75, 130
Union of Soviet Socialist Republics (USSR), 13, 92
UNITA, 84
United Nations (UN), 65, 72, 82, 86, 167
United States
  business ethics, 21, 44, 46
  consumer price index inflation, 69
  Declaration of Independence, 87
  dollars, 114–15, 225, 229, 233
  economy, 21, 94, 100, 121
  gold reserves, 116, 225
  government, 62, 108–9, 119, 121, 125
  outsourcing to China and India, 213
USSR. *See* Union of Soviet Socialist Republics
usury, 118, 123, 142, 185, 187, 218, 230, 251
  prohibition of, 144–45, 173, 196, 201, 211–14, 257
  and virtual economy, 104–9, 112
  See also riba
Uzbekistan, 89

V

value
  definition of, 52, 99, 103, 119, 181, 185
  of products, 50–51, 53
  virtual or real, 51–54
Vietnam, 85
virtual economy (VE), 52, 95–99, 122, 213
  and banks, 104, 106
  and gold/silver standard, 112–14, 116–18
  and stock markets, 100–101, 107

W

Wall Street, 17, 21, 128, 133, 247
Washington Mutual, 102
Watt, W. Montgomery, 264
WB. *See* World Bank
wealth
  in Islamic economy, 171–74
  partnership with labor, 216–18
  provided to poor, 198–99
Wealth of Nations, The (Smith), 30
Wells, Herbert George, 266
Williams, Rowan, 22
Wilson, Woodrow, 109
Wolf, Martin, 20
Wolf, Richard, 211, 276
World Bank (WB), 49, 65–66, 68, 72, 81–83, 111, 229
World Health Organization (WHO), 73, 80–81
World Hunger: Twelve Myths (Rosset), 49, 70
World Trade Organization (WTO), 82
World War I, 82, 87, 112–13, 159, 223–24
World War II, 57–58, 83, 113–14, 223, 225, 230

Y

Yarmouk (river), 159
Yathrib. *See* Medina
Yemen, 161, 222, 239
Young, Ardis Armstrong, 71

Z

zakah, 145, 152, 170, 179, 239–43. *See also* charity
Zallum, Abdul Qadeem, 157
   How the Khilafah Was Destroyed, 157
Zenawi, Meles, 89
Zimbabwe, 89

Edwards Brothers,Inc!
Thorofare, NJ 08086
24 June, 2010
BA2010175